THE LAIRD OF ABBOTSFORD

UNA POPE-HENNESSY

THE LAIRD OF ABBOTSFORD

An Informal Presentation of
SIR WALTER SCOTT

PUTNAM

LONDON & NEW YORK

First Published, February, 1932

1583

Made and Printed in Great Britain by the KEMP HALL PRESS LTD.
in the City of Oxford

1606

TO
LADY GREGORY

PREFACE

NO definitive biography of Sir Walter Scott can be written until the complete collection of his Letters (now being edited by Professor H. J. C. Grierson) has been published, and the Abbotsford Papers (recently acquired by the National Library of Scotland) have been sorted and made accessible to students. For the substance of the present study I have gone first to Sir Walter Scott himself; secondly to Sir Walter Scott's friends, acquaintances, and enemies; thirdly to the monumental biography written by Sir Walter Scott's son-in-law. In this magnificent ten-volume tomb the Laird of Abbotsford has reposed in urbane dignity for nearly a century. Perhaps it is time that he walked the earth again and reassumed some of the characteristics of which Lockhart in his protective love divested him.

It would render an unpretentious book unreadable to give the reference for every statement made, but derivations, acknowledged or unacknowledged, from pioneers in the enterprise occur on every page, and to these my predecessors I hereby declare my grateful sense of indebtedness.

UNA POPE-HENNESSY.

Hurworth-on-Tees. January 1932.

CONTENTS

My dear Mrs. Slade

I have just seen the card with which Miss Mant has honoured me. As I am not the author of Waverley nor in any way connected with these very successful novels I am sure Miss Mant will be aware that with every desire to oblige a friend of yours it is quite impossible that I can have the honour of accepting the flattering inscription which she proposes & also that I have it not in my power to grant or refuse the request which she prefers. I regret it very much as nothing would give me more pleasure than to do whatever might be agreeable to a friend of so old & so valued a friend as yourself. I am with great regard

Yours most faithfully

Walter Scott

Facsimile of letter from Sir Walter Scott to Mrs. Slade in which he denies authorship of the Waverley Novels. [See p. 149]

THE LAIRD OF ABBOTSFORD

CHAPTER I

THE WAY TO LIFE

ON summer evenings in 1777 a loiterer on the links at Prestonpans might have watched a small boy with long, sand-coloured hair limping across the flats. Evening after evening the resolute figure in the short scarlet jacket stumped to its perch of observation—a mound from which, in comparison with the short-cropped turf around, the grass grew long and rank. Sometimes a woman walked with him who would often speak of the officer she had seen cut down by the sword and buried on that very spot thirty years agone ; sometimes a man appeared and pointed with his stick to the old thorn tree and other landmarks on Prince Charlie's battle-field ; sometimes the child sat alone on the mound until he was fetched for bed.

A miniature of this boy " Wattie " Scott, if compared with the portraits made of Sir Walter Scott the famous author, reveals how little the essential features changed with maturity. We note the same domed forehead, the same long upper lip, the same almost innocent expression of wonder at the world. And when we see the lad seated on the soldier's grave beside the sea we are confronted, as it were, with the foreshadowing of Scott's great achievement in a life begun in dreaming over a dead and half-forgotten Scotland, and spent in recalling to his native land a past more vividly than monument could commemorate it.

From babyhood everything in Walter Scott's experience conspired to make the child the father of the man : even apparent afflictions " happened lucky." Infantile paralysis precluded his parents, who had already lost six of their children, from keeping their second Walter to fade in Edinburgh wynds, and induced them to send him to the place, under forty miles away, where his father had spent his childhood—his grandfather's farm Sandyknowe. And there, remote from urban influences and in the delightful company of shepherds and their lambs, the infant grew to boyhood.

With a grandmother who sat over the fire and repeated stories of the Border raids she had been told as a girl, with an uncle who could describe the fighting at Culloden and the cruel executions of Scotsmen he had witnessed at Carlisle, with an aunt willing to croon ballads of the old days, Wattie Scott's waking life became a sort of reverie which even the emaciated minister who visited his grandmother could not disturb. Indeed, Dr. Duncan, with his Don Quixote countenance, may be said to have added to the bewitchment of the surroundings for had he not seen Alexander Pope the poet, who had made the translation of Homer which his mother kept beside her chair, a book on which every little boy in Scotland was brought up ?

In this halcyon graduation to a life in which past and present were equally substantial we may discern the seeds of Scott's later miraculous success in transmitting his own perceptions to the world. History never appeared to him as a ghostlike abstraction ; since the events had never died they formed part of the living texture of existence and were always tangible at first or second hand.

There were not many books at Sandyknowe. One or two lay on the window seat in the living-room, among them Ramsay's *Tea Table Miscellany*. Out of this book came the ballad *Hardyknute* read to the child by his aunt Janet. Wattie knew its verses by heart in no time and roared the lines :

> Stately stept he east the wa'
> And stately stept he west,

as he stamped his feet on the cobbles by the window to the aggravation of chance visitors. The lilt awoke in him something that struggled for expression and leapt up at the call of romance. He was to murmur the same verses in Italy when a second childhood was dawning in which the response to new impressions was the re-awakening of old ones.

From the people who went haphazardly across the Sandyknowe horizon Wattie seemed to get just what he wanted to help him with his dream-pictures ; and luckily for him there were no other children to jeer at his singing and tease him for his lameness. Close to the farm was a lake and beyond it the ground broken by an outcropping of limestone rocks rose sharply to a hill sur-mounted by a peel-tower of time-defying solidity. Could any more favourable playground be devised for an imaginative child than the foursquare grey tower with the strange blood-red stones outlining angles and doorways and window, the tremendous walls, the dark interior, the winding stair, the ruined bartizan ? Warding the quiet tarn among the rocks and the little homestead below, Smail-holm Keep was in itself an epitome of Border history.

The shepherd who carried the lame child out in

the morning and set him down among the rocks
at the foot of the fortress, told him gravely, as to
an equal, legends of the country spread before
their eyes.   From that rough eminence they
could watch flocks moving by " velvet tufts of
loveliest green " to other pasturing grounds, and
could gaze away across the Tweed to the house of
Scott, the Laird of Raeburn, to Dryburgh Abbey
—the burial place of the Haliburtons, to the three
peaks of Eildon, and the mists surrounding
Melrose, to bleak Lammermoor and the blue
Cheviots—the scenery later to be described in
Marmion.   During all the years of his fame his
heart never strayed far from this landscape.

From these early days Scott's adoration for the
Border country dates.   Two propensities gradually dominated him and became the very essence
of his being—a passion for Scotland and all that
Scotland signified, and a passion for the past that
was his past—things that his grandsires had seen
and done, things that the cow-bailie and the
shepherd could " mind."   As he developed he
realized history more and more clearly as the
tissue of life, and he exulted to find the name of
Scott running like a bright thread through the
weaving :   Michael Scott the Wizard ; Walter
Scott of Buccleuch killed by Kerrs in the streets
of Edinburgh ; " Auld Wat " Scott of Harden,
husband of the Flower of Yarrow ; " Auld
Wat's " son William Boltfoot, who though lame
had yet survived " to be a man " ; Minstrel
Scott of Satchells, with his " extraordinary poetical performance," *A True History of Several of
the Name of Scott*[1] ; Sir William Scott who in
Stuart times wrote on Roxburghshire ; his own
amber-bearded grandfather, who had been out in

[1] 1688.

Dundee's wars and in 1715. And the ultimate outcome of all this concern with the clan of which he felt himself the heritor, was to be the *Lay of the Last Minstrel*, that apotheosization of Scotts in Border history.

The blissful yet thrilling existence at Sandy-knowe was for a while interrupted when he was sent to Bath with his aunt Janet for a course of treatment. At Bath he could observe and listen to the talk of Scotland's leading dramatist John Home, author of the popular play *Douglas*. This may have given his latent patriotic feeling a further fillip, but the grand new experience was entering a theatre. With the spectacle of *As You Like It* began his worship of Shakespeare and familiarity with his works. In later years the common feature of their comprehensive humanity was to lead men to compare them together.

From Bath there was a return to Sandyknowe; but in the autumn of 1778 the quiet setting of Wattie's life was rudely and for ever changed, for he went to live with his parents at the family residence in George Square, Edinburgh. It was a good stone house with area and basement. From its doorstep one may still look down on the Meadows and it is obvious that an ingenious boy could rig up mirrors by his bedroom window in which the men moving across that grassy slope would be reflected in miniature. Though the Writer to the Signet had a comfortable home the fraternal company into which his little son was now pitchforked was noisier and rougher than that to which the child had been accustomed, and except for the pleasure of his mother's reading, he would far rather have remained at the farm; education however was the reason for bringing him back, and he was

entered to Edinburgh High School.   The family
to which he was at this time restored consisted
of his father Walter Scott, a strict Calvinist and
hard-working attorney with many Highland
lairds among his clients ; his mother a daughter
of Dr. Rutherford, Professor of Medicine at
Edinburgh University ; four brothers Robert,
John, Thomas, Daniel ; and a sister Anne. When
as quite a youngster Walter became interested in
heraldry and the combining of devices, it pleased
him to know his mother to be of old Roxburghshire stock, and his maternal grandmother a
Swinton of Swinton, and that he himself could lay
claim to their boars-heads and martlets as well
as to the mascles of Haliburton and the crescents
of Scott.   By virtue of his great-grandfather
" Beardie," who had married a Campbell, he
dared in later life to parade in a Campbell tartan
when he welcomed George IV to Scotland.   Mr.
Scott, W.S., who brought up his family to
venerate the head of their sept, Scott of Harden,
perpetuated the old traditions by taking his wife
and children to Harden at Christmas time " in
token of vassalage."

It was not till the successful author began to
decorate the armoury at Abbotsford, that he
could express his boyish pride in being connected
with so many Border families, and then twelve
shields with coloured devices were affixed to the
corbels of the ceiling, and in the glass windows the
painted achievements of the Clan Scott effectively
diluted the sunlight.   One of Wattie's childish
dreams came to life in that entrance hall.   People
who do not appreciate heraldry as the epitome of
medieval history have reproached Scott for his
snobbery and subservience to men of great estate,
but pride in pedigree and pride in armigerous

families was in the blood of all true Borderers, and Scott was nothing if not a Borderer.

The Smailholm atmosphere at times was revived in George Square. Mr. George Constable, the spectator of the Prestonpans battle, was often in the house, and among Mr. Scott's clients was Stewart of Invernahayle who had been " out " in '45. A frequent guest, he was welcomed by Wattie who hung breathless on his words. One day when he was recounting the exploits of youth, an earnest little voice was heard asking, " O, Inver, were you ever afraid ? " " Troth, Gurdie mavourneen," he replied, " the first time I gaed into action when I saw the red coats' rank opposite to us and our people put their bonnets to say a bit prayer and then scrug their bonnets over their een and set forward like bulls driving each other on and beginning to fire their guns and draw their broadswords, I would have given any man a thousand merk to insure me I wadna' run away." At the end of his life Scott looked back on these days and said, " What a godsend I must have been as a boy to the old Trojans of 1745, nay 1715, who used to frequent my father's house, and who knew as little as I did for what market I was laying up the raw material of their oft-told tales ! "

Walter Scott's school career was not remarkable, for he was self-educated in everything in which he afterwards excelled. As an example of this we may look at a lanky lad of twelve, fair-headed and dishevelled, lying reading under a plane tree in a Kelso garden. The book in his hands is a volume of Percy's *Reliques of Ancient Poetry*, and as he turns page after page it is clear from his expression that he finds the perusal an enchantment. Unheard the dinner bell summons him to food; he reads on until hauled out of his retreat by his good angel, Aunt Janet. In another country an older youth Gottfried Bürger had read the *Reliques* with the same ecstasy and fired by their music set about writing a ballad himself. The result was *Lenore* which, in its turn when it reached Scott many years later, was the spur that set him off on his rhyming career.

At longest his official education lasted some seven desultory years between 1778 and 1785. And all the while the interludes were what signified most, the tramps to old castles, the climbs on Salisbury Crags with John Irving, the endless weaving of chivalric story they indulged in together, the books they read perched side by side among the rocks. Two little girls, Jane and Anne Porter, sometimes played with Wattie, and to them too he told stories, awakening in them the powers of fancy. Anne was precocious and published *Artless Tales* at the age of twelve, an impressive proceeding in the eyes of her contemporaries. Later she was to write a book, *Scottish Chiefs*. Jane, who published *Thaddeus of Warsaw* in 1804, ten years before *Waverley* came out, often boasted that in her initiation of the historical novel, she had no less a follower than Sir Walter Scott !

In the summer of 1783 we find Walter Scott preparing for the autumn term at Edinburgh College by attending the Grammar School at Kelso, where he met the three Ballantyne boys, two of whom were destined to entangle their lives so fatefully with his own. In 1784–5 he attended College and then fell suddenly ill with an internal hæmorrhage which obliged him to lie in bed for months, a whispering cereal eater,

Like Goethe, who as a law student was overtaken by the same calamity, he read voraciously, racing through all the folios, romances, and chronicles that Sibbald's circulating library could produce. Sometimes he watched men drilling in his window mirror, sometimes he played chess for a change, but at no period in his life did he think games anything but sad waste of brains. During this intermission from active life the harvest of information gathered was heavy, for at this time and for long afterwards " to read was to remember." The omnivorous intake of material at an impressionable age makes it easy to account for the enormous output of his middle years.

After months of invalidism he recovered of his bloody flux, and was sent again to Kelso to regain the uses of muscle and limbs. Some say that he went back to College for a short time, others that he never returned. It is quite immaterial whether he did or not, for he had lost so much academic time that he could not hope to compete successfully for any academic distinction. It became obvious to his father that Wattie would never make a scholar ; it was unlikely even that he would make anything of a career, for his queer unsatisfactory habits of collecting ballads and nicknackets were fatal alike to ambition and concentration. He was an idle fellow and no mistake ! Intensive education on classic lines was clearly waste of time and money ; but since the boy's Latin and general information were good enough for an attorney, Mr. Scott decided to harness him at once as prentice Writer to the Signet. Wattie was forthwith invited to enter his father's office, and at the age of fifteen signed his indentures. Thus began an important initiation—though who was to guess it?—the initiation to quill-driving. Never in his most creative mood was he to cover one hundred and twenty pages of foolscap without food or rest, as he did in one day in his father's office. Rapid penmanship became, after this training, second nature, and those who scrutinize Scott's writing must attribute its equable, featureless character to the drudging discipline at an attorney's desk. It is probable, however, that he was made to cross his t's and dot his i's, a refinement he afterwards abandoned. The small sums he gained from copying were mainly spent in learning Italian and purchasing books and broadsheets. Evans' *Old Ballads* were acquired, among them was *Cumnor Hall*, one day to reappear as the core of *Kenilworth*. At sixteen he was sent by his father to the Highlands to supervise an execution for non-payment of rent on tenants of Stewart of Appin, brother-in-law to his old friend " Inver," with whom he stayed. Mr. Stewart repeated all his stories and told of the sword-and-target duel he had fought with Rob Roy in the dim past. During this excursion Walter gazed for the first time upon Loch Katrine, and in that tenacious brain was registered the setting of the *Lady of the Lake*. From this time forward he devoted all the time he could get off work to walking or riding into the country to examine old buildings and talk over old days with the oldest people he could find. Mr. Scott, who disapproved of his " strolling pedlar " habits tried in the third year of his apprenticeship to pin him more tightly to toil by entering his brother Thomas to the family office, and arranging for Walter to become a barrister. Conforming with the parental wishes Walter, in company with his friend Willie Clerk of Eldin, began to work for his law examinations. In

spite of the extra study involved, the young man
still found leisure in which to exercise his imagination and his legs. Rather wearily his father had
to accept the fact that it was not possible to keep
this third son on the leash, whatever happened he
would go his own gait and squander the profits
of bondage in books and antiquarian objects.
Mr. Scott, whose chief diversion was theology,
had to console himself as best he could in his
study, and try to forget what a mess his foolish
Wattie was making of the semi-basement allotted
to him below. Study did he call it? It was
more like a scrap heap with its old bits of iron
and wood and books out of their bindings!

As the vacations came round Walter made
ready for a tramp into the wilds. In the summer
of 1791 we find him settled snugly at a farmhouse
in the Cheviots examining with close attention
Flodden, Otterburn, Ford and Chillingham, " all
within the compass of a forenoon's ride." The
Marmion tombs at Tanfield made an indelible
impression on that ductile mind, and it is certain
that the foundations of his greatest poem were at
this time well and truly laid, though sixteen
years were to elapse before the structure was to
become visible to other eyes. In 1792 we find
him exploring round Hexham, talking enthusiastically with country folk who answered in Chau-
cerian English. In this way he became familiar
with the Cat-Rail and the Roman Wall and all the
roads and by-paths leading into Scotland. In
1792 he also spent some time at Kelso, cogitating
about we know not what as he lay in a nest of his
own construction high in a tree overhanging the
river. The west wind rocked the branches, the
Tweed rolled beneath him, and the great boy of
twenty-one cut Latin words upon the bole, or

made " embrasures " through the leaves so that he might fire at cormorants and gulls.

A friendship made at this time with Robert Shortreed, Sheriff of Roxburghshire, intensified his natural love of ballads. Shortreed not only gave him all the fragments he had collected, but also for several successive years led him on excursions into Liddesdale to hear songs and stories of the old days.   To preserve these before they were forgotten became for him a sacred duty. So fast was the world moving that even the tales and rhymes of 1745 were fading from men's minds.   If stories but fifty years old were hard to come by, what of the older traditional verses handed down through the generations ; was there still time to rescue them ? To Dr. Johnson ballads were ridiculous rubbish to be parodied out of existence. To Scott they were the music of history, and therefore with all resolve he set himself to listen and record but without thought of publication.

The weariness of studying for the Bar was diversified in other ways than travelling. He began to take a serious interest in German literature.   Like all his contemporaries he had read *The Sorrows of Werter*, for young people of his day were brought up on Goethe's melancholy tale not only in book form but in pictures. Describing a middle-class sitting-room of this date Crabbe writes :

> Four prints along the papered wall are spread
> There Werter sees the sportive children fed
> And Charlotte here bewails her lover dead.

Werter however had not stimulated Scott to learn German as did a lecture on German drama given by Henry Mackenzie in Edinburgh in 1788.

The " Man of Feeling " took his examples from French versions of selected plays, but even at second hand Scott suddenly realized that there was something akin to his own unformulated aspirations and sentiment in the subject matter of *The Robbers* and *Goetz von Berlichingen*. Here at least was a return to medievalism and an emancipation from the unities and the remote conventional world of Racine. With his close friend, Willie Erskine, he became the pupil of Dr. Willich, who did his best to ground him in grammar before letting him loose to browse on plays. Too eager to extract the kernel from the nut Scott decided to familiarize himself with the language by translation. After all, young Fraser-Tytler despite little knowledge had made a version of *The Robbers* that had gained some popular favour, surely he could do as well. The standard was not high, for the future Lord Woodhouselee had made but a feeble rendering of the short acting version of Schiller's play. With zealous emulation Walter applied himself to forcing dramas by Steinberg and Meier into English. The results were read aloud to long-suffering friends : a translation of Schiller's *Fiesco* reduced an audience to tears. One day he told Mrs. Hughes, " I used to read *Fiesco* to sobbing and weeping audiences, and no wonder, for whatever may be thought of the translation the original is sublime."

The most exciting of the plays was that of a German lawyer[1] which, though written in the year of his own birth, Scott found a complete novelty. The hero was a free-knight, a kind of Borderer, not actually lame, but one-handed and therefore greatly to his taste. He found it not

[1] *Goetz von Berlichingen*, Goethe.

so much a play as a sort of dramatized chronicle, and it suggested to him the kind of way that medieval history might be presented to a contemporary audience. His translation of *Goetz* does not pretend to be literal, though it achieves a rough and ready success in giving the spirit and sense of the original. Some of his renderings show how little Dr. Willich's advice had been heeded. Brother Martin's line, *Mein Kloster ist Erfurt in Sachsen*, was rendered " The cloister is involved in business," and another of his lines, *das ist nun ihr Bienenkorb* (meaning bee-hive or field of labour) is given as " where they have raised beans." Some of his adaptations are presumably arranged to suit his audience. *Kroch er zum Kreuz* is given as " pulled in his horns," " *Wir wollen ihnen die Hölle heiss machen*," " we will cook their porridge for them," while others arise from ignorance or carelessness, such as making " *weiten Naslöchern*," " white locks," " *Arbeit*," " fatigue," " *munter*," " alert," and " *gefangen*," " conquered." It was turgid enough in style. " Never did I experience such a depression." . . . " Come let us to the big-wigs. They have had time to deliberate, let us take the trouble upon ourselves ! . . . Help us first to drub the Bambergers ! . . . If we durst but once serve the princes in the same manner who drag our skins over our ears. . . . It is horrible warfare ! . . . The haughty vindictive man ! I hate him ! His power waxes like a mountain torrent . . . let it but gain a few brooks and others come pouring to its aid." As an older man he laughed over his mistakes with Mrs. Hughes (who through copying his *Goetz* could not help finding him out). " I remember among other comical blunders," he said, " I gallantly translated *Glatze* (bald head) into ' glasses ' and made a landlord's drunken customers threaten his crockery instead of his noddle ! "

At no time could Walter Scott be bothered with too much exactitude. He would take a certain amount of trouble, but only a certain amount, about anything. The chief value of these translations does not lie in their intrinsic merit but in the meditations they set going in his brain—meditations which led to the conception of *Marmion* and *Ivanhoe*. If we are looking for spiritual genealogies we have them here in this world of battlemented keeps, swart men at arms, swift action and deaths on the field of battle. It is the problem of the reanimation of history that concerns Scott and those who study Scott.

The House of Aspen, which long years afterwards was put into rehearsal at Drury Lane, dates from this period, but in spite of Scott's enormous vogue it was never produced. His interest in German brought him to the notice of James Skene of Rubislaw who became a life-long friend. Skene had been educated in Saxony, and had a number of German books which he put at the student's disposal. It was difficult to obtain foreign books in Edinburgh, but Scott had managed to purchase Adelung's dictionary through a Scottish monk in Ratisbon (the monastery to which he banished Redgauntlet). Later, when his kinsman Scott of Harden brought a German bride to Edinburgh, the problem of obtaining books from abroad was simplified.

All his life Scott was an eager and rather undiscriminating reader of novels. Some of those he read as a young man had a very deep influence on his development and give the key to many passages in *The Abbot*, *The Monastery* and

Marmion. Two novels in particular, *The Castle of Otranto* and *The Monk*, entranced him at every reading. From Horace Walpole he no doubt got the idea of accounting for some of his stories by inventing " authentic manuscripts," a tedious device that can only be occasionally condoned. From Lewis he derived many of his Catholic scenes, and his conception of the excessive lewdness of the lives of monks and nuns. When weak women to whom he read the canto describing the judging of Constance, entreated him not to wall her up, he with his mind fixed on the terrible fate of Agnes and the goings on in the vaults of St. Clare's convent, would show no mercy. Had he not a good precedent for his severity ?

At the earliest age a peculiar individual quality is to be observed in Scott, a something in him that rushes out to meet the past and falls as it were overcome by it. The reading of a ballad, for example, would cause such quiverings in his mind that with it he seemed to reach a new kind of affective existence. His perceptive impulses were potent, and he derived emotions of the most pervading, shattering kind from dungeons, battle-grounds and objects that recalled earlier days, such as a thumbscrew, a ring, a horn. Impelled by the inspiration that came to him from the handling of antiquarian odds and ends and the musing on them, he was from boyhood a collector. In the strength of his manhood the unpacking of the Scottish Regalia overwhelmed him, for might not Bruce have worn the crown ? He was incapable of speech, though to some spectators it was the occasion of a joke. This sensibility to the suggestive power of relics, which others did not understand, he kept to himself, for it was the deepest adventure alike of his boyhood, early manhood and middle age. He found he could not share these secret thrills with anyone. He who was most insensitive in other respects was hypersensitive in this, and one surmises that it was the same feeling of reserve about Scottish history that kept him in the first instance from acknowledging *Waverley*. He did not want to have to discuss the book with everyone, or to have dumb eyes prying irreverently among his imaginations. The rough criticism to which his poems had been subjected may perhaps have been an additional motive for anonymity.

In Walter Scott we have a human being with the rare faculty of suffusing the objects he took cognizance of with his own emotions. Things came to life because he cared for them, and acquired import because he understood them. We are all aware that there is no value in anything apart from some appreciation of it, and in appreciation lies the root and essence of all Scott's excellence. In boyhood he was always eager to transmit his perceptions by the natural method of story-telling, and later in life, when he had found a medium to his use, in verse and then in prose. Not only did he find keen pleasure in perception, but he also found an equal pleasure in transmitting his perception. His books are the expression of his peculiar emotions, and the beauty of his work originated in his human sensibility. His contemporaries accused him of venality, and judged him harshly ; but there are two Scotts, and since every pleasure is in one sense disinterested, the Scott who wrote the poems and the novels was not writing for pay but for intuitive satisfaction. What filled his mind was not calculation, but the image of an object or event tinged with feeling, and the pace, the

c

furore, with which he wrote proves this. There was a Scott who dealt in manuscripts and played off one publisher against another, who sought for place, and within moderate limits, power and wealth ; but this Scott, had very little to do with that other self which was the vehicle of romance and the servant of the past.

" There is nae ganging thro' the warl without a wee tate o' fauset," says a Scottish proverb ; and Scott, who began by disguising his own sensibility, ended by having to lie on every occasion on which his authorship of the novels was challenged, and, owing to his secret business connections, on many other occasions as well. Possibly he was of the same opinion as his idol, Thomas the Rhymer, when he declined the fairy's gift of " the tongue that can never lie," as an entirely useless gift for a romancer.

CHAPTER II

LIFE AT THE BAR

THE old Scottish Parliament House, in which Walter Scott was to spend so much of his time, was the great centre of Edinburgh life. For the purposes of the Law the old building had been partitioned into two sections, one of which, a room thirty-five feet square, was known as the Inner House. In this dark and grimy chamber fifteen judges took their seats at ten o'clock on working days. On Mondays they did not sit, as this day was reserved for the criminal business of the High Court : on teind or alternate Wednesdays they did not sit, for then another set of officials assembled to hear another set of problems arising out of tythes ; but with these exceptions the routine of the Court went on from the twelfth of October till the twelfth of March, except for a short Christmas vacation, and from the twelfth of May until the twelfth of July. It was to this schedule that Scott, both as advocate and Clerk of the Session, worked.

The Judges or Lords Ordinaries, who presided over the Inner House, were dressed in purple velvet coats, blue cloth breeches and silk gowns ornamented with knots and reminded strangers more of Presidents of the French Parliament than Judges of a British Court of Law.[1] All were venerable and some were old, though not as antiquated as the Lord Ordinary seen by Hogg

[1] *Peter's Letters to his Kinsfolk*, Vol. II, p. 16 *et seq.*

and Shelley during their visit to Edinburgh. Below the Bench at a table sat the principal Clerks of the Session, a fraternity so intimately linked that they all played the part of uncle to each other's children. It was their duty to record their lordships' decisions, and we may conclude from the amount of private correspondence transacted by Scott during office hours that the work was not continuous.

The Outer House, a much larger chamber, was crowded with men practising or wishing to practise the law. Its stone walls were sprinkled with portraits grimed with age-old dust. Mr. Scott, W.S., had often taken his son Walter there during his apprenticeship and had familiarized him with the ways of solicitors and their clients. If we are to accept Saunders Fairford (in *Redgauntlet*) as an accurate picture of Walter Scott senior— and Mr. Clerk assured Lockhart that it was exact— we may visualize a neat man in a bob wig, small cocked hat, stock, snuff coloured coat and breeches, woollen stockings, and black shoes with buckles of silver. Most barristers, including his big son, donned the legal wig and gown, but some young advocates went wigless. Under their robe they wore knee-breeches, trousers, or indeed any sort of raiment ; and when the Napoleonic scare kept volunteers on the alert, bright uniforms were to be seen peeping out from the folds of black drapery. In winter time the hall was thick with haze, and the stream of advocates and solicitors moving along the tracks on the floor, which ancient custom had assigned to them, appeared as in a mist. Much as Walter Scott adored the freedom of the country, he came to share with all his colleagues an affection for that Outer House, which in point of fact combined the advantages

of office, forum and club. George Ticknor,
after pacing its floor with Scott, alluded to it as
" that Babel." All the news and gossip was
thrashed out there, and members of the legal
profession, who frequented the courts day in
day out, became welded, as it were, into a
real brotherhood. Never was any society more
intimate than that of the lawyers of Edinburgh.

In July, 1792, the new-fledged advocates, Walter
Scott and Willie Clerk, swept with considerable
satisfaction through the Parliament House in
their black bombazine robes. It was their first
and only appearance before the summer recess.
Friends hailed the neophytes, and one Writer to
the Signet gave young Scott a guinea for luck,
because he was his father's son. When the Court
closed the two friends strolled down the High
Street with something of a swagger. " This is a
sort of wedding-day," said Walter to Willie, " I
think I must go in and buy me a new nightcap."

The life, to which they that autumn as advocates found themselves committed, obliged them
to make an appearance in the Parliament Buildings at nine o'clock with the Writers to the Signet
and other solicitors. It was only the aspiring
barristers who turned out as early as this ; those
with briefs strolled in a little before ten. The
newly-called had nothing to do but hang about
and wait for jobs and thought themselves lucky
if some Writer to the Signet requested them, in
the absence of a Senior Counsel, to address a few
words to the Judges. For this no fee was given
or expected. Much, however, might depend on
these few words, for if the Writer was pleased with
the way his commission was carried out, he would
give further employment.

Briefless advocates had to walk the boards till

two in the afternoon. Some young men were fit
to perish of boredom ; but Walter Scott was never
in any circumstances bored, and his laugh, which
was very loud, could be heard above the talk as
he promenaded the floor for pastime before the
Judges made their appearance. In cold weather
discussion raged round the big stove of the Outer
House, and the young politicians of Scott's day
were known as " the Mountain," for the principles
of the Revolutionaries in France were eagerly
debated, by the glowing coals. Though other
youngsters might display interest in, even enthusiasm for, a future state of society, in which the
perfectibility of man might be made manifest,
Scott infinitely preferred the vanished world,
made perfect in his eyes by the glamour of
chivalrous romance ; and whenever he got the
chance, told a story recalling old events. Gradually Duns Scotus, as they nicknamed him, made
himself a position as a *raconteur*, and young men
looked to him to enliven the tedium of waiting
away the hours. It was here that Scott learnt
that habit of narration, which made him in later
years almost impenetrable to the conversation of
others.

Mr. Scott, W.S., did what he could to put work
in the way of his son, but it was of a quite
unimportant kind, and there are but few instances
of the younger man's pleadings on record. One
of the first was defence of a minister who had been
dismissed from his post for drunkenness. Scott,
who never was to learn to speak well in public,
began to plead in a shy voice, but when he came
to repeat the speeches alleged to be indecent,
from sheer nervousness he raised it almost to a
shout, and a Judge called him to order. Abashed,
the young advocate lowered his voice again in

order to repeat the words of a drinking song. His
friends tried to put fresh heart into him by shouting *Encore!* but the case was lost. We learn that
he attended the Michaelmas Circuit Court at
Jedburgh in 1792, while representing a client of
his father's. But taking all in all, his legal work
was not onerous, and though some ardent admirers
have gone so far as to say that Scott might have
made a success of the bar, had he but stuck to the
work, fees do not bear this contention out. In
his fifth year he earned £144, £50 of which came
through his father's office. In his seventh year
he earned still less, and after his father's death
fees fell even lower. According to Lord Cockburn,
Scott unconsciously militated against his own
success as a lawyer by secretly despising the law
and all its activities. The truth was that he
never put his back into legal work, his enthusiasm
being expended on other interests. He spent
hours in searching through rolls and genealogies,
and in deciphering parchments in the Advocates'
Library. In time he became its Curator ; and
when he had made friends with Southey earned
his gratitude by sending books to him in England,
though such a proceeding was strictly forbidden in
the regulations. It was a red letter day in his
calendar when he lighted on the Auchinleck
manuscript in the library, for it contained among
other metrical romances one professing to be a
copy of that written by Thomas the Rhymer on
Sir Tristrem. As a child he had listened fascinated to stories of this Border prophet, and as
a man one of his greatest satisfactions lay in
acquiring the localities he believed to be the scene
of True Thomas's encounter with the Queen of
the Fairies. In the beginning Scott was a slow
worker, but by degrees he built up about the

poet an elaborate theory which he was to make public ten years later when he published his own edition of this Arthurian romance.   Thomas the Rhymer and everything connected with him continued to interest Scott till his dying day.

It is observable that the matters in which Scott interested himself as a young man bore fruit later in life : none of his activities ran to waste. Shortly before becoming an advocate he joined the Speculative Society, a debating and literary club.   In the usual way papers were read by one member and criticized by the others.   For this society he refurbished essays on the same subjects he had dealt with at the Literary Society in previous years.   They consisted of dissertations on Feudalism, Ossian and Northern Mythology, and cannot have given occasion for very lively debates.   But this much may be noted, that Scott stuck persistently to his themes and that all embody the germ of future publications.   He became secretary of this society, and the first time a dark young man named Jeffrey attended a meeting, he saw Scott sitting miserably at the table, his head enveloped in a woollen night-cap against the tooth ache, but in spite of this disadvantage reading an article on Ballads. Next day Jeffrey called on him at his parents' house in George Square, and found the lecturer in the semi-basement room, in which he read, and assembled his antiquities.   Jeffrey described it as " a small den on a sunk floor, surrounded by dingy books."

To this period of Scott's life belongs the tenuous romance, of which so much has been made by Scott idolators.   The story is of the simplest.   One wet Sunday outside Greyfriars Church he offered the shelter of his umbrella to his young and

distant kinswoman Williamina Belsches, whom he
had not previously met. Brought up in a very
different milieu from his own, Green Mantle, as
he called her afterwards, struck him as ideally
beautiful and high-born enough to be worthy of
chivalrous devotion. She was but sixteen when
they met, and it seems that after this encounter
he chose to regard her as his liege lady and
metaphorically to pin her favour in his bonnet.
After all there was nothing peculiar in that, for
Dante had deified Beatrice at fourteen, and other
troubadours had selected very young ladies to
whom to pay allegiance. Elated by the meeting
and its reverberations within himself, he breathed
the secret of his attachment into the ears of some
twenty confidantes, and continued for three
years to regard Williamina as the object of his
devotion, to write to her and to seek her out at
every rout and assembly. Then, for some reason
or another, he felt he must bring her out of the
dream-sphere to earth and proposed marriage.
The whole story is so pallid that one can hardly
bring oneself to believe that it was a flesh and
blood affair. There is nothing to show that
Williamina either regarded him in a romantic
light or as a possible husband, and some of Scott's
friends were apprehensive that he was subject to
some illusion as to the lady's attitude towards
him. After all, Miss Belsches was an heiress, and
whatever Walter and his parents may have
thought, there was never any question of a penniless young man being seriously regarded as a
suitor for her hand. The well-born banker
Sir William Forbes was a much more eligible
match than the son of a solicitor, even though he
was a third cousin ! When she married, Scott is
supposed to have addressed to her a set of verses

accusing her of falseness. The verses are futile enough, but even Miss Belsches with her large bovine eyes could not have been particularly pleased to hear that to Scott they shone through " a watery lustre." The story, although it is supposed to have furnished material for the romantic interludes in *Redgauntlet* and other novels, is of such very faint interest that we can afford to let it lie, and marvel how much Scott sentimentalized over it in his later age, just as we may also marvel at the way he belittled his hot, heady courtship of Charlotte when recalling his past to Lady Abercorn. But then he was more than half in love with the exquisite, enthusiastic lady whose superior attractions he could acknowledge but by inference.

We must for a moment return to Green Mantle, and record that the chief effect of his first courtship was to make him more careful of his clothes and hands. Before the attachment he used to wear corduroy breeches for so long at a time that they became shiny on the right side by the rubbing of the stick that marched in unison with the leg and close against it. His hands were rough and red and his nails uncared for. Through devotion to Williamina, whom at any time he might meet in any Edinburgh with-drawing room, he became almost a dandy, and adopted the deliberate method of dressing himself, which has so often been remarked on by those who have chronicled his habits.

At the time this transformation took place, Scott was a very powerful-looking fellow, six feet high, massive in the torso and with hard, muscular arms and legs. His hair was light brown, his complexion high-coloured, his forehead domed and unusually lofty, his nose fleshy. He gazed out upon the world from under eave-like eyebrows with smiling expression when animated, but in repose his face had a stolid look, the look Raeburn has preserved for us in the 1808 portrait, which Scott himself disliked and called " chowder-headed." His jaw was firm and his upper lip very long. Chantrey, when measuring him with the callipers, said that the distance between nose and mouth and mouth and chin tip were equal. He had facial tricks ; one of them Willie Clerk called the " hautboy player expression." His underlip was sucked into his mouth, the upper lip was drawn down over it and a sort of blowing took place. This curious habit was observable through life and it generally indicated concentration.

The verses provoked by Williamina's behaviour give no indication that Walter Scott was ever to achieve fame as a poet ; indeed he never knew an inner compulsion to lisp in numbers and was twenty-four years old before he felt the obligation to versify. Willie Clerk told Mr. Ticknor that Scott never could write verse as a young man. When they were both twenty-two they were in a boat together, and tried to make up verses. Walter finally gave up in despair saying, " well it's clear you and I were never made for poets ! "

His genius, it would seem, was always liberated by impact with something outside himself. The occasion that turned him into a rhymer was an evening party in Edinburgh, at which he was not even present. Professor and Mrs. Dugald Stewart entertained in honour of their house guest, Miss Laetitia Aikin. During the tea-drinking ceremony, Miss Aikin drew from her reticule a manuscript translation of *Lenore,* a ballad by Gottfried Bürger. It had been made by her friend, William Taylor of Norwich, the philosopher, whose name at least must have been known to those present. After a few preliminary words, Miss Aikin proceeded to proclaim the clattering stanzas. The onomatopœic lines :

> Tramp, tramp across the land they speed,
> Splash, splash along the sea,

were found specially stimulating, and the delight of the audience was in no way marred by the fact that no corresponding lines exist in the original poem. George Cranstoun, Mrs. Stewart's brother, repeated them to his friend, Walter Scott, who was excited to frenzy by them.

The lines jigged away in his head. This was the sort of poetry he could write himself. Indeed it was the sort of poetry that might almost be said to write itself. He must persuade Countess Brühl, bride of his kinsman, Hugh Scott of Harden, to obtain Bürger's poems for him immediately. When the volume arrived Scott worked himself up into a passionate state of excitement over translating them. It is not really fair to call *Lenore* a translation, it is an adaptation. " Judah's Wars " are substituted for the Battle of Prague, and Taylor's lines are used three times. Knowing little German, the rendering, must have required on Scott's part great labour and zeal ; it was on the whole a success, though it is easy to show that he did not get, owing to his defective ear, the eerie effect of Bürger's repeated vowel sounds :

> Lass sausen durch den Hagedorn
> Lass sausen, Kind, lass sausen
> Der Rappe scharrt ; es klirrt der Sporn
> Ich darf allhier nicht hausen.

> Let the wind howl through hawthorn bush
>> This night we must away ;
> The steed is wight, the spur is bright,
>> I cannot stay till day.

And again when the skeleton in chains is invited to dance at the wedding, a good deal is lost in the translation :

> Und das Gesindel, husch, husch, husch
>> Kam hinten nachgeprasselt
> Wie Wirbelwind am Haselbusch
>> Durch dürre Blätter rasselt.

> And hurry, hurry, clash, clash, clash,
>> The wasted form descends
> And fleet as wind through hazel bush
>> The wild career attends.

While adjusting his outlook to the morbid imagery of the German original, he dwelt on Mat Lewis' horrible ballad *The Brave Alonzo and the Fair Imogene* :

> The worms they crept in and the worms they crept out
> And sported his eyes and his temples about,
> While the spectre addressed Imogene.

Inspiring as these lines proved, he yet felt the need of contemplating some tangible emblems of mortality. From a surgeon he acquired a skull and cross-bones,[1] and hurrying back to his basement with these treasures under his arm was inspired to write :

> The eyes desert the naked skull,
>> The mouldering flesh the bone,
> Till Helen's lily arms entwine
>> A ghastly skeleton.

---

[1] In spite of the accepted story the bones were obviously acquired before the completion of the poem.

These lines were reminiscent of Lewis but they did not exist in Bürger's ballad. As for the bones they remained part of Scott's permanent equipment, though never used again for like purpose. Visitors to Abbotsford noticed that when he was feeling humorous, he wound his day tie about a skull which stood in his dressing-room.

Once the thirty-two stanzas had been turned into sixty-six quatrains—a work that must have taken not one night but many—he was impatient to read them aloud. Running round to the Cranstoun's house soon after dawn, he asked for his friend Miss Jane. She rushed downstairs, thinking some catastrophe must have happened but it was only Walter, wild eyed and excited, who wished to read her some verses. His earnestness as he intoned the concluding stanza :

> E'en when the heart's with anguish cleft
>   Revere the doom of Heaven,
> Her soul is from her body reft ;
>   Her spirit be forgiven.

quite took her breath away. She hardly knew what to say to this new Wattie—might she keep the manuscript ? and read it through quietly to herself ? It was most wonderfully impressive ! Certainly she might keep it, for he was just off to the country to see the lady of his attachment, and away the rhymer sped.

Later that day Miss Jane talked over the episode with Wattie's friend, Willie Erskine. Could they not get the poem printed and post it after him to the Belsches' house in Kincardine-shire ? It might help him with his apparently hopeless suit, one never knew. Miss Jane, who shortly afterwards married Count Purgstall, was fond of telling guests in her Styrian Castle that the printed poem reached Walter Scott just in time for him to read it aloud at tea and present it to the fair Williamina. If this is true, *Lenore* seems to have served to alienate rather than to attract affection.

A few months later *Lenore* and *Der Wilde Jäger*, which was even more of an adaption than *Lenore* and shows signs of boredom and haste, were published as *William and Helen* and *The Chase.* Though private friends were encouraging, the thin quarto did not sell, and its unbound sheets were eventually disposed of as waste. The really important thing to note about these trivial experiments is that they revealed to Scott his aptitude for what he called " pleasure in literary labour," and put the notion into his head of writing modern ballads such as *Glenfinlas* and *The Eve of St. John.*

At the height of his fame "Monk" Lewis came to Scotland to stay with the Argylls, and Scott made his acquaintance through lovely Lady Charlotte Campbell, the toast of the moment. This introduction, he says, altered " the Scottish ballad-maker's future prospects in life." For him it was a great moment when he dined with the diminutive novelist at an Edinburgh hotel. Though three years younger than his guest, Lewis was a Member of Parliament and a novelist of much renown—moreover except for Henry Mackenzie he was the first author Scott had met, though he had seen Burns for a moment as a boy. Lewis invited his guest to contribute to the anthology he was planning, and Scott enquired whether there might not be a public in London for his translation of *Goetz von Berlichingen.* Mr. Lewis opined that there might be and undertook to enquire. He then talked volubly of versification and the structure of poetry. When Scott submitted his ballads to him he received criticism and advice on his defective rhymes.

" I do not despair," wrote Lewis, " of convincing you that a bad rhyme is no rhyme at all ! . . . How can anyone think that ' soil ' rhymes with ' aisle ' ? ' Head ' with ' descried '? ' shower ' with ' roar ' ? ' within ' with ' strain ' ? . . . What can Mr. Scott have in his mind to perpetrate such line endings ? Then again he must point out that ' grace ' and ' bliss,' ' o'er ' and ' star,' ' steed ' and ' bed,' ' door ' and ' flower ' are not rhymes at all. However it is always possible for Mr. Scott to learn to do better and he may rely on his mentor for guidance."

Though always humble about his own work— and Scott remained throughout life the least conceited of men—he faintly resented Mr. Lewis' superior tone, though possibly he may have derived benefit from his instruction.

The discussion over Lewis' anthology made Scott realize that he had in hand the material for a far more interesting anthology of legitimate not bastard ballads. All his life he had been collecting them ; copies made in a childish hand testify to this. Ballads literally were always in his mind. This natural enthusiasm he suddenly realized could be turned to account, he could do a great deal better than Lewis now he had been shown the way. Again one notices that his genius was always liberated by something outside himself, and often by a chance contact.

A young man with Scott's enormous physical energy did not exercise himself on words alone, whether spoken or written. He was an enthusiastic volunteer in the Edinburgh troop of Midlothian cavalry.[1]   It was a glorious outlet for his tribal fancy for war—and for his rather noisy conviviality. What a relief from the pacing of the Parliament floor to mount black Lenore and gallop and wheel and turn and brandish a sabre. What he specially enjoyed was charging at a turnip on a pole and shouting : " Cut them down, the villains ! Cut them down ! " as he swung his weapon at the supposed Frenchman's head. What others enjoyed was seeing him fall off as he delivered a specially vicious blow. In after years he would canter along with his children at Abbotsford, brandishing a stick and shouting : " Schlachten, meine Kinder ! Schlachten ! " It was bad German, but very exhilarating to him, as was the war song he produced for the use of the Edinburgh Dragoons :

> To horse ! to horse ! the standard flies,
> The bugles sound the call ;
> The Gallic navy stems the seas,
> The voice of battle's on the breeze,
> Arouse ye, one and all !

The verses of this poem never caught on with the troop and never, as we can well guess, superseded " Hey ! Johnny Coape " and other popular songs. Scott's German period however was nearly at an end.

---

[1] Formed at the beginning of 1797, for not till this year were voluntary forces in Scotland exempted from being drawn on for drafts for the regular army.

D

CHAPTER III

COURTSHIP AND MARRIAGE

WITH his head full of Arthurian legends emanating from the Auchinleck manuscript, Walter Scott, accompanied by his brother John and his friend Adam Fergusson of the 73rd Foot, set out on horseback in August, 1797, for a tour in Cumberland. Before crossing the border they stayed with Dr. Adam Fergusson at Halyards in Peeblesshire. In proof of Scott's unusual suggestibility we must notice the effect produced on him during this visit by a dwarf recluse reputed to be something of a wizard. The young men entered his hut for a talk and they heard him doublelock the door behind them. Fixing his attention on Walter Scott, the dwarf seized his wrist, and asked earnestly, " Man, hae ye ony poo'er ? " Scott shook his head. Pointing to his big black cat the mannikin then said with a grin, " He has poo'er, ay he has poo'er." When the party got out into the light again Fergusson noticed that Walter Scott was ashy pale and trembling in every limb. The unsuccessful story of *The Black Dwarf* is supposed to have originated in this incident.

From Halyards the three young men made their way to the Valley of Ulpha, which was still the home of legends connected with King Arthur, and thence by way of Windermere and Ullswater to Penrith. Towards the end of the month they decided to go and see something of fashionable life at the Spa of Gilsland on the confines of Cumberland and Northumberland. On approaching their destination they passed a dark, smart-looking girl on horseback. As they walked their horses up the hill leading to the Wardrew House, Scott remarked on her foreign beauty and wondered where she came from. Gilsland was but sixteen miles from Carlisle, and since it had become a modish Spa it was patronized by the county people and the clerical society of the Cathedral town. Its hotels were well sited to obtain a wide view southwards over the country. The Shaws Hotel, a large and modern building, provided music and a ballroom, besides facilities for card-playing, and well kept gardens full of flowers. It stood on the summit of a leafy gorge through which the Irthing tumbled. The policies were neatly kept, and visitors could clamber down by graded paths to the river-level and turn down stream to the medicinal well, or up stream to enjoy the rocky and secluded loveliness of the glen. High up across the gorge the Roman Wall projected, and a well trodden path led from the village to its eminence. It was the habit of hotel guests to ascend the slope and enjoy the salubrious breezes which the more sheltered position of the hotels with their deep screen of trees denied them.

Wardrew House was the smallest of the three hotels accommodating perhaps a dozen guests, but it had the advantage over the Orchard House of being within a few steps of the Shaws Hotel, so that even ladies could walk there in the evening for the entertainments without wetting their feet. As Walter Scott entered the dining-room to take his place at the ordinary he recognized the dark beauty he had seen out riding. Bowing to the company he and his companions were shown to seats next the party of Canon Bird from Carlisle.   The Canon was accompanied by three ladies—Mrs. Bird, his cousin Miss Nicolson, granddaughter of the Bishop famous for his history of Cumberland, and the dark beauty Miss Carpenter.   As no introductions had been made the meal began in silence.   Mrs. Bird, who was out to enjoy polite society, jogged her husband to enquire if the newly-arrived gentlemen had heard anything of the rioting at Tranent, or failing that, did one of them perchance know her friend Major Ridell ?   Walter Scott rose eagerly to the fly and a pleasant talk ensued, so pleasant that on the conclusion of the meal Mrs. Bird invited the trio to drink tea in their private sitting-room.   Walter Scott could not take his eyes off Miss Carpenter ; she was the first French girl he had met, and seemed so lively and arch compared with the rather homely young women (Williamina always excepted) with whom he associated in Edinburgh. He must see more of this utterly charming person, perhaps Mrs. Bird would permit him to accompany them on their forthcoming picnic on the Wall ?   Guests at the hotels always included a drive in wagonette or four-in-hand to Birdoswald Crags, an attractive spot from which to investigate the Roman fortifications.   The excursion was easily arranged and Scott found himself escorting the ladies on their outing.   Stirred out of his usual solemnity by Miss Carpenter's kindling glance he showed himself an eager gallant, offering heather to the object of his devotion, accompanied by lines which still retain their spontaneity and charm.

Take these flowers which purple waving
    On the ruin'd rampart grew,
Where the sons of freedom braving
    Rome's Imperial standards flew.

    .   .   .   .   .

Warriors from the breach of danger
    Pluck no longer laurels there.
They but yield the passing stranger
    Wildflowers wreaths for beauty's hair.[1]

He was not Miss Carpenter's sole admirer ; there
were other young men seeking her favour, and
these he viewed with a jealous and disapproving
eye.   One was " a puny fop," another sported
"Hessian boot and pantaloon," and yet another
was " a wordy youth trained early for a statesman's part."

The big hotel was full of smart visitors.   The
suitor views a foreigner, with whom foreign
Charlotte is inclined to flirt, as " a walking
haberdashery of feathers, lace and fur."   Then
the fashionable rhymsters who " recited their
lays by waxen light," while " the *chasse-café*
glides around " were also suspect, the truth being
that he felt very provincial in these sophisticated
surroundings.   Shortly after he arrived there was
a ball at the Shaws Hotel, and for it he dressed
with a scrupulosity he had never practised before.
The barber shaved him smooth, pomatumed his
head, powdered it and arranged his locks so neatly
that he was almost unrecognizable.   After staring
in the glass at the figure he cut he decided to have
himself immortalized in a miniature.   His features looked enormous and rather plebeian when

[1] These lines were obviously written at Gilsland and local tradition
assigns Birdoswald as their place of origin.   Until Mr. Russell the
accountant gossiped to Lockhart thirty-five years later about other
flirtations taking place at this time, they were always assumed to be
addressed to Charlotte.   Mr. Russell's story fits in with nothing we know
of Scott and may be disregarded.

his hair was combed back, but the deep directoire
collar, high cravat and the one silver epaulette
on the sabre shoulder, to say nothing of the
scarlet coat with its blue facings and the white
doeskin breeches, made him look so smart and
well-groomed that mere plainness of feature did
not matter at all.   Walter's companions danced
with many girls, but he limped after one alone
and sat out with her as long as in those days was
considered decorous.   It was very diverting for
Miss Carpenter, she loved the bright uniform and
felt flattered by the complete surrender of the
big Scotsman to her charms.   Mrs. Bird and Miss
Nicolson began to discuss the situation taking
shape under their noses ; it was all very well for
Charlotte to flirt with this " hot heady young
man," but what did they know about him or his
antecedents ? Mrs. Bird thought it would be wise
to write to Edinburgh to make enquiries about
the creature ; after all Charlotte had come to
Gilsland to escape from an undesirable love
affair, they did not want to be involved in another
mistake.

Triermain Castle was but two miles from the
Spa, and Scott, who never could resist a ruin even
if he were seeing it for the tenth time, carried the
Bird party with him to investigate it.   On this
excursion he discovered that Miss Carpenter
loved with him :

> . . . to tread enchanted ground
> And thread like him the maze of fairy land
> Of golden battlements to view the gleam
> .   .   .   .   .
> Such lays she loves . . .

For her he began to make *The Bridal of Triermain*,
that story within a story of the Vaux bride from

the magic fortress. With delight he saw her hang upon his words as he told of Gynneth who had lain for five centuries invisible in the vanishing castle of Ulpha. Roughly, incompletely, passionately was this courtship poem drafted, to be polished, enlarged, completed and published anonymously sixteen years later.

It has been the Scottish convention to accept Walter Scott's calf-love for Miss Belsches as the great love of his life,—a convention which makes him out to be much less of a live man than he really was, and there has been a systematic effort among Scott's curiously sentimental admirers to orchestrate a tinkling tune as if it were a theme of deep passion. There has also been an assumption that Scott went to Cumberland heart-broken and that the designing Charlotte caught him on the rebound. Scott who always liked covering up his tracks gave support to this school of interpreters by talking of his " pieced " heart, and worse, when dazzled by Lady Abercorn's fascinations, almost denied that he had ever been in love with Charlotte at all. Anything more untrue can hardly be conceived but it is the conventional view. Lockhart knew better but he did not tell. He was perfectly aware of the inner history and significance of *The Bridal of Triermain*. He drops a hint—a hint no biographer has taken, but then possibly no biographer has gone to Shaws or read the poem over in the valley of the Irthing, or visited the site of Triermain or made contact with the Roman Wall at Birdoswald. Lockhart knew a great many things he never told, and if genius for selection is the hall-mark of the artist, Lockhart was a consummate artist and his great biography is a consummate work of art. Scott was very much a man and to make him out to be anything less is to misrepresent him entirely.

As we read *The Bridal of Triermain* we feel that Scott in this poem impersonated his characters, that he was Arthur blowing his bugle horn, the hero beguiled to dalliance, and Roland discovering and wedding the enchanted maiden. It is the poem of all others in which he reveals himself. In the rôle of story teller he feared no rival lover. He could take his time over *Triermain* and like Arthur let :

> The silence of that ancient place
> Sink on his heart.

Every day saw him more deeply in love. His one ambition was to be alone with Charlotte. Most of the hotel guests rose late after a night of gambling and dancing. Walter Scott lured Charlotte early to the gorge and conducted her by stepping stones across the river, or even lifted " the burthen dear," " the form so slender light and fine," over the water to a retreat where stood some mossy grey boulders conspicuous in their water-worn shape from the jagged fragments that strewed the river bed. The introductions to the cantos of the *Bridal* furnish us with the descriptions of their wanderings :

> And now we reach the favourite glade
> Paled in by copswood, cliff and stone,
> Where never harsher sounds invade
> To break affection's whispering tone
> Than the deep breeze that waves the shade.

He discerned in her the secret sorrow of the orphan, for :

> . . . quicker far is lover's ken
> Than the dull glance of common men,

" She for whom lords and barons sigh " has no
parents " to command " but " guardians whose
contending voice press each his individual choice."
Charlotte told him something of her story, of
her nationality, of her noble guardian and of her
Protestant baptism, of her brother in India ;
but Scott cared for none of these details. Whatever her history she was peerless and perfect.
As lovers will they shunned the regard of other
guests, especially at the hour of noon when
" the courtly inmates " of the grand hotel strayed
occasionally " beyond the gravelled maze " and
roamed to " kill the goodly day." Many times
he urged Miss Carpenter to marry him and make
an end of secret meetings :

> . . . Say how long
> We still must dread this trifling throng
> And stoop to hide with coward art
> The genuine feelings of the heart.

He tries to persuade, but she is silent when he
suggests " a golden annulet," " a landaulette
with four blood bays " and " a drive to the
Northern land : "

> I ask but one—a simple sound
> Within three little letters bound
> O, let the word be Yes !

Miss Carpenter was coy, and would not declare
herself during those lovely summer mornings
spent by what the crowd now calls " the Popping
Stone," the grey old glacial boulder standing
quietly by the seething stream. They show the
big rock from which the lover bent towards Charlotte as she perched on a lower rock listening to
her minstrel's tales. A ledge has been chipped
out of her seat by past generations of tourists

who believed it brought them luck in love to
secure a splinter to sleep on.

It is amusing to note that Scott, who invented
nothing but always allowed his imagination to
play with his recollections, and always made use
sooner or later of his experiences, used the name
Shaws as the home of Clara Mowbray in *St.
Ronan's Well* ; and it seems more than probable
that several of the guests, such as Lady Penelope
Penfeather and Sir Bingo and Lady Binks in
that novel, were caricatures of the persons he
observed at the Shaws Hotel. For him it was a
unique plunge into fashionable life.

In due course Mrs. Bird received an answer to
her enquiry regarding Mr. Scott's character.
He was reported to be a respectable young fellow
and likely to rise at the bar. By the same post
came another letter asking her what sort of a girl
it was who was going to take Wattie Scott. This
was perhaps a more difficult letter to reply to
than the enquirer guessed.

When Charlotte at length engaged herself to
Scott he was in a seventh heaven of delight, and
wrote to his mother that he was going to marry a
foreign orphan, " without relations and almost
without friends." . . . " Her guardian is, I should
say was, Lord Downshire to whom I must write
for his consent."

It was a surprising kind of announcement to be
received at the family breakfast table. Wattie
had obviously been caught by a designing young
female and a foreigner too. They made up their
minds to disapprove, and wrote at once to this
effect. On receiving their letter Walter wrote to
his aunt Christian Rutherford, telling of his
parents' hasty prejudging of his case and giving
further details of his capture. He explained that

Charlotte was " a very amiable young woman
. . . born in France—her parents were of English
extraction—the name Carpenter. She was left
an orphan early in life and educated in England
. . . Miss Carpenter is of age but as she lies
under great obligations to the Marquess of
Downshire, who was her guardian, she cannot take
a step of such importance without his consent
. . . though born in France, she has the sentiments and manners of an Englishwoman, and
does not like to be thought otherwise. A very
slight tinge in her pronunciation is all which
marks the foreigner. . . . She was baptized and
educated a Protestant of the Church of England."

This letter, though it elucidated nothing, at
least relieved the family fear that he was engaged
to a Catholic.

After incising his name on a pane of glass in
the Birds' sitting-room at Wardrew, Scott returned to Scotland at the end of September,
triumphantly happy that he had at length persuaded his exquisite sylph to marry him, and
caring less than nothing about anything so
mundane as parentage or dowry. Immediately
he found himself in difficulties, for it was awkward
not to be able to reply to all the questions with
which his family bombarded him. What was
Charlotte's nationality? What was her father's
profession? What was her brother's position in
Madras? How old was she? Why was the Marquis of Downshire her guardian? Why did she
live in England? His relations were not easy to
satisfy, and they indicated that it was stupid of
Walter not to have found out all that parents
must wish to know before welcoming a daughter-
in-law into their house. Mr. Scott specially
deplored the absence of a family tree and the

precarious nature of the girl's income, which was
apparently dependent on her brother remaining
a bachelor.

Charlotte had no parallel difficulties. She
had written to her guardian explaining that
Walter Scott was of good family and that she
desired Lord Downshire's consent to her marriage
with him. In the first days of October " the
very best man on this earth " informed her that
he would be happy to hear from Walter Scott.
She advised her suitor to write to the Marquis
at once to ask for her hand.[1] He did so in the
deferential style of his day. Lord Downshire
intimated that he did not consider the letter " an
intrusion," and that Miss Carpenter, though of
age, having referred the subject to him, he feels
bound as " her friend and guardian to try to
secure her happiness . . . and to prevent her
being left destitute. . . . Her good sense and
good education are her chief fortune ; therefore
in the worldly way of talking she is not entitled to
much. Her brother who was also left in my care
at an early period is excessively fond of her . . .
he is doing very well in India where I sent
him some years ago. . . . I am endeavouring to
secure the happiness and welfare of an estimable
young woman . . . for whom I have the highest
regard, esteem and respect."

The letter pleased the lover as it raised no
objections to the marriage. He replied to it in
terms which struck his correspondent as " manly,
honourable, candid and full of good sense." " I

[1] On October 8th, Scott writing to Shortreed states that he has
received a letter from Lord Downshire couched " in the most flattering
terms," giving his consent to his marriage with his ward. Lockhart
does not print this letter which must have been the missive addressed
to Charlotte and forwarded by her to Walter. Another letter printed
by Lockhart, dated October 15th, is obviously the first indited by
Lord Downshire to the pretendant.

think Miss Carpenter's friends," wrote Lord
Downshire, " cannot in any way object to the
union you propose. Its taking place when or
where will depend upon herself . . . any pro-
vision that may be given to her by her brother
you will have settled upon her and her children."
Thus did the noble guardian dissociate himself
from any responsibility for his ward. His feelings
may have been kinder than he allowed them to
appear for though he did not offer to give Charlotte away he did send her a Cashmere shawl.

Harassed by family cross-examination Walter
wrote to his " lovely friend " to say that though
the matter was of little consequence to him, he
felt awkward at not being able to answer precisely
on matters of fact connected with her family.
Charlotte's vagueness is inexplicable unless she
had something to conceal and we find her telling
Scott[1] that she is waiting for Lord Downshire
to write before giving a full answer " to your
very proper enquiries about my family." " Miss
Nicolson says that when she did offer to give you
some information you refused it—and advises
me *now* to wait for Lord D's letter." Charlotte[2]
was provoked into scolding Scott for suggesting
that her " silence gives an air of mystery " to her
story.

" I have no reason that can detain me in ac-
quainting you that my father and mother were
French, of the name of Charpentier, he had a
place under government ; their residence was at
Lyons, where you would find on enquiries that
they lived in good repute and in *very good style*.
I had the misfortune of losing my father before I
could know the value of such a parent. At his
death we were left to the care of Lord D., who

[1] October 22nd.   [2] October 25th.

was his very great friend ; and very soon after I had the affliction of losing my mother. Our taking the name of Carpenter was on my brother's going to India, to prevent any little difficulties that might have occurred. Lord D. could have given you every information, as he has been acquainted with all my family."

There was nothing in this narrative letter to encourage Mr. and Mrs. Scott to assume that they were getting a normally bred daughter-in-law. They continued to worry, and the more they worried the more anxious Scott became to set up a house of his own and live his private life. The controversy must in the face of an accomplished fact be set at rest. Charlotte's letters reflect some of his troubles and apprehensions. " What reason have you for so many fears you express ? . . . they perhaps don't like me being French ? . . . at your father's age prejudices are not easily overcome. . . . If he has an objection to my being French, I excuse him with all my heart, as I don't love them myself."

When Walter left Gilsland Charlotte had threatened to seclude herself on the sea coast at Allonby with Miss Nicolson, but this did not come off, and he learnt that his orphan angel had retreated on Carlisle to enjoy the autumn season of assembly meetings and hunt balls. Fearful of fresh rivals he caused a miniature in uniform to be executed and despatched it to her by express for had she not told him she " adored the stylish cavalry " ? In return a lock of hair reached him and a mysteriously worded note alludes to more hair having been cut off and sent to London " for another purpose." It was the age of hair chains, lockets, rings and miniatures.

The small likeness painted of Charlotte at this

time shows a young woman in a pale pink
decolletée satin dress. The slightly powdered
hair is piled on top of her head while ringlets
curl on her neck. She is quite the modish
grande dame. This portrait was evidently done
by some local English artist and probably at
Carlisle. It is in sharp contrast to another
miniature made of her as a much younger girl,
in which large, dark, child-like eyes look at one
from a white small face, and a tiny figure is
depicted in a high waisted organdie frock with
blue vest and ribbons. The hair is grey and
frizzed and the artist obviously French. These
miniatures and an oil-painting made by Saxon in
1805 are all we have to go on in making our own
picture of Charlotte. In the oil-painting we see a
dark woman of almost typically French expression
and intelligence and from it we surmise that as a
girl Miss Carpenter could not have been really
pretty, though she had an engaging lively expression, an everchanging face, hair so dark as to look
black by candle-light, a pale complexion, sloe-like
eyes and a little figure, very slight and " fay-like."
Scott said to his friend Patrick Murray a day or
two before he was married, " her figure is not very
frappant, a smart looking little girl with dark
brown hair would probably be her portrait if
drawn by an indifferent hand." Hogg who was
told by Walter Scott that Charlotte was " dark
as a blackberry " was astonished to be introduced
to " one of the most beautiful and handsome
creatures " he had ever seen " . . . a brunette
certainly " with " raven hair and large black eyes,"
but in his estimation " a perfect beauty." She
was very French in manner, always spoke with
a noticeable accent, had no aspirates, and though
at one time an industrious copyist of her husband's

poems, loathed writing letters in English, was terrified of thunder and of *ennui* and very given to quizzing. Scott, who was rather a heavy-weight as a wooer, was chaffed for making sentimental allusions to the place where his bones were to lie, and for trying to envisage all the troubles they might have to meet. He really could be very depressing at times, but then young men in love may be anything from mutes to buffoons. She laughed at him and his grave-yard letter and he tried to play up to her moods. " I admire above all things your laughing philosophy and shall certainly be your pupil in learning to take a gay view of human life." He even ventured to versify on the subject of *ennui*.

Once Lord Downshire had signified that he raised no objection to the wedding, Scott hastened to the Birds' house at Carlisle to persuade Charlotte to marry him forthwith, but she put him off with, " My dear Sir, No ! You must not think of it this great while ! " the real truth being that she had no money to purchase a trousseau and was waiting for her brother's remittance from India. Two months later on Christmas Eve, 1797, the wedding took place in Carlisle Cathedral, no Scott witnessed it, but Canon Bird and Miss Nicolson appended their signatures,[1] and on a cold winter afternoon the little French girl and the big Borderer made their way northwards in a postchaise. The bride expected her lover to go

[1] " 1797. Walter Scott of the parish of St. Andrews in Edinburgh Esqr Bachelor and Margaret Charlotte Carpenter of this parish Single woman were married in this church by License this twenty-fourth day of December in the year one thousand, seven hundred and ninety-seven

" This marriage was solemnized between us
{ Walter Scott
M. Charlotte Scott late Carpenter by me J. Brown."

" In the presence of
{ Jane Nicolson
John Bird."

on with his story telling.   He refused for a reason
he gave later, in *The Bridal of Triermain* :

> . . . loveliest when thou first didst pray
> Continuance of the knightly lay,
> Was it not on the happy day
>   That made thy hand mine own ?
> When dizzied with mine ecstasy,
> Nought past or present or to be,
> Could I or think on, hear, or see,
>   Save, Lucy, thee alone.
> A giddy draught my rapture was
> As ever chemist's magic gas.

Inclined to be insistent and then irritated by
Scott's protracted silence and endearments :

> When twice you pray'd I would again
> Resume the legendary strain
> Of the bold Knight of Triermain.
> At length a peevish vow you swore,
> That you would sue to me no more,
> Until the minstrel fit drew near,
> And made me prize a listening ear.

In after years the poem was finished during
blissful married days at Lasswade and at Ashestiel
when he could assure her :

> . . . these flowers,
> That wailing brook, these lovely bowers,
>   Are, Lucy, all our own
> And since thine Arthur called thee wife,
> Such seems the prospect of his life,
> A lovely path on-winding still,
> By gurgling brook and sloping hill.
> 'Tis true that mortals cannot tell
> What waits them in the distant dell ;
> But be it hap or be it harm,
> We tread the pathway arm in arm.

During the early days of marriage, there was
much talk about Charlotte, since lack of

E

information as to her antecedents had to be supplemented by conjecture. James Hogg gave voice to some of the gossip he heard, and suggested that Walter Scott's children might be allied to the peerage. Lockhart gives an account of Miss Carpenter's origin with which every one is familiar ; this is but another aspect of the tattle of the time,though possibly it was the story favoured by Walter Scott himself. Lockhart states that Jean François Charpentier, Charlotte's father, was a respectable loyalist in Lyons who had foreseen the Revolution and hedged against it by consigning his wife, children and fortune to England to the care of a kind hearted Irish nobleman who had allowed him to invest his savings in a mortgage on his estate. An odd and flimsy story which carried no conviction to the people of his day, and which subsequent researches have proved to be untrue.

The only facts known to the people of Edinburgh when the young couple first made their appearance, were that Mrs. Scott was a foreigner who had been protected in some way by a Marquis and companioned by a Miss Nicolson, whose salary the Marquis presumably paid. How Lord Downshire came into the picture nobody could explain. It is possible that Scott himself did not know everything. For example, if he had known his wife's exact age, he could quite easily have stopped some of the gossip by stating that Lord Downshire was but seventeen years older than Charlotte, who was born at Lyons ten months after her parents' marriage, and that as Lord Hillsborough he had gone abroad for the first time in his twenty-second year, that is when Charlotte was five years old. When Lady Scott died Sir Walter did not cause

her exact age to be graven on the coffin plate and
at Gilsland he seems to have looked upon her as
very much younger than himself, though in fact
she was nine months older. Chambers' story
may of course be true that Lord Hillsborough
ran away with Madame Charpentier, and that
Monsieur Charpentier forthwith repudiated his
children, and that the lover made himself responsible for them. Scott in writing to Lockhart
in 1827 said that Miss Jane Nicolson, "a woman of
great cleverness and at one time of great personal
beauty came from France with Madame Charpentier and her children," but this is less likely
than that she came over with the Dumergues in
1785. Scott added that he had never enquired
into his wife's family history. "There was
I believe domestic distress betwixt Madame
Charpentier and her husband—at least I have
conjectured so much." From this letter it would
appear that Charlotte told him nothing and that
he was either too kind to probe into her story,
or knew too much to ask questions.

As far as can be ascertained the real facts are as
follows : Charlotte was the daughter of French
parents, who were married in Paris in February,
1770. She was born and baptized in Lyons in
December, 1770. The next definite thing we
learn about her is that she was re-baptized in
May, 1787, at St. George's, Hanover Square, in
company with her brother John David and her
friend Sophie Dumergue the daughter of the
King's surgeon-dentist Mr. Charles Dumergue.
Mr. Dumergue had come to England in 1785,
heartbroken at the elopement of his wife, and
bringing with him a letter of recommendation
from Louis XVI to George III. It is possible,
and seems probable, that the unfaithful Madame

Dumergue was a sister of the flighty Madame Charpentier, but as Mr. Dumergue never mentioned his wife's name or allowed his family to admit her existence there is no proof of this. As far as Mr. Dumergue was concerned, she had never lived. It seems clear that he brought little Charlotte Charpentier over from Paris at the same time as his own daughter. With him also appeared Miss Sarah Nicolson, an English lady who acted as his housekeeper in London. From Scott we learn that Miss Jane Nicolson, her sister, had in 1797 been in charge of Charlotte for " many years." Miss Jane also appears to have come with the party to England and to have received a salary for chaperoning Charlotte who only lived part of the year in Piccadilly. The presumption is that this salary was paid by Charlotte's guardian Lord Downshire, but there is no certainty of this as there may have been some family arrangement into which Canon and Mrs. Bird (who were cousins of the Nicolsons and old friends of Lord Downshire) may have entered. Charlotte's letters however give one to understand that she was in some measure dependent on her " noble friend." Between the years 1787, the date of her re-baptism, and 1797, the date of her marriage, we know nothing whatever about her ; and yet from the affectionate way she spoke of Lord Downshire to Scott she must have been constantly in his company.

A miniature of Monsieur Charpentier exists at Abbotsford. It is that of a good-looking man in a red coat and powdered hair. As conductor of an Academy of Equitation at Lyons he was much in contact with young Englishmen who came there for instruction and probably Lord Hillsborough was recommended to him by Canon Bird. Sir

Walter seems to have been vague about Monsieur Charpentier : when he asked Fenimore Cooper to institute a search at Lyons for Lady Scott's birth certificate[1] he also enquired for the death certificate of Charlotte's father and did not appear to know whether his demise had taken place before or after 1776. Madame Charpentier who had had her children baptized as Catholics in Lyons must be assumed either to have died or to have been living apart from her family in 1787 the year in which they became Protestants. We have Charlotte's own statement that she lost her mother very shortly after her father's death and that he died when she was too young to appreciate a father, a curious tale to tell when he is registered as being still in charge of his Academy in 1785. Nothing that Charlotte said at this time can be relied upon but no doubt more information will one day come to light. The few dates cited are not much to go on if one wants to reconstruct a person's life, and when we think that the people of Scott's day had no facts at all presented to them except the indisputable one of Charlotte's existence, French accent and foreign ways, is it any wonder that the town gossiped at the time, as posterity still gossips, of illegitimacy and foreign mistresses ?

Two years after marriage Walter Scott was introduced to Lord Downshire at the Dumergues' house in Piccadilly West and found him charming. He promised to be godfather to their expected child —an undertaking he fulfilled some months later.[2]

[1] May, 1828.
[2] " 24to die Octobris 1799.—Margareta C. Scott, filium apud Edinburgum edidit. 15o Novembris 1799, in Ecclesiam Christianam recepta fuit per baptismum dicta filia nomenque eni adjectum Carlotta Sophia, per virum reverendum Danielem Sandford ; sponsoribus praenobile Arthuro Marchione de Downshire, Sophia Dumergue, et Anna Rutherford matre mea."—Extract from Sir Walter Scott's family Bible.

In considering Charlotte and her ways we must not forget that she was an alien in Scotland and probably never cared much for her adopted country and people. It is to be observed that she showed up in quite a different light when she had foreigners to entertain, and that she read French books and was an admirer of Charles Nodier's works.

A great deal had been surmised about this marriage ; it began with much tenderness, as we see from the manner in which the young parents shared their grief over the death of their first baby boy, and the way in which the devoted husband refused invitations when the second was on its way. In declining to go on some jaunt he says : " You must be married yourself before you can conceive in the slightest degree the interest one takes in an event which is likely to perpetuate his memory *tel qui soit* (*sic*)." For years they got on extremely well, were gay and happy enough and delighted in their children ; and even when the glamour had worn off they remained good friends. It seems that Scott was proud of her in the beginning, that she was all elegance and grace to him until the unlucky day when he took her to stay at Stanmore Priory and saw what smart ladies of the great world were like. In experiencing the heady flattery of Lady Abercorn he lost his simple faith that Charlotte embodied the acme of all perfections. In speculating about their ultimate relations we must remember that Scott never made the love interest paramount in his novels, it was always subordinated to the general trend and setting of his book, and he never made love the paramount interest of his life—indeed like many men, after a few years he took his wife as much as a matter of course as the furniture in his house. Charlotte, so far as we can see, looked after him beautifully, cut his untidy hair, saw that his fire did not go out when he was writing, fussed over him generally, provided good food, ran the house or rather the houses very comfortably and extravagantly and effaced herself. Quite naturally she got bored with the hordes of strangers attracted by her husband's fame and with the heavy entertaining which she was compelled to undertake.

When they settled into their first home at South Castle Street they were fêted and asked to parties at every legal house. The Yeomanry dinners, however, were greatly preferred by Charlotte to all other feasts, for every guest wore uniform and all were gay and young, and toasted the bride the first time she appeared at any of their tables. She enjoyed herself hugely and her husband rejoiced in her success. As she was fond of the theatre, Scott took her to every new play. Then since she proved the best lady whip in Edinburgh he procured for her a low phaeton from London which she drove gallantly into Liddesdale over tracks so rough that Scott wondered they did not upset. With this good-humoured, gay young woman Scott idled away the first idyllic summers at Lasswade.

CHAPTER IV

BALLAD MAKING AND BALLAD TAKING

BALLADS as we know had for years formed the undertone of Scott's life, the pulsating rhythm of his advance. Though the little boy who had stumped shouting up and down the paths at Smailholm had disappeared, a powerful young man, who struck his stick on Edinburgh pavements to a hidden air had taken his place. Friends said that this young man had enough rhymes in his head to fill two or three entire days with recitations, but then his memory was unusually capacious. One dark night on the banks of the Tweed, James Hogg was astonished to hear the eighty-eight stanzas of his *Gilmanscleugh* repeated without halt. It had never been printed, and Scott, as far as he knew, could have heard it but once. This faculty enabled him to introduce the unpublished *Christabel* to Byron and repeat to Campbell his *Turkish Lady*. When George Ticknor fresh from Spain visited him and talked of Spanish ballads and metrical romances Scott repeated an English translation of *The Cid*. The visitor asked for a copy. Scott said he had never seen one but that it had been made by Hookham Frere who had read it aloud to him.

His memory was not so tenacious of short lyric poems or sonnets. A moral sequence or else a bony structure of tradition or history had to be discernible within a poem for it to leave a deep impression on him or even make

72

an appeal. From his paramount interest, the romance of history, Scott was not easily shaken, and the permanence of his interest is one of the satisfactory things about him. In his day ballad collecting was a kind of romantic sport; it had not yet been reduced to a science. No one at that time knew how many there were, but now anyone who takes the trouble may learn that but three hundred and five genuine English and Scottish ballads exist, and that all but five of them have more than one version. One, indeed has twenty-seven.[1] Further we may learn that but eleven ballads are extant in manuscript older than the seventeenth century, and that the Percy Folio, on which the Bishop based his *Reliques*, was written in a hand of about 1650. Percy found it under a bureau in a country house; and in Scott's day it was permissible to believe that one might at any moment light on other manuscripts in other country houses and it was certain that one could take down ballads that had never been transcribed before from the lips of the old.

We have seen how Scott devoured the *Reliques*, and we know that as a lad he took from Mrs. Irving, mother of his friend John Irving, all the verses she could recite to him. Then with Short-reed he had gathered ballads from shepherds and old women in Liddesdale, Ettrick, and other districts. His meeting with " Monk " Lewis had determined him to publish some of them, and he told James Ballantyne[2] that he thought he " could with a little trouble put together such a selection as might make a neat little volume to sell for four or five shillings." The size of the book

[1] *The Twa Sisters.* See *The English and Scottish Popular Ballads,* by Professor Child, Boston, 1882-98.
[2] In 1798.

was eventually governed by his own copious introduction and notes and *Minstrelsy of the Scottish Border* was finally published in two volumes in London in 1802.

A great deal has been written about the way in which Scott edited ballads. People of scholarly conscience have disapproved of the free manner with which he treated his material. The explanation is that he loved his material more than he loved accuracy of transcription. His familiarity with the various versions of one song gave him the feeling that a ballad was a fluid thing—and might be dealt with freely by an editor. He felt that people who read ballads for enjoyment do not want to be confronted with the oldest or most accurate, but merely with the most satisfactory version. He renovated, restored, replaced one word by another, until he considered he had a version rendering the spirit if not the letter of the ballad.

Scott's methods are really unassailable, because he was Scott and felt the honour and beauty of being in his own way a disciple of Homer. "*Doch Homeride zu seyn, auch nur als letzter, ist schön.*" He speaks of himself to the Duchess of Buccleuch as "the only minstrel of the clan," and in his heart was a moss-trooping bard ready to celebrate the exploits of his kinsmen. Nothing else explains *Kinmont Willie*, which is suspected of being mainly his work. It is a recasting of one of the best ballads known—*Jock o' the Side*—and has been adapted to celebrate a deed of Bold Buccleuch.[1] It is so good that it emphasizes the badness of other efforts, the almost universal failure of the ballad maker.

[1] It has been suggested that Scott changed this ballad enough to make Scotts take the place of prominence that had been held by the Elliots in the original form of the story.—*Edinburgh Review*, October, 1906.

To Scott it was a positive duty to refurbish a theme connected with clan or country. Not only *Kinmont Willie*, but *Jamie Telfer* and *Otterbourne* testify to this. In ballad-editing circles Ritson[1] alone stood for accuracy. Percy was shown to have been a manipulator when his book was compared with the original folio. Scott claims to have observed a " more strict fidelity " to his originals than Percy ; but, as James Hogg would say, " Sure no man will think an old song the worse for being somewhat harmonious ! " We know that Scott called tradition " a sort of perverted alchemy which converts gold into lead."[2] It is not impossible that in altering whole lines in old ballads and writing new ones Scott may have thought he was turning lead into gold. He held, as we know, to the minstrel origin of the ballad, for to him a song implied a singer : " All that is abstractedly poetical, all that is above the comprehension of the merest peasant is apt to escape in frequent repetition ; and the *lacunae* thus created are filled up either by lines from other ditties or from the mother wit of the reciter or singer. The injury in either case is obvious and irreparable." He considered that Burns had a genius for patching up old Scottish songs, and it is to be inferred that Scott thought ballads were only getting their right due when a skilful hand touched them up and restored to them their original lustre. Scott was a master of ballad phraseology, but could hardly ever resist the impulse to improve rhythm, rhyme

[1] Author of *Pieces of Ancient Popular Poetry from authentic MSS. and Old Printed Copies* (1791), *Ancient Songs from the Time of Henry III to the Restoration* (1792), *Scottish Songs with Genuine Music* (1793), *Ancient English Metrical Romances* (1802).

[2] Review of Gromek's *Reliques of Burns*, *Quarterly Review*, February, 1909.

and often sense. He thought his versions truer than those he gathered from recitation.[1] He sometimes made what he called " conjectural emendations." In the *Dowie Dens of Yarrow*[2] he altered twenty-eight of sixty-eight lines. For example, he turned :

> A better rose will never spring
> Than him I've lost on Yarrow.

to :

> A fairer rose did never bloom
> Than now lies cropp'd on Yarrow.

and again he substituted for :

> As he gaed up yon high, high hill,

the line :

> As he gaed up the Tennies bank,

presumably because Tennies was a farm belonging to Buccleuch and therefore worthy of a place in epic poetry. Lockhart gives him just the sort of praise that would have pleased him, " From among a hundred corruptions he seized with instinctive tact the primitive diction and imagery."

Scott prided himself on an infallible sense for distinguishing a genuine from a spurious ballad. " I scarce know anything so easily discovered as the piecing and patching of an old ballad ; the darns in a silk stocking are not more manifest."[3] Yet an antiquary acquaintance, Robert Surtees of Mainsforth,[4] was able to palm off on him three ballads of his own[5] as ancient. Scott included them in the *Minstrelsy* and Surtees never dared confess his imposition.

[1] Out of two versions of *Earl Richard* he selected the best verses from both.

[2] Henderson's edition of *Minstrelsy of the Scottish Border*, Vol. III, p. 173.

[3] C. K. Sharpe, Vol. II, p. 424.

[4] Noted for *History of Durham*, 1816-40. He did not meet Scott till 1802.

[5] *Lord Ewrie, The Death of Featherstonhaugh, Barthram's Dirge.*

The work of preparing the ballads for the press was enthralling to Scott. It seemed to canalize all his ardours of adolescence, and he experienced the unction of delight in fingering the proofs as they issued from the press of James Ballantyne. In the *Introduction* he dealt with the life of the people among whom such poetry flourished; but remembering the fate of Bishop Percy at the hands of Ritson he was careful to explain that the Editor did not intend " to enter upon a history of Border Poetry; a subject of great difficulty and which the extent of his information does not as yet permit him to engage in." The admirable *Remarks on Popular Poetry*, which now preface the *Minstrelsy*, were not written till thirty years later, when his judgment was surer and his fame established.

Scott's main consultants in the preliminary venture were Ritson, Heber, the aged Percy and a new young friend, John Leyden, who helped him considerably with the notes. It was not until the Ballads were set up at the Ballantyne press that fresh enthusiasts were drawn into the Scott orbit. And then Mr. Andrew Mercer, a Selkirk man in Edinburgh, asked his friend Willie Laidlaw to look out for ballads, and Laidlaw passed the request on to a man who had once been his father's shepherd, James Hogg. It is improbable that Scott and Hogg met before June, 1802, and it is certain that neither Hogg nor Laidlaw had any finger in the first edition of the *Minstrelsy*, though in the second they may have influenced some alterations. Hogg talks of a summer day in 1801 (which must be meant for 1802 since he had already seen the first volume of the *Minstrelsy*) and of copying a number of ballads from his mother's chanting and sending them to Scott preparatory to the publication of a third volume. This was the beginning of their friendship, though they were not to meet for some months.

Minstrelsy of the Scottish Border had been beautifully printed by James Ballantyne at Kelso. Eight hundred copies were sold,[1] but as the publishers, Cadell and Davis of London, refused to bring out a second edition, Longman was able to buy the copyright from them for £500. Scott made about £80 out of the first edition. The money was nothing, but the fame accruing to the editor was everything. George Ellis, Ritson, Miss Seward, the Duke of Roxburghe, himself a collector of ballads, and Lord Spencer wrote to compliment him. James Hogg alone took up his pen to criticize Scott for departing from some of the old traditions. Only those who have suddenly woken up to find that they have struck sympathetic echoes in unknown hearts realize what this appreciation meant to the inexperienced editor. Above all it convinced Scott that the chief object of his life must be literature.

In the summer following the publication of the *Minstrelsy*, Scott and Leyden set out to visit Laidlaw, Hogg and, above all, Hogg's mother, who, as the shepherd said, was " a living miscellany of old songs."[2] Laidlaw had told Scott of a ballad *Auld Maitland*, which the shepherd's grandfather could repeat. When the collectors reached Blackhouse, Laidlaw flourished a written copy of the ballad in Scott's face. Scott read it aloud. Leyden got fearfully worked up, paced the room, and clapped his hands, while the Sheriff

[1] Fifty of which were on large paper embellished with a drawing of Hermitage Castle by Scott and improved by W. Clerk.
[2] *Familiar Letters*, Vol. I, p. 12.

keeping his feelings under control, read with ever greater emphasis and burr.

Another visit to Blackhouse followed shortly after, when Laidlaw acted as guide to Ettrick. They visited James Hogg in his thatched cottage, an occasion celebrated by the shepherd in verse. The authenticity of *Auld Maitland* and of the *Border Widow* have been questioned, but the effect they had on Scott at that time was over-powering :

> Scarce grew thy lurking dread the less
> Till she the ancient minstreless,
> With fervid voice and kindling eye,
> And withered arms waving on high,
> Sang forth these words in eldritch shriek,
> While tears stood on thy nutbrown cheek :
>   Na, we are none o' the lads o' Frence,
>   Nor e'er pretend to be ;
>   We be three lads of fair Scotland
>   Auld Maitland's sons, a' three !
> Thy fist made all the table ring ;
> " By ——, sir, but that is the thing ! "

Mrs. Hogg did not mince matters with Scott. " There were never ane o' my sangs prentit till ye prentit them yoursel', an' ye hae spoilt them awte-gither. They were made for singing and no' for reading ; but ye hae broken the charm now, an' they'll never be sung mair. An' the worst thing of a', they're nouther right spelled nor right setten down."

The old lady spoke sense ; culture kills the ballad. Once these wild flowers are gathered to the *hortus siccus* of the antiquary they cease to bloom on their native soil.

One of the effects of reading ballads was to infect people with the idea that they could write them. Their specious air of simplicity led many

people to put pen to paper. It was suggested to
Scott from various quarters that he might perhaps
edit a collection of modern ballads and bring it
out as a third volume of the *Minstrelsy*. Amused
by the idea he decided to carry it out. As soon
as his intention was known ballads rushed like
fish into his net. Some of the contributors were
more distinguished than their verses. Seeing
this, the Ballantynes urged him to be inclusive
rather than exclusive in his selection : it was
better business. The consequence was that some
pure rubbish was interspersed among the better
compositions. Mat Lewis weighed in with *Sir
Agilthorn*, a ballad of a sleekly sentimental sort.
The knight takes leave of his lady before spurring
off to Flodden Field in these words :

> Flow, flow, my tears, unbounded gush !
> Rise, rise, my sobs, I set ye free ;
> Bleed, bleed, my heart ! I need not blush
> To own that life is dear to me.

As he does not return, his lady sends her little
foot-page to seek him ; he comes back, with a
bloody scarf ; the lady goes to dig her knight's
grave and dies upon his breast.

It is amusing to read Scott's anonymous opinion
of the spurious ballad as " the last refuge of those
who can do nothing better in the shape of verse,
and that a man of genius should disdain to invade
the province of those dawdling rhymsters."[1]
His experience in dealing with the rhymes sent
to him seems to have soured his natural
sweetness.

The ballad mania was almost like a contagion,
such unexpected people caught it. In peaceful
Lichfield Anna Seward felt the fever, and sat

[1] *Edinburgh Review*, October, 1806.

down to write *Rich Auld Willie's Farewell*;
the Willie in question being a freebooter taken by
the English and condemned to be executed.
The authoress takes language from both sides of
the Border; a glossary is necessary to make her
lines intelligible.

> Farewell my sheep that sprattle on
>   In a lang line sae braw;
> Or lie on yon cauld cliffs aboon
>   Like late left latch o' snaw!
>
> .   .   .   .   .
>
> Farewell my brook that wimplin rins
>   My clattering brig o' yew,
> My scaly tribes wi' gowden fins
>   Sae nimbly flickering through!
>
> .   .   .   .   .
>
> Farewell my winsome wife sae gay!
>   Fu' fain frae hame to gang,
> Wi' spunky lads to geck and play
>   The flowery haughs among!

Scott complimented her in his letter of thanks by
saying it was hard to realize that she came from
the wrong side of the Border.

Mr. Morritt of Rokeby contributed a Highland
tale, *The Curse of Moy*; it was in the fashionable
tone of gloom:

> The raven screamed and a slogan yell
>   Burst from Glen Iran's sable wood.
> They heard in the gale a bugle swell
>   They saw in the shade a man of blood.

The Reverend Dr. Jamieson, a specialist on
Danish ballads, sent in *The Water Kelpie*. C. K.
Sharpe wrote two ballads and so did Leyden.
Colin Mackenzie of Portmore sent a contribution,
and the Reverend John Marriott (of whom Scott
became fond enough later to address to him one

F

of the introductory epistles in *Marmion*) composed *Archie Armstrong's Aith* and *The Feast of Spurs*. The latter ballad was after Scott's heart, for it was a tale of Wat of Harden and his wife the Flower of Yarrow When the last bullock was killed and devoured, it was the custom of this lady to place on the table a covered dish containing a pair of spurs, a hint to the riders that they must foray for their next meal. These are the words of Harden to his followers, who are to collect cattle from the Southron.

> Intull your saddles scour away
> And ranshackle the Southronie.
>
> Let ilka ane his knapsack lace
> Let ilka ane his steel jack brace ;
> And Deil bless him that shall disgrace
>
> Walter o' Harden's liverie !

Scott himself was the biggest contributor. *Thomas the Rhymer*[1] ; *Glenfinlas* ; the *Eve of St. John* ; *Cadyow Castle*, and *The Gray Brother* were all from his pen. There was no poem in the three volumes which did not do honour to Scotland, and the collection was dedicated, in words not his own, to the soil from which Scott sprang.

> To thee, for whom my purest raptures flow,
> Kneeling with filial homage I devote
> My life, my strength, my first and latest song.

[1] The first part was by Thomas the Rhymer ; the second and third by Scott.

CHAPTER V

OLD MEN'S SHOES

NO one realized more clearly than Scott himself that apart from the peculiar sensibility that made him the spokesman of romance he was very far from being a fanciful or poetical person. Both the *Familiar Letters* and the *Journal*, as well as such of his talk as has been preserved, go to manifest the earthy quality of his humour and his lack of imagination in the affairs of daily life. It made him very approachable and very lovable to dependents and country folk, for he could share both their jokes and their outlook. A man who could compare Melrose Abbey with a ripe Stilton, a Scotch mist with a hysterical wife, and the editing of historical memoirs to the dragging of dung-carts had, it must be admitted, his commonplace side. Except for the one great creative faculty, that differentiated him from all other Scots, he was a cautious man scheming to get comfortably established in life and not ashamed of it either. " ' I'd rather be a kitten and cry Mew ! ' than write the best poetry in the world on the condition of laying aside common sense in ordinary transactions and business." There were two worlds for Scott—the work-a-day world and his private romance world. He stepped from one to the other as if he lived in two rooms. At no time did he hold literature to be as fine or manly a pursuit as soldiering or statesmanship. He said that if either of his sons showed signs of becoming a poet he would " inculcate the duty of cultivating some honourable profession and qualifying himself to play a more respectable part in society than the mere poet." He never thought much of his own work and did not really care for poetry of the higher kind. Among contemporaries he would have awarded the palm to Crabbe or Joanna Baillie.

Scott moved tentatively along the paths of Parnassus. By thirty-three he had apparently accomplished nothing but in reality he had done all, and his equipment for his life work was complete. Once he had discovered his own capacity he began to cast about him for regularly paid employment that would set him at liberty to write as much as he wanted. In loafing through Liddesdale with Robert Shortreed he had found out how delightful was the often itinerant work of a Sheriff, and how congenial to himself would be a post that brought him into contact with all sorts and conditions of men. But at the age of twenty-six could one secure such a position? It was to be observed of all that Mr. Andrew Plummer, the Sheriff-depute of Selkirkshire, was getting past his work, but even in that happy-go-lucky age of patronage, sinecures did not fall into the mouths of poor young advocates unless some powerful hand were induced to toss them there. Judicious wire-pulling, however, in those days was inherent in the very notion of advancement, and the more intelligent you were the better could you pull wires. Fortunately for the aspirant, Mr. Plummer, a scholar and antiquary, had proved most willing to be consulted in the matter of ballad collecting and had allowed his brain to be picked over contributions to *Minstrelsy of the Scottish Border*. His name figures more than

once in the notes to that anthology. The sick
man liked Walter Scott and his enthusiasms
and had the power of indicating, if not of
nominating his own successor. Clearly he was
a person to be cherished. The Sheriff lived
with his three spinster sisters and spent most
of his time in his library, walking from
the parlour to the garden but once a day,
saying no one but a fool or a fox-hunter would
do more.

In a letter written during courting days Walter
Scott said he had " every reason to hope that a
post occupied by a gentleman in a very precarious
state of health " might soon fall to his lot. If he
wanted the reversion of the Shrievalty before
marriage, he wanted it twice as badly afterwards,
for the young couple were very badly off and must
have been hard pressed to find the rent of their
house in Edinburgh and their cottage at Lasswade.
Charlotte had no money except what her brother
allowed her from his pay in India,—a possible two
hundred a year. Walter had what he earned at
the Bar, and it is unlikely that his father could
help him as he lay paralysed in bed. During
the year following his marriage, as he watched
Mr. Plummer becoming increasingly feeble, the
bridegroom discussed with his bride the best
method to adopt to ensure stepping into Mr.
Plummer's shoes when the right moment came—
in other words he sought how to get his name put
forward officially for the post before the Sheriff-
depute resigned or died. When appealed to for
help in this matter the Duke of Buccleuch reminded his kinsman that all Crown patronage in
Scotland was best come at through his neighbour
in the Esk valley, Henry Dundas of Melville
Castle, then Secretary at War in London. The

Duke begged to enclose a letter of recommendation to this Minister.   It was the most natural
proceeding in the world for a Tory to ask an
appointment from Mr. Dundas, for both in Scottish and Indian affairs he was supreme and could
" recommend " to all vacant offices.   He was
the unquestioned ruler of his country, and in the
general election of 1796, of the forty-five commoners and sixteen peers elected to Westminster
he could assure Pitt that thirty-six commoners
and thirteen peers were at his beck.   Families
like that of Henry Mackenzie who lived close to
him at Auchendinny, battened on his friendship.
In this case a father and three sons received
lucrative posts from the uncrowned King of
Scotland.   So universally was his beneficent rule
recognized that Mrs. Siddons in her childish hand
had begged him to obtain the Edinburgh
theatre for her son Henry.   Nothing was too
small and nothing too great to ask of him.

An interview with Mr. Dundas being so obviously necessary to Scott's cause, the spring
vacation must certainly find him in London.
He had plenty of excuses for going south, publishers to see and Charlotte to please   Expenses
would not be heavy, as one of the great assets
brought to him by marriage was the hospitality
of kind Mr. Dumergue in his well-situated house
in Piccadilly West.   At all times was he ready
to welcome Charlotte and her husband.   For
the rest, Scott reflected that being a Tory
gave him an advantage, since his more brilliant
contemporaries at the Bar were for the most part
Whigs who stood no chance of patronage under a
Conservative administration.   It was unfortunate
that his old father should be lying on his death-
bed in Edinburgh, but vacations were short and

the lives of paralytics sometimes unexpectedly
long. It was probable that he would be back
home again before the end. He dared not wait
upon the event as he might be too late to influence
the nomination to the Sheriffship.

It was the first time Scott had been to London
since childhood, and as he set out with an excited
Charlotte he made up his mind that they would
enjoy all the fun they could command, besides
making the most of the opportunity for advancement. Soon after their arrival they met Lord
Downshire at dinner with the Dumergues. He was
most pleasant to his ward and her husband, but
of intimate conversation that might illuminate
the past we hear nothing. It is to be deduced,
however, from this arranged meeting, the charm
of his conversation and his interest in the forthcoming baby, that Lord Downshire still felt a
kindly interest in his ward and in meeting the
man of her choice.

"Monk" Lewis was a prompt caller and reported
on his dealings with publishers over the translation
of *Goetz von Berlichingen*. He had extracted £25
from Longman, but *Goetz* had fallen as flat as
Coleridge's *Wallenstein*, and had not sold though
it had been out six weeks. He therefore declined
to act as intermediary for " an original melodrama " *The House of Aspen*, which Scott wished
to see in print. In other ways, however, he was
useful, introducing his Scottish *protégé* to a rich
bibliophile—Richard Heber—owner of two hundred thousand volumes distributed in eight houses
and interested like everyone else in ballads. To
him Scott was able to pour out his enthusiasm
for Scottish verse, his anecdotes of Thomas the
Rhymer, and his theories concerning the Auchinleck manuscript in the Advocates' Library.

Caught by his eager talk Heber decided to winter
in Edinburgh. It was at this time that Scott
got into personal touch with Ritson, the un-
impeachable authority on legendary poetry, who
was living in the village of Hoxton near by.
Scott had pored over his works and presently
under the veil of anonymity was to venture to
defend the methods of his beloved Percy of the
Reliques from the invective poured out on him
by this learned, vegetarian critic.

The great world, he found to his delight, was full
of students of poetry. The work of George Ellis
interested Scott particularly for he was attempting
to popularize the Anglo-Norman Romances. With
him he discussed and afterwards at great length
corresponded over the version of *Sir Tristrem*
which he had found in Edinburgh. Later he
reviewed Ellis's work in an amusing article in
which he could not resist quoting improbable
stories of Richard Cœur de Lion. What mat-
tered it that Richard never eat a fat young Sara-
cen instead of pork, or served to the Sultan's
ambassadors the heads of their countrymen at a
banquet, or said that there was no flesh so nouris-
sant unto an Englishman ? Scott's point was that
the Crusades changed European character, for
the worse, and that listeners in baron's hall and
courtyard learnt to expect sensational tales from
wandering minstrels.

Stimulating as were the literary contacts to be
made in London, more important in a way than
these excitements was an interview with the
Secretary at War, upon whom Scott bestowed his
recommendatory letter from the Duke of Buccleuch. The minister proved easy to deal with ;
he had heard of his Eskdale neighbour at Lasswade ; his sons in the Yeomanry had spoken of

their Quartermaster, "Earl Walter," and he agreed without demur to nominate Mr. Scott as Mr. Plummer's successor. Seven months later Mr. Plummer died, and on December 16th, 1799, Scott was appointed Sheriff-depute of Selkirk-shire. A year later he had the honour of being made a Deputy-Lieutenant of the county. After these favours Scott was in the habit of referring to Henry Dundas as " the architect of my fortune." So far, so good ; the unsuccessful advocate had by his prescience and promptitude made sure of an income of £300 a year for life. The work was light enough and can hardly have interfered with other occupations except on the rare occasions when his presence was required at the Court itself. We see that during the thirty-two years during which he held this appointment he gave judgment in one hundred and fourteen legal processes, all of them common sense judgments requiring but little knowledge of the law's intri-cacies. His custom was to have the process sent to him at home, where he read and considered it at leisure and wrote his judgment or " deliver-ance." Most of the cases were between landlord and tenant, buyer and seller, and Scott used to say that very few of the cases that came before his Court ought to have come anywhere. He was lucky to secure the appointment but he owed it to his opinions. A Whig like Jeffrey might whistle long for such a post and had to risk marriage on £100 a year because of his political principles. Scott, however, was a Conservative from the cradle.

Once Scott had made sure of his objective he returned to Edinburgh only to find his father dead and buried. With the little patrimony inherited from him he moved from South to

North Castle Street, though not to the house which was finally to become his home.

Having made his first move in extricating himself from the toils of advocacy, Scott looked around for further openings. To become a Clerk of the Session would be the means of securing complete independence. As he watched the old gentlemen file in through the Outer Hall of the Parliament House a few minutes before ten each morning, in order to take their seats below the Judges in the Inner Hall, he wondered how he could join himself to their company. If only it could be managed he would be free of competitive work and financial worry for ever. The more he thought about their automatic recording of judgments, their short working hours, their four and sometimes five day week, their excellent salaries, the more desirable did the appointment seem. Some of them were getting infirm and must in the course of nature retire in a year or two. Scott kept his eye especially focussed on one of them, Mr. George Home, as the man most likely to go, and made up his mind one fine day to step into his shoes. His proceedings did not become discernible till about 1804, when he made overt moves to propitiate the old gentleman, going so far as to offer to do his work for him without remuneration. If only he were lucky enough to secure the assignment he could give all his spare time to writing. No sacrifice could be too great to achieve this end. When the auspicious moment arrives we shall see Scott once more hurrying to London to solicit patronage, once again pouncing with determination on the reversion of an official post.

There was a shrewd instinct of self-protection in Scott. It is manifested not only in his efforts

to secure salaried appointments, but also in the
habit of anonymity he eventually developed.
His first two long poems excited much criticism,
at least the kind of bludgeoning that was held to
be criticism in those days, and the fame accruing
to him through these verse romances never made
up for the mortification he secretly endured.
Such feelings—and on the romantic side he was
full of sensibility and feeling—were something
to be protected ; he must either grow a hard shell
or conceal his identity. The self-protective
instinct innate in Scottish people grows stronger
as life goes on, and Scott developed it to a peculiar degree. The fecklessness and self-exposure
of a rich Shelley or a poor Keats or Poe were
completely alien to his nature. He did nothing
without consideration of a most careful kind. His
first country cottage, for example, was close to
Melville Castle, a situation that must soon
rather than late have brought him into the
Dundas orbit.

At Lasswade, where the first lovely summers
were spent with his bride, he was intensely happy.
The cottage they lived in was but six miles
from Edinburgh ; it nestled under a thick bee-
hive shaped thatch and was what was known in
those days as a *cottage orné*, that is to say
that it had a very humble aspect outside and very
comfortable, spacious rooms and stairway inside.
The Scotts' bedroom on the first floor has a strange
little passage running round it between the lath
and plaster and the thatch. The room below
may have been then as now the dining-room; out
of it opens a small room that Walter called his
oratory. The house was very bare when they
arrived, but was soon converted into a lovers'
bower of honeysuckle and roses. The wooden

stem of an old jasmine planted by Charlotte still
entwines the door. By day they linked crooked
trees together to form an archway and laughed at
the romantic turn they were giving to things.
By night they linked arms and sauntered through
the moonlit garden out to the hawthorn-hedged
track that led to the main road and "classic
Hawthornden." Laidlaw and Scott returning
one evening to Lasswade about sunset found
"the Sheriff's young and beautiful wife looking
on at the few shearers cutting their crop in
a near-by field." Mrs. Scott seemed to Laidlaw
"a lovely interesting creature" and the Sheriff
met her with undisguised tenderness and affection. If Scott ever knew the sweet folly of love
he knew it at Lasswade.

The Gray Brother, that slightly ridiculous adaptation of the story of a Scottish preacher who,
sensing the presence of evil, could not proceed
with his discourse in the barn until the source of
evil had been removed, was written at Lasswade.
Scott moves the scene to Rome where :

> The Pope he was saying his high, high mass
>   All on St. Peter's Day
> With the power to him given by the saints in Heaven
>   To wash men's sins away.

Dropping the chalice at the moment of consecra-
tion the Pope sensing the presence of evil speaks
from the altar :

> Up, up, unhappy ! haste, arise,
>   My adjuration fear.
> I charge thee not to stop my voice
>   Nor longer tarry here.

This ballad, which Scott himself had a very poor
opinion of and wished to suppress, contains the
well known often quoted lines :

Sweet are the paths, oh passing sweet
By Esk's fair streams that run
O'er airy steep, through copse-wood deep
Impervious to the sun.

There the rapt poet's step may rove
And yield the muse the day ;
There Beauty led by timid love
May shun the tell-tale ray ;
From that fair dome where suit is paid
By blast of bugle free
To Auchendinny's hazel glade
And haunted Woodhouselee.

Who knows not Melville's beechy grove
And Roslin's rocky glen,
Dalkeith which all the virtues love
And classic Hawthornden ?

When Gillies[1] visited the young couple he was
met by a groom in livery, who took his horse
and leading it away from the village where he
had dismounted preceded him along the cart-
track between the hawthorn hedges at this
time bright with scarlet berries. He found his
host at a table by a window transcribing from
an old manuscript volume into his commonplace book. This was probably the famous
Auchinleck MS., a thick quarto of three hundred
and thirty-three leaves. He was carelessly attired " in a widely made shooting dress with a
coloured handkerchief round his neck." The
guest was received with great cordiality, offered
luncheon and a walk. Scott extolled their happy
life. " No man," he said, " can thoroughly
appreciate the pleasure of such a life who has not
known by experience what it is to rise spiritless
in a morning and dawdle out half the day in the
Parliament House."

[1] R. P. Gillies.

Gillies noticed that even the Lasswade cottage had been turned into a kind of museum, for a lay figure wearing a coat of mail and holding a rusty sword in its hands presided over the living room, and above the marble chimney-piece there hung a Highland targe. Seeing these objects, Gillies suggested to Scott a secret excursion to Roslin Chapel at dead of night to dig up one at least of the twenty coats of armour that are said to lie mouldering under the chapel flag-stones :

> Each Baron for a sable shroud
> Sheathed in his iron panoply,

but nothing so exciting was afoot and he was taken by Mr. and Mrs. Scott to see a cave cut into a precipitous rock face, the entrance being concealed by overhanging greenery. Later on when *Waverley* came out, Gillies was inclined to think that Scott must have had this cave in his mind when he was describing the hiding-place of the Baron of Bradwardine.

Lasswade cottage stood on Clerk of Pennycuick property. One day his great friend Willie Clerk (of Eldin) took Walter Scott to call on his kinswoman at Pennycuick House. Lady Clerk on the tenth of June each year wore pinned on her breast a cockade yellowed with age together with a white rose. She had been born Mary Dacre at Rose Castle the very day the Scottish Army had marched into Carlisle town. A Highland chief asked to quarter himself and his men at Rose Castle but hearing of the new-born baby he withdrew, not before pinning his own cockade to the infant's frock.

At this time the author was working on the *Lay of the Last Minstrel* and on his edition of *Sir Tristrem*. By the summer of 1802 the *Lay*

was sufficiently advanced for him to read from it
to his cronies, Willie Erskine and George Cranstoun, at Lasswade. They were so cold about its
merits that he threw the manuscript on one side ;
but by 1803 he had re-written it and it was advertised for publication in the third volume of
Minstrelsy of the Scottish Border.[1] Even after this
there was a delay of nearly eighteen months.
Scott felt insecure as to its merits, he knew it to
be monotonous in metre, for he read it aloud to
critical ears in Windsor Forest in April, 1803,
George Ellis, Hookham Frere and Richard Heber
being among his auditors. It was at this time he
discovered that if he accepted and acted on all
the advice given him there would be nothing of
the original framework left, but at first he found
it difficult to trust his own judgment. Meanwhile he determined to publish *Sir Tristrem*,
if only Constable could be cajoled into accepting
it. It is evident that to the editing of this
manuscript Scott gave scrupulous care. His
long introduction and notes witness to this,
but as we know, it was not in his nature to
deal dispassionately with any subject connected
with Scotland, and therefore he was at pains to
prove Thomas the Rhymer collected this tale in
far Strathclywd, a British province, and that it
was derived from Celtic tradition without recourse to any foreign minstrel—an untenable
theory, which took no account of the fact that the
story of Tristrem was popular in France at least
thirty years before the probable date of Thomas
the Rhymer's work. " I am determined," wrote
Scott to Ellis, " not only that my Thomas *shall*
be the author of *Sir Tristrem*, but that he shall be

[1] " In the Press and will speedily be published *The Lay of the Last
Minstrel*, also *Sir Tristrem*."

the author of *Hornchild* also.   The date does not greatly frighten me as I have extended Thomas of Ercildoune's life to the three score and ten years of the Psalmist and consequently removed back the date of *Sir Tristrem* to 1250.   The French translation might be written for that matter within a few days after Thomas's work was completed—and I can allow a few years.   I have made Thomas to use a military phrase *dress backwards* for ten years."   Constable saw no money in this book and published but one hundred and fifty copies.   The great success of the *Lay* however enabled him to sell two larger editions later.   With *Sir Tristrem* off his mind Scott could devote himself to re-writing the *Lay*.

William Wordsworth and his sister Dorothy walked up the hawthorn lane at Lasswade very early one September morning in 1802 to call on Mr. Scott ; they were made welcome by having the first four cantos of the *Lay* recited to them. To dainty Charlotte they must have looked an odd couple ; tanned Dorothy very plainly attired, and her brother with a flapping straw hat to shade his weak eyes ; in both indeed " their exterior semblance did belie their souls' immensity."   The Wordsworths had planned to walk back to Roslin, where they had slept the previous night, and then to make their way to Melrose. Scott eagerly proposed to join them at Melrose and show them the sights on his way to the Circuit Court of Jedburgh.   This was joyfully agreed to, and the Wordsworths were duly introduced to the pale red stone Abbey by its lover. They noticed as they dined with Scott that night at the inn with how great respect he was treated as Sheriff of Selkirk.   " I could not persuade the woman to show me beds," wrote Dorothy in her diary, " or to make any sort of promise till she was assured from the Sheriff himself that he had no objection to sleep in the same room with William."

Next morning Scott went off early to Jedburgh in his gig, and the Wordsworths followed him in their phaeton, halting at Dryburgh to see the Abbey. The day was wet and cold, and they arrived at Jedburgh just as the Judges were expected out of Court for dinner. Directly Mr. Scott was freed from official duties he rushed to see them, causing supper and wine to be sent from the inn at his expense. He stayed late and again recited portions of the *Lay*; but when asked for passes to the Court he seemed none too anxious that they should see him tricked out as a Sheriff. However, on the following day they went " to hear the scarlet-robed Judge pronounce his charge," then stood in the street to watch the procession advancing to the sound of a trumpet, their eyes fixed themselves on one member of the group, Walter Scott, in his large cocked hat, as he limped with all dignity to the judges' lodgings. The show, Dorothy recorded, " was not much calculated to awe the beholders." Directly Scott could get into plain clothes they all went to spend the night at Hawick. Scott's servant drove his gig, and his master shared the phaeton with the Wordsworths. The Sheriff was happy showing Teviotdale to the English visitors, and next morning he walked them up a bare hill to get an extensive view of Liddesdale and the Cheviots. To Wordsworth he confided that he had given up all hope of rising in his profession and said he knew he could get more money than ever he could wish from booksellers. He had earned £202 in

G

the last year at the Bar, and he had made £600 from *Minstrelsy*, and there could be no question which was the more profitable avocation, but he did not care to be dependent on literary earnings, and therefore was glad of the Shrievalty. Wordsworth, who was exceedingly poor, possibly wished someone would give him £600 for anything. His own earnings had been minute.

Among the many feet that tramped the hawthorn lane were those of Scott's Edinburgh friends, Willie Erskine, George Cranstoun, Fraser Tytler, and John Stoddart. The last named had come home on leave from Malta and is credited with having repeated to Scott a poem by Coleridge, the newly arrived secretary to the Governor of the Island. The poem was *Christabel*. Judging by internal evidence this may well be true. When Scott heard the magic of the lines he felt he was listening to a metrical wonder. It will be remembered that Shelley fainted on hearing *Christabel* for the first time, and Walter Scott in his degree was strongly affected by its strange incandescent beauty. With this creation in his mind he could surely re-model his own work. The couplet :

> The lady has gone to her secret cell,
> Jesu Maria shield her well

delighted and excited him beyond measure. It set his mind arace as once had done the jingle of Taylor's *Lenore*. The inspiration of his earlier work *Love and Age* with its opening lines :

> The night was dark, the wind blew cold,
> Anacreon grown morose and old,

could now be supplemented by lovelier scenes.

It is not improbable that the tryst between
Margaret of Branksome and Henry of Cranstoun
may have been suggested by *Christabel* going out
at midnight to pray for the soul of her lover, and
that

> Deadly to hear and deadly to tell
> Jesu Maria shield us well

originated in

> Hush, beating heart of Christabel
> Jesu Maria shield her well.

In any case Coleridge thought that " in the
Lay " an unavowed endeavour had been made to
catch his tone, and had succeeded just far
enough to recommend to unbounded popularity
what had nothing in common with it."[1] Later
in life Scott could adapt lines even from Coleridge
without giving offence. When he likened the
Picts to a stream that disappears

> . . . in caverns measureless to man
> And sinks in silence to a sunless ocean

no one was injured ; such unacknowledged
borrowing was not sufficiently like the original
to signify.

It is well known that Scott had begun the
Lay in obedience to the wishes of Lady Dalkeith,
who desired that some Gilpin-Horner legend
should be embodied in a ballad. The theme
imposed on him by this charming person proved
intractable and gradually subordinated itself to
his own narrative, wherein he satisfied his debt
of gratitude to Duchess Anne of Buccleuch and

[1] Leigh Hunt's Autobiography, p. 267.

Monmouth, who after 1715 had saved his great-grandfather from being hung.[1]

In pondering over the poem Scott discovered that in it he could unload his mind of the ideas and stories which " from infancy have rushed upon it," and could expel " from his brain the fiend of chivalry." Rivalries of families on both sides the Border, forays, jargon of device, and shield and armour, tressured fleur de luce, sheaf of spears, azure star and crescent, golden field, medieval manners, all were worked in. He did not forget *Homeride zu seyn* and to sound the fame of his clan. Paraphrasing Satchells' " Four and Twenty Knights " he sang of " Nine and twenty Knights of fame," all Scotts, of William of Deloraine, a Scott who rode the Roman road. Again he praises :

> The Scotts of Eskdale, a stalwart band
> . . . Who scattered the Beattison clan.

and recalls that while :

> Ettrick boasts the line of Scott
>
> .   .   .   .   .
>
> The havoc of the feudal war
> Shall never, never be forgot.

[1] There was no one but Walter Scott to recall to Scotts the romance that attached to their name and lineage. Stories of " good Earl Francis dead and gone and of Earl Walter, rest him God " lingered in Tweedside, but there was no one to sound them in the ears of the lineal descendants of the Laird of Branksome. After the death of Anne Duchess of Monmouth the family continued to live obscurely and lethargically in England, the Monmouth Rebellion still disqualifying them for politics and the Darien scheme having impaired their fortune. Charles Townshend's stepson the English-bred Duke of Buccleuch, came of age in 1767, married Lady Betty Montagu and then went to live in Scotland at Dalkeith. It was this Duke Henry's son and daughter-in-law who were Scott's friends. Lady Dalkeith was " my lovely chieftainess."

Lockhart says, " Next and almost equal to the throne in Scott's eyes was Buccleuch."

He tells of :

> Scott of Harden whose
> . . . wood embosomed mansion stood
> In the dark glen so deep below—
>
> .   .   .   .   .
>
> A braver knight than Harden's Lord
> Ne'er belted on a brand.

It is evident that Scott gave time and care to his metre in this poem. It is more varied than the narrative of *Triermain*, for he manipulated his octosyllabic lines, altering them by tricks of equivalence, like the ballads he had dealt with. Except for two lines :

> The pi / tying Duch / ess praised its chime

and

> He had play'd / it to King Charles the Good ;

the Introduction beats carefully and regularly, but in the first canto he gets away with many changes. Trochees for iambs in

> Nine and twenty knights of fame
> Hung their shields in Branksome Hall,

and short lines too such as he had noticed that Coleridge made use of.

> They carved at the meal
> With gloves of steel.

The variety in quatrains, couplets, and irregular rhymes, make it likely that in his anxiety to avoid monotony he was trying to approximate to the ideal standard he had caught a glimpse of in *Christabel*. The *Lay* represents two to three years of desultory work. His perseverance was rewarded by immediate success. The poem made its appearance in January, 1808, dressed in an expensive quarto, the " rivulet of verse flowing through a meadow of margin," so dear to the hearts of printers of that day. The public rushed to buy it as they had not rushed to buy *Lyrical Ballads*, *Thalaba*, or the *Village*. Though it was but a series of episodes strung together by a minstrel voice it was at once recognized for fiction in verse. It rattled away at a good pace and much of it was charming. Soon the lines on Melrose Abbey and the opening stanzas of the sixth canto, " Breathes there a man " and " O Caledonia " were on all lips. Three quatrains of the thirty-first canto are an adaptation of the *Dies Irae*, *Dies Illa*, those other octosyllabic lines which haunted Scott till his last unconscious moment.

Pitt and Fox agreed as to the high merits of the *Lay*. It is curious that a poem which is not a great poem should triumph over all contemporary art of the same nature. Perhaps it was because it perplexed nobody. But a short while earlier the copyright of *The Ancient Mariner* and some of Wordsworth's shorter poems had been returned to their authors as entirely without value. It is not unnatural that Southey getting £3 17s. 0d. for *Madoc*, which had cost him so much labour and for which he had collected such waggon-loads of material, should record with a sigh of wonder that 4,500 *Lays* had been sold and that Scott had netted over £1,000.

Southey of course could produce nothing half so readable. He called the *Lay* a very amusing poem of exciting novel-like interest. Words-worth thought of it as a novelette in verse and William Taylor[1] frankly owned he did not take to

[1] *Memories of William Taylor of Norwich*, Vol. II, p. 104.

stories like Pilpay's fables in nests of boxes, one within the other, a minstrel singing a story and in that story more minstrels singing more stories. Crabbe was rivetted by the *Lay* in a bookseller's shop at Ipswich. He read it standing and said, " a new and great poet has arrived." He was heard repeating again and again the couplet :

> " The lady has gone to her secret cell,
> Jesu Maria shield us well."

Neither praise nor blame had any effect on the sale of the *Lay* which was phenomenally rapid. The fortunate author had attained popularity at a bound.

Till the spring of 1804 Scott had lived outside the boundaries of Selkirkshire. If he wished to retain the Shrievalty he had to set up house within the borders of the county. The Lord Lieutenant was firm about this, and in consequence the family transferred to Ashestiel, enthusiastically described to his new friend Lady Abercorn as a paradise for coursing, fishing and shooting. He tells her how he has to go and shoot a bird in order to obtain a quill with which to write to her, and she sends him a packet of Bramah nibs so that he may have no excuse for not writing. The Scotts' new home was a wonderful place for sport. Situated on a high bank of the Tweed over-looking one of the most charming of the river reaches, it remains as retired and delightful spot now as it was then. The low house stands round three sides of a gravelled space facing a garden that slopes upward to the high road. Probably it is the nicest place the Scotts ever lived at, and the walks by the flowing water must have made the composition of *Marmion* a delight. Ashestiel was the property

of Walter Scott's aunt Mrs. Russell, [and when
her son a soldier from India came home, the
Scotts had to find another dwelling. If Scott
could have become the owner of Ashestiel, he
certainly would have done so.

The fishing there was perfect. One day he
and John Richardson were out after trout.
Richardson hooked something big and the top of
his rod broke, but he held the butt down and
finally steered his fish round a peninsula towards
the bank. Walter Scott jumped in and seizing
the fish, a huge river trout, such as Tom Purdie
had not seen for twenty years, brought it safely
to land. Hogg used to say that when he was
wading in the Tweed up to his waist " his glee
exceeded that of all other men."

Though Scott was fond of legitimate fishing he
had a weak corner in his heart for spearing salmon
or " leistering " by torchlight at night. His
hilarity on these occasions was ungovernable.
" The more mischief, the better sport for him,"
noted Hogg. One January night they went out
in a craft that soon showed signs of being water-
logged. " Oh ! she goes fine," said Scott, and as
the boat began to sink he roared out,—

> An' gin the boat were bottomless
> An' seven miles to row !

All went down into the deep pool. " It was no
sport at all for me," said Hogg, " but it was a
glorious night for Scott." Sometimes the bard
was an uproarious host and even the staid and
unsporting Southey was dragged out leistering
when he stayed at Ashestiel.

Like Lasswade, Ashestiel was the scene of
much domestic happiness. The children, Sophia,
Walter, Anne and baby Charles, were all taught

to love dogs and horses.   Scott adored all animals
himself, and hens, pigs, dogs and horses attached
themselves to him with enthusiastic fidelity.
When teaching the children to ride he was
fond of quoting from the Cyropaedia, that
maxim of Persian training : " Without courage
there cannot be truth and without truth there
can be no other virtue."

During this summer of 1805 Scott inherited his
uncle Robert Scott's house at Kelso.   Unable to
make personal use of it, he sold it for £5,000, and
for the first time in his life was the master of
capital.   What to do with this money became
an important question.   In talking it over with
James Ballantyne to whom he had once lent
£500 to move his presses from Kelso to Edinburgh, he realized that since James had paid
good interest on this advance there might be
money to be made in fine printing ; and Ballantyne said he had work enough from Constable
to keep twelve machines going and that *Minstrelsy of the Scottish Border* had been a good
advertisement for his press.   What better use,
thought Scott, could his money be put to than
invest it at fifteen per cent. in this business ?
Having no capital at his back, James Ballantyne
welcomed the suggestion, and by Whitsunday
1805 the two men entered into partnership with
each other.   As Scott was still an advocate he
was by the rule of his cloth precluded from
entering into any trading agreement whatever ;
if it came to be known that he had made one he
would be disgraced.   He was well aware of this,
but the fact that he was so soon to cease being an
advocate seems to have influenced him in his
decision, for in his mind a gulf was evidently
fixed between clerk and practising advocate,

Somehow he felt his fortune safe since he had a letter in his despatch box assuring him that " his business " with Lord Melville " was in good train," a dark reference to his desire to be appointed to succeed Mr. George Home of Wedderburn, Clerk of the Session.[1] Months earlier he had made his compact with the old gentleman, who had agreed to cede his patent in return for the full salary of £800 a year. This was an unusually generous arrangement, as the outgoing Clerk was in the habit of stipulating with the incoming Clerk for a lump sum down, or for an annuity amounting to half the salary. Scott however took no chances and outbid all possible competitors from the start. He had, as we have seen, excellent reasons for acting in this way, and Mr. Home did not delay in applying for a new conjoint patent for himself and Mr. Walter Scott. By inadvertency the new patent was drawn up for Scott alone, which in the event of the younger man's death would have left Mr. Home penniless. All such patents had to be approved and endorsed at the Scottish Office in London, so Scott once more set out for London regretting that the Tory " architect of his fortunes " had retired from office pending a charge against him of malappropriation of public funds during his term at the Admiralty.[2] He carried with him a letter from Lord Somerville, recommending him to Lord

[1] Scott to Dundas (undated) refers to the Clerkship as a matter which without Mr. Dundas' kind and active patronage would never have advanced so far. Melville MSS.

[2] The Tenth Report of the Commissioners of Naval Enquiry ordered by the House of Commons to be printed February 13th, 1805, was the foundation of the impeachment of Lord Melville. " I feel truly savage about the whole affair," says Brougham (*Autobiography*, Vol. II, p. 317), " and only lament most sincerely, as every admirer of Pitt must do, that he has been so long coupled with such a nasty dog." So much for the Whig point of view.

Spencer, who was ruling at the Home Office. A little tremulous at the idea of a Whig Fox-Grenville cabinet being in power, Scott waited on Lord Spencer and put forward his application. Lord Spencer made no trouble over the patronage and ordered the patent to be issued in the form Scott required. He wrote at once to Lord Dalkeith, who replied : " I do most cordially and sincerely felicitate you on having obtained your commission at last from the Secretary's office. I should have said ' *Gratulor* ' sooner had I not been somewhat more occupied lately than usual with a variety of avocations. . . . Lord Spencer (as a professed Patron of Literature) has done what he ought to have done in regard to you, independent of the fairness of the request. You are now to snap your fingers at the Bar. But you are not to be idle. We shall expect much from your leisure."

Scott was extremely pleased at the result of his ten months' negotiation, for it culminated in his taking his seat in the Inner Parliament House on April 6th, 1806. A letter to Southey reflects his state of satisfaction.

" I have been in London, ' pursuing fortune's slippery ball ' and have been fortunate enough notwithstanding the change of men and measures to secure the reversion of a considerable patent office which was destined for me by Mr. Pitt and Lord Melville. I venture to hope my success has given some pleasure to my friends at Greta Hall and Grasmere. It is particularly acceptable to me as it enables me without imprudence or indeed injustice to my family to retire from the Bar which I have always thought and felt to be an irksome and even hateful profession." At last he was " completely withdrawn from the Bar " says Gillies, and " seemed like a voyager who had got into port."

To Lady Abercorn he also wrote out of sheer pleasure and pride : " When I came to town I had to take possession of my new office, which your ladyship will hardly suppose a very difficult one when you are informed that I am actually scribbling at my bureau amidst the clamour of the lawyers—' the drowsy bench, the babbling hall,' being my immediate neighbours."

To other friends he wrote : " I took possession of my new office on my return. The duty is very simple and consists chiefly in signing my name and as I have five colleagues I am not obliged to do duty except in turn, so my task is a very easy one as my name is very short." . . . " The situation is most desirable besides being consistent with holding my sheriffdom." . . . " A few hours' labour in the forenoons and the whole evening and vacation open for literary pursuits. . . ." A literary reputation was certainly a help in soliciting patronage. Except for the fact that in future he would have to work four hours a day for nothing Scott was enchanted with the prospect opening before him. As he told Crabbe, he was " a sort of pluralist as to law appointments " and had " two gowns and everything handsome about him."

The nomination of a Tory to the Clerkship caused tongues to wag in Edinburgh. Had Walter Scott truckled to a Whig Ministry, if not, what was the reason of his success ? And since every appointment was in those days a proper subject for a political attack, it surprised no one that the grumbling should eventually culminate in a speech made by the Whig member for Lanarkshire in the House of Commons in a

debate on the Scottish Judicature Bill. It was
pointed out that if a Clerk of Session had any
real business to do, it could not very well be done
by a man who found time for more literary
enterprises than any author of the age, undertook
and wrote more books than anyone could find
leisure to read, and also disported himself largely
in society.

To prove himself still a vehement Tory Scott
wrote a song for the banquet held to celebrate
Lord Melville's acquittal from the charges of
corruption brought against him. Writing to
Melville's son on " the glorious decision of the
House of Peers," Scott says, " Our *gaudeamus*
went off splendidly. I got Ballantyne to holloa
forth with the voice of a Stentor." In this
song, " Here's to old Harry and long may he
live ! " was one of the toasts, while another was
the Princess of Wales, around whom the Con-
servatives at that time rallied :

> Be damn'd he that dare not—
> For my part I'll spare not
> To beauty afflicted a tribute to give
> Fill it up steadily,
> Drink it off readily—
> Here's to the Princess and long may she live !

Some people took offence at the line " Tallyho
to the Fox." Lady Rosslyn said it was " an
uncalled for mark of personal disrespect to Mr.
Fox." Scott did not much mind this criticism ;
he continued for some months to flaunt a rather
aggressive Toryism, but after a while settled
down soberly to the duties of his new office. A
conveyance, known as the Clerk's Coach, picked
up the six clerks in turn at their homes and
conveyed them each morning to the Parliament
House.

One of the advantages of his new sedentary post was that he could write and even read there. Indeed he soon learnt to work at the Clerk's table as conveniently as he did at home. To quote his own words, " I can get on quite as well from recollection while sitting in the Parliament House as if wandering through woodland wold ; though liable to be roused out of a descriptive dream now and then if Balmuto, with a fierce grunt, demands, ' Where are your cautioners ? ' " So far, so good. From the platform of steady employment and steady income great things might yet be achieved. The *Lay* had been a success, *Marmion* must be a still greater success.

CHAPTER VI

EDITORIAL WORK AND POETRY

FROM the time that Scott determined to make writing his main interest he tried his hand consistently at prose. A field in which he could both educate himself and earn money was opened to him in a newly founded quarterly, *The Edinburgh Review*, published by Archibald Constable.

This organ of liberal opinion had originated in the minds of the Whig advocates, Francis Jeffrey and Henry Brougham, who in collaboration with an English curate, Sydney Smith, had planned a periodical which though critical in character should not be as crushing as the *Anti-Jacobin*. The reviewers, who had decided that all contributions should be anonymous, met in the attic dwelling of dark, alert little Jeffrey to draw up the first number.[1] Each member of the group as well as Lord Webb Seymour and Mr. Horner, who had been added to it, worked hard to make the *Review* a success. Sydney Smith consented to act as editor—and contributed eighteen articles to the first four numbers, whereas Brougham wrote twenty-one and Jeffrey sixteen. No wonder that Smith laid down a policy of " Secrecy," and ordered contributors to go separately and incognito to the printing office to correct their proofs !

When Sydney Smith, a few months later,

[1] October, 1802.

dropped out of the editorship Jeffrey took his place, and in the next sixteen numbers wrote fifty-nine articles, while Brougham also wrote fifty-nine. No anonymous review could carry on long in this way, and even at the cost of employing Tory pens fresh contributors must be found. Walter Scott was invited to write on Southey's *Amadis of Gaul*, for no one knew more than he about chivalric custom and history. Even Amadis bore on Scotland for this unwanted child of Elisene and Perion, placed on the sea in a cradle, was found on the Scottish coast by a knight of Scotland who educated him as his son. Scott praised Southey for having made accessible to other than students of black-letter this wonderful romance. This, the first of his articles, was long and carefully constructed. It is easy to trace in it the foundations of his later article on Romance for the *Encyclopædia Britannica*.

Thus was Scott offered the opportunity of exercising himself in prose and gaining experience in presenting a case. Though never so voluminous an essayist as Jeffrey and Brougham he contributed fifteen articles[1] between 1803 and 1806 on such diverse subjects as Froissart, Cookery Books, and Ossianic Poetry. His critical

[1] Southey's *Amadis of Gaul*.
Sibbald's *Chronicles of Scottish History*.
Godwin's *Life of Chaucer*.
The Life and Works of Chatterton.
Ellis's *Specimens of Ancient English Poetry*.
Johne's *Froissart*.
Thornton's *Sporting Tour in Scotland*.
Various Cookery Books.
Todd's edition of *Spenser*.
Godwin's *Fleetwood*.
Ossianic Poems.
Poems of the Hon. W. Herbert.
Ellis's *Specimens of Early English Romances*.
Ritson's *Selection of Ancient English Metrical Romances*.
The Miseries of Human Life.

faculty never developed much either in relation to his own work or to that of other people; but the variety of subjects with which in reviewing he was obliged to become familiar enlarged his grasp and widened his mental horizon.

From 1805, the date of his partnership with Ballantyne, he was much occupied in scheming out work for the Ballantyne Press. We find him touting for orders for the printing office. For example, he asks Southey to have his work executed by Ballantyne, " The convenience would be pretty near the same to you, as all your proof must come by post at any rate. If I can assist you about this matter command my services." For the sake of the Press more than for any other reason, he undertook to edit *Dryden* (for the London firm of Miller) in eighteen volumes at forty guineas apiece. It was not a particularly congenial task, and he was more interested in providing copious historical notes than in giving a correct text. Hunting up in the British Museum all the old pamphlets bearing on Dryden's political poems, he expended enormous industry on this aspect of his subject, as he laughingly said : " From my research the boldest spiders fled. And moths retreating trembled as I read." Owing to his obsession with the historical illustrations, he left James Ballantyne to wrestle with a common uncollated edition of the text, and allowed him to make what conjectural emendations he fancied. Ballantyne, who was a conscientious worker, complained sadly to William Taylor of Scott's textual carelessness.

When Dr. Johnson came to write on Dryden he found to his surprise that nothing had been composed on him by contemporaries, a singular fact when one remembers that for forty years

H

Dryden was the leading literary figure in London. As all know he wrote for bread and changed with the fashion. For example, he wrote to animate public feeling against the Dutch in the Dutch Wars, to welcome Charles II, to welcome William III and to please Charles II's supposedly French taste for the theatre ; all of which changes gave great scope to Scott in his commentary. Any life of Dryden must be a rehash of existing lives, and Scott naturally leant on Malone and Johnson, even to the point of adapting some of the latter's sentences and quoting from the same poems. Yet he took infinite pains and his style is better than usual. Matter and manner make it the best of his critical biographies. He devoted eight of his eighteen volumes to the plays and, possibly by an oversight, instead of giving Dryden's own text of Virgil printed one with the pedantic improvements of a forgotten scholiast.

By a single word he was unfortunate enough to attract the dislike and contempt of Leigh Hunt. In an historical gloss on *Absalom and Achitophel* Scott stated that Charles II, out of spite, sent Mulgrave to Tangier in an unseaworthy vessel, believing that he must perish on the voyage. The editor called this an " ungenerous attempt to destroy him in the very act of performing his duty." To speak of deliberate wickedness as mere want of generosity infuriated Leigh Hunt, and made him distrust Scott's integrity of mind and not only where Stuarts were in question. Many times in after years did the Minstrel wince under the flagellation of this critic. The animosity evoked in literary breasts by Scott was often bitterly expressed.

There was nothing acute about Scott's way of summing up ; he probably felt this himself.

Speaking of Dryden's style he says[1], " Dryden's poetry was gifted in a degree surpassing in modulated harmony that of all who had preceded him and inferior to none that has since written English verse," (*sic*) which really means nothing in particular.

Concurrently with the *Dryden* he edited the *Civil War Memoirs* of Slingsby and Hodgson, Carleton's *Memoirs of the War of Spanish Succession* (fictitious), the *Memoirs of Robert Carey Earl of Monmouth*, *The State Papers* of Sir Ralph Sadler for Archibald Constable, and *Strutt's Queenhoo Hall* for John Murray. All these works have a bearing on Scott's future career, but *Queenhoo Hall* more than any, for through studying it he learnt what to avoid and what to aim for in composing historical novels. He seems to have shouldered more work than any other literary man of his time. One day when he and Lockhart were felling larches Lockhart observed that he must feel " something like what a locomotive engine on a railway might be supposed to do, when a score of coal waggons are seen linking themselves to it and it rushes on its course regardless of the burden." " Yes," said he, laughing and making a crashing cut with his axe, " but there was a cursed lot of dung carts too."

His enormous activity in editing and writing was in London in 1807 combined with many social contacts, the most important of which was the ripening of his intimacy with Lady Abercorn, the lovely third wife of Lord Abercorn, who had eclipsed Charlotte when they had stayed at the Priory in 1803. This charmer, an inveterate lion-hunter, had taken an immense fancy to Scott, and wrote to him as " my dearest friend."

[1] *Dryden*, Vol. I, p. 405.

He frequently claimed her patronage, sometimes for himself, sometimes for others. She helped him to become Secretary to the Parliamentary Commission on Scottish Judicature, and he thanked her for " kind intercessions " on his behalf. She also interested herself and some Treasury officials in a pension superannuation scheme which would enable him to enjoy the fruits of his work as Clerk during Mr. Home's life-time.

Rather new to London life and the ways of the great world, he was flattered to be taken by his old friend Lady Louisa Stuart and her sister Lady Lonsdale, to dine at Montagu House, Blackheath, with the Princess of Wales. "I had the honour," he told George Ellis, " of dining with a very fair friend of yours at Blackheath, an honour which I shall very long remember. She is an enchanting princess who dwells in an enchanted palace and I cannot help thinking that her prince must labour under some malignant spell when he denies himself her society."[1]

One night Grenville was dining with the Princess in " her equivocal exile at Montagu House." Walter Scott was there. After dinner the party was grouped round the Princess's chair when she abruptly said, " They tell me, Mr. Scott, you relate the prettiest Scotch stories in the world ; do have the goodness to relate me one." "This," commented Grenville " was making a little of a mountebank of the great bard to be sure but his deference for royal rank was so great that he merely bowed and said ' Yes, Madam,' and began. In the reign of King such-a-one there lived in the Highlands of Scotland such a laird, going on with his legend as if he were reading it from a book. The story was short and neatly

[1] *Lockhart*, Vol. I, p. 450.

told and produced a good effect. 'Dear me, Mr. Scott, what a clever story,' exclaimed the Princess, 'pray be so obliging as to tell me another.' 'Yes, Madam,' said he, and without a moment's hesitation went on with another as a schoolboy would go through his task."[1]

The Princess was most kind to him, so kind that he was half-scared by her odd flirtatious manner. After all he did not want to get himself into the predicament that Thomas Lawrence had slipped into and be cited as a possible lover. No duologues in greenhouses for him. In some ways it was a comfort to be introduced by Sotheby the poet to demure Joanna Baillie for he could take refuge in her correct sitting-room at Hampstead and talk with someone whose ways he thoroughly understood. A few years later when the Prince Regent began to take notice of him Scott's admiration for the Princess evaporated in an access of loyalty to the throne.

No one who saw the way Scott at this time drudged at the Museum or at his desk would have guessed that nearing completion in his mind was a narrative poem that would reverberate from Calcutta to New York. *Marmion* was begun in the autumn of 1806.[2] Before that date Scott had composed *Six Epistles in Verse from Ettrick Forest*, which were in design very like the introductions to the cantos in *Triermain*. They were addressed to six of his friends ; and Lockhart says that Scott had the intention of publishing them separately, but that for some reason he changed his mind and used them as introductions to the six cantos of *Marmion*. Ellis thought the plain author displayed in these Epistles a poor

---

[1] *England*, Fenimore Cooper, 1837.
[2] Published February 23rd, 1808.

substitute for the Minstrel with his cloak and beard and harp.   Nine out of ten persons now-a-days as then peruse them separately and are charmed by their simple cadences.

Marmion is the greatest of Scott's poems.   His peculiar force in telling a story, in piling incident on incident, in getting effects without atmosphere is remarkable.   The cameo-like pictures, the excitement, intrigue, pomp and circumstance, swift movement, tragedy, love-songs are most deftly woven into the story.   There is no wide horizon, one is pinned down to the event, the fight, the charge or whatever it may be, but it makes an indelible impression.

It was the description of Flodden more than any other passage that gave the poem its immense success.   The drumming objectivity of the lines which recommends them to plain men is apt to stupefy the less plain.   It is to be noted that Scott's versification proceeded from the natural imitative power of his own mind, and not from great practice in that kind of composition, and for this reason is often blatant and banal. The fifth canto was supposed to have been hammered out during yeomanry exercises on Portobello Sands.

Being at this time in ingenuous thraldom to the Princess of Wales, the poet begged Skene to illustrate the poem for presentation to her, since it mentioned her father, the Duke of Brunswick.   The Princess duly received her pictured version and in acknowledgment sent Scott " a most elegant silver cup and cover " with a compliment upon *Marmion*, particularly on the part respecting her honoured parent.

It should be borne in mind that for the *Lay* and for *Dryden* Scott had chosen a London publisher, and that up to this time Archibald Constable had had no dealings with Scott except with regard to the editing of *Sir Tristrem* and sundry volumes of Memoirs. This publisher, who was given the nickname of " the Czar " because of his magnificent and autocratic ways, felt when he read the poet's manuscript that it was time for him to exploit Scott's growing reputation. With a fine gesture he offered what at the time was considered the fantastic sum of £1,000 for *Marmion*, and twice as much for an edition of Swift's works as Miller had given for the edition of Dryden.[1] Scott had gratefully accepted both offers.

Constable's courage was justified. *Marmion* sold wonderfully well ; the first edition was gone in three days,[2] the second[3] in fourteen. The delighted publisher arranged to have the poet painted, at his expense, by Henry Raeburn. He also presented the author with a hogshead of excellent claret. Scott had every reason to be pleased with his success. And yet the approval of those from whom he most desired approval was never to be tendered to him. Jeffrey gave an unfavourable, almost a hostile account of the poem, balancing this against that, and the *Lay* against *Marmion*. He thought it an anachronistic composition, as if one were to revive Gothic architecture, and he stabbed Scott by saying that throughout he had neglected Scottish feelings and Scottish characters. Wordsworth damned the poem with faint praise. Leigh Hunt was specially objectionable, talked of the worn-out sword he used for pen and wrote Scott down a snob. Byron thought even worse thoughts, though they were not made public till two years

[1] £1,500,   [2] 4to, 2,000 at 1½ guineas,   [3] 8vo, 3,000,

later. He gibed at the *Lay* and at " golden
crested haughty Marmion . . . a mighty mixture
of the great and base." Successful Mr. Scott
was always deeply hurt by unsympathetic criticism and gladly threw himself into the study of
Swift for, as he explained to a correspondent, it
was a rest " after such a scourging crop as
Marmion." Three editions of Swift were already
available, so there could have been no urgent call
for a fourth ; however Scott and his volunteer
helpers managed to net about thirty more poems
and sixty more letters than other editors had
done, not all of them of accepted authenticity.
The most important additions made were the
twenty-eight letters from Swift to Vanessa, and
the sixteen from Vanessa to Swift, of which only
a fraction had been published. Jeffrey found
fault as usual and expressed great dissatisfaction
at Scott's too kind treatment of the Dean's
" failings," but added a sop in saying of the
biography it was more like the tolerant work
of a man of the world than the production of a
mere man of letters—praise of the sort Scott
approved.

In editing *Dryden* Scott had had recourse to
Lord Somers' Collection of Tracts. They struck
him as of extreme interest, and he persuaded his
London publisher Miller to commission him to
edit them. The Collection had been accessible
to historians some fifty years and consisted of
pamphlets of every reign from Elizabeth to
George I. It is amusing to note that Scott did
some of his editing at home, and caused scarce
pamphlets to be forwarded to him, directing " that
those of great rarity should be set under a trans-
parent horn case so that not even a compositor's
thumb shall sully them." The object he set

before him in his thirteen quarto volumes was " by his annotations to make the reader independent of reference books." If the task involved much hard work in obscure regions, we may reflect with satisfaction that it contributed liberally to his store of information and thus indirectly to his ultimate renown. Both Lady Louisa Stuart and Lady Abercorn protested against this hackwork. He excused his industry by dubbing it " little more than an amusement," and worth £400 a year for three or four years.

After glancing thus cursorily at Scott's editorial work, we must return for a moment to Jeffrey's review of *Marmion,* which produced reverberations of an unexpected kind. It was, of course, the sort of criticism that authors have to steel themselves against, and must have been to some extent softened by the editor's letter explaining that though he had said what he thought, he would be mortified to feel he gave pain to a friend. Charlotte, always jealous of Scott's fame, took up an implacable attitude towards Jeffrey ; and while he was saying good-bye to her after dining in Castle Street on the very day they had read of the review, she said : " I hear you have written a cruel article on Scott. I hope Mr. Constable paid you well for it ! " Except for this incident Scott probably would have disregarded the article, but Charlotte's fury combined with a defeatist article on the Peninsular War disgusted Scott utterly with the *Edinburgh.* This article, " Don Cevalhos on the Usurpation in Spain," was ascribed to Mr. Brougham and gave infinite offence both in London and Edinburgh. It was really by Jeffrey though no one at that time seems to have suspected that he was the author of it. The writer doubted the patriotism and efficiency of the Spaniards, thought the enthusiasm caused in England by the national rising against Napoleon uninformed and exaggerated, and took a despondent view of British prospects in the Peninsula. He expected Napoleon to land in Ireland and asked how England was then to be preserved ? Looking upon the conquest of the whole continent by France as a practical certainty he was for peace at any price, and non-interference whatever happened elsewhere. Lord Grey deprecated the public use of such language since the Spaniards required encouragement. To deplore our intervention in Spain was little short of treason to Scott, and " Brougham's " pronouncement infuriated him as a patriot. Scott and twenty-four other well-known people stopped their subscriptions to the *Review*. Lord Buchan had his copy laid on the lobby floor of his house in George Street and then kicked it out through the wide open door.

In London John Murray read Jeffrey's review and the Spanish article very carefully and drew his own conclusions therefrom. As " a gentleman, an author, and a Tory," Walter Scott's feelings must be wounded to the quick. Surely his confidence in his publisher must be shaken ; might it not perhaps be a judicious moment to plumb the situation by a personal visit to the North ? Acting on this impulse he wrote to James Ballantyne about fresh work and " estimates for same." So important to the Canongate Press were the proposals contained in this letter that James Ballantyne decided to meet Murray at Ferrybridge in Yorkshire. It was snowing hard, and as they sat in the inn parlour they discussed the setting up of a Tory organ in Edinburgh, and the plan of establishing a bookseller there in opposition to Constable. Sufficiently excited by what he heard, Murray travelled on to Scotland with James Ballantyne and called on Scott at Ashestiel. He found him sitting over the fire discussing "Brougham's" article with Richard Heber. Scott was angry and intended to cancel his subscription to the *Edinburgh Review*. " Imagine !" he said, " the d——d thing has a circulation of 9,000 copies and penetrates into the houses of every family of the slightest distinction ! " Indeed, Constable was apt to boast that the articles in his *Review* were read by 50,000 thinking people within a month of publication. The influence of *The Times* was not to be compared with it for the circulation of this newspaper in 1816, seven years later, was but 8,000.

Murray was delighted at finding Scott disturbed after this fashion. Here indeed were the troubled waters in which he hoped to fish. Entering into the spirit of the conversation he asked whether it would not be a good plan to establish a Tory Review in London. Of course it would have to be well staffed, literarily and politically sound. Money for such a purpose would be easy to find ; Mr. William Gifford might edit and Mr. Ballantyne print it. Scott took up the proposal and said he could find a dozen good reviewers immediately. There was Richard Heber, for example, present in the flesh, and his friends, Stewart Rose, Willie Erskine, Ellis, Malthus, Hookham Frere, to name only the first people who jumped to mind. The scheme attracted him, and his own plan of an Annual Register seemed provincial by comparison. A London Quarterly was a very different proposition ; he would be glad to support it and write at once both to Gifford and to Ellis. Gifford, who was in the confidence of

Canning and other important persons, should be in a position to write well-informed political articles, and literary ones were easily purveyed. As the wine circulated after dinner Murray was regaled with Scott's grievances against Constable, the unfavourable review of *Marmion*, the scandalous article on the war in Spain and the rudeness of Constable's new partner, Mr. Hunter, who seemed to him " a sort of Whig run mad." Before Murray left it was agreed that Scott should come to London at the close of the winter session and help with the preparation of a New Tory organ, to be known as the *Quarterly Review.* Shortly after Murray's departure Scott observed to Ballantyne that Constable seemed very cool— did he think it had anything to do with Murray's visit ? He also noticed that Hunter became more and more obnoxious, had indeed actually urged that when an author had engaged himself to a publisher on a literary undertaking such as an edition of Swift, he should exclude other work until the first was ended. What was this he heard about *another* long poem and about articles for the new *Review*? And why did he want to foist Miss Seward's poems upon the house of Constable ? They had no value whatever, commercial or literary ; it was patent that Scott's judgment was bad. Irritated beyond bearing at Hunter's consistent disapproval, Scott demanded the cancellation of the Swift contract, and as " a parting favour " requested that the portrait by Raeburn, for which he had sat at Constable's invitation, should be considered as done at his debit and for himself. This was quite unacceptable to Constable ; he apologized for " our Mr. Hunter " and preferred to keep the Raeburn. Whereupon Scott ordered a facsimile portrait from

Raeburn, the only picture he ever had made at his own charge.

After receiving the apology Scott regained his usual buoyancy, and wrote to Miss Seward that Constable should be " careful not to kick down the ladder by which he had climbed till he was sure of his footing." Though Constable had apologized as a private friend, he was stamping the ground and growling, " Ay, there is such a thing as rearing the oak until it can support itself," and in his heart was meditating hostility.

It came rather as a surprise to Scott that after this quarrel had been to all appearance patched up, Constable should threaten to withdraw all orders from James Ballantyne's Press. " By this false step," said Scott, " he will probably establish a formidable rival in his own line of publishing . . . which will be a most just retribution."

In consultation with the Ballantyne brethren he decided to forestall Constable's possible action by setting up John Ballantyne as a bookseller or publisher. Resentment of Constable's threat made him dip his hand deep in his pockets for money, and provide his own half share of the capital required to establish the new business, and probably also the quarter shares of the Ballantyne brothers. The deed of partnership became operative in July, 1809, but there was much preparatory work to be done beforehand. Irresponsible little John Ballantyne was the figurehead, receiving a salary of £300 a year and a share in profits ; but behind him in real control of the business was the powerful form of his creator. "Jocund Johnny" was set up in South Hanover Street and dealt in old books as well as new. Cheerful parties assembled under his roof at which Walter Scott,

Henry Mackenzie, Willie Erskine, and John Kemble were frequent guests. Whenever Mrs. John Ballantyne presided Scott played his lion part dressed as a member of the Border Club, in uniform coat, scarlet waistcoat, knee breeches and white silk stockings.

Scott told Southey the story of his quarrel with Constable and said : that " being out of a publishing house, he had no interest to be of any service to Coleridge's intended paper,"[1] but he added casually that Ballantyne, the printer, " who is opening a shop for his brother " might favour the work. A fortnight later he wrote again, saying that from his regard for James Ballantyne he meant to give the young publisher any assistance he could, more especially as " he is understood to be starting against Constable and the Reviewers " and to be publishing the *Quarterly*. " Indeed he is in strict alliance with J. Murray." Thus did Scott conceal his business ventures from his friends.

John Ballantyne was despatched to London in February, 1809, on *Quarterly* business, and directly the winter session was over Scott followed him, and busied himself hatching out the new *Review* in conjunction with Canning, Ellis, Gifford and Murray. The first number appeared while he was lodging in Half Moon Street, and in it were three literary articles from his own pen, one of them on the *Battles of Talavera*.[2]

[1] *The Friend*, 1809.

[2] Articles written by Sir Walter Scott for the *Quarterly Review* in 1809 :

Campbell's *Gertrude of Wyoming*.
Croker's *Battles of Talavera*.
Reliques of Burns.
Southey's *Chronicles of the Cid*.
Sir John Carr's *Caledonian Sketches*.
Cumberland's *John de Lancaster*.

It must have amused him to review Croker's poem. " It is written," he said, " in that irregular Pindaric measure first applied to serious composition by Mr. Walter Scott," he goes on to compare the description of the fighting to Flodden, and disapproves the couplet :

> Full fifty thousand muskets *bright*
> *Led* by old warriors trained to fight.

Everyone agreed that the *Review* had made a flying start and that it was well up to Edinburgh standards—though except for its Toryism, without any characteristics of its own. A few Whig critics said that it was very dull, but Scott was delighted with it : " The *Quarterly* is beyond my praise," he said, before returning for the summer session to Edinburgh.

When he got home he found himself in the usual way jostled by schemes and ideas—the predominant one being a new long poem. When the July vacation came round he took Charlotte and Sophia to Loch Katrine in order to compel himself to finish *The Lady of the Lake* which he intended to bring out for Christmas. The party stayed in hereditary castles, and Scott declaimed portions of the poem, such as the Stag Chase, to admiring house-parties within them. His tour was somewhat disturbed by reading a satiric poem, *English Bards and Scotch Reviewers*. It had been written by a versatile young man of twenty-one. It was disgusting to be baited in this way, really he had no luck with the critics. How he loathed reviewers and their like ! 'Twere better in future to be anonymous. But had anyone the right to apostrophize a fellow writer in this fashion ?

And thinkst thou, Scott ! by vain conceit perchance
On public taste to foist thy stale romance ?
Though Murray with his Miller may combine
To yield thy Muse just half-a-crown a line.

No ! when the sons of song descend to trade
Their bays are sere, their former laurels fade.
Let such forego the poet's sacred name,
Who rack their brains for lucre, not for fame ;
Still for stern Marmion must they toil in vain !
And sadly gaze on Gold they cannot gain.
Such be their meed, such still the just reward
Of prostituted Muse and hireling bard !
For this we spurn Apollo's venal son,
And bid a long goodnight to Marmion.

To be told by this young puppy that if he
insists on writing for hire he must do his best for
his paymasters, but not disgrace his undoubtedly
great genius by a repetition of black letter
imitations ! This was indeed an insult.

It was entirely untrue to say he wrote the poem
for money, Byron must be apprised of that
forthwith by letter. It was horrible to be made
a butt of. If his patron Lord Melville were
appointed Governor-General of India he would
certainly jump at the chance of going out as his
secretary. At any rate he would do as well as
poor Leyden who had slipped into a Judgeship
and he would not be the first Scott to go to India.
These thoughts were destined to come to nothing,
for within a few months Lord Melville was to die
suddenly. That autumn it was almost a comfort
to get back to routine work and editing the
Memoirs of Grammont ; even the secretarial work
of the Scottish Judicature Commission[1] was
better company than one's thoughts, and with

[1] 1809-10.

luck one might derive benefit from this unpaid work, possibly a Barony of the Exchequer Bench or some such reward. Scott's luck however was out owing to a step he took to advance his brother Thomas's welfare.

Each Clerk of the Session had charge of a department of the Great Register House of Scotland, to which he had power to nominate the employees. A post worth £400 a year had become vacant in Scott's department towards the end of 1809. He promoted a clerk to the vacancy, and in the clerk's place appointed his brother who, having failed in his father's business of Writer to the Signet, resided in the Isle of Man. The appointment was called an Extractorship, and a substitute was to do Thomas Scott's work and give him a share in the salary.

Disagreeable people chose to consider this a job on the part of Walter Scott, more especially since as secretary of the Judicature Commission he must have been aware that Extractorships were to be abolished and compensation given to all holders of the same. The Scottish Judicature Bill passed the House of Commons; and during its third reading in the House of Lords Lord Lauderdale pointed out that the Secretary of the Commission had perpetrated " a perfect job " in appointing his brother to a post which he knew was to be done away with, so as to secure him £130 a year for life as compensation for duties he had never performed. It was a jobbing age; Lord Melville defended Scott by saying that he had been " so disinterested " as to have appointed his brother to the " inferior " instead of the " superior situation "; the noble Viscount saw no injustice in the case and " there was no partiality but what was excusable." Lord Holland, while confessing a great esteem for the literary character of Walter Scott, deemed it an unjust and improper proceeding " that a man should be placed in a situation which he and his brother knew at the time would be abolished in order to claim from Parliament an indemnity for what could not be pronounced any loss." Lord Lauderdale's anti-compensation amendment was lost, and the Bill became law without further objections being raised. Scott chose to look on Lord Lauderdale's criticism as " a most unworthy exertion of private spite and malice," and said he made charges which could neither be understood nor refuted. When Lord Holland next dined with the Friday Club in Edinburgh, Scott " cut him as remorselessly as an old pen." His perfervid admirer, Lady Abercorn, congratulated him on his action, but Jeffrey was sad ; it was the only time he had seen him really rude to anyone.

It is probable that this affair destroyed any chance Scott may have had for preferment to a Barony of the Exchequer.

CHAPTER VII

" THE LADY OF THE LAKE " AND " ROKEBY "

THE *Lady of the Lake* was launched magnificently in May, 1810, by the new firm of John Ballantyne. Two thousand quarto copies at two guineas apiece disappeared instantaneously, and four octavo editions were called for within the year. Scott paid himself two thousand guineas for the copyright. Printer James had read stanzas to selected audiences as it passed through the press. Publisher John had touted it to all travellers. It excited an extraordinary sensation and even Jeffrey praised it. The world of fashion hurried to the shores of Loch Katrine and expressed an almost frenzied enthusiasm for Scotch scenery. Post-horse prices doubled, and innkeepers did homage to their benefactor. The poem was dedicated to his dear Lady Abercorn's husband. He hopes, in writing to her, that she will like the fourth canto for his sake. They had talked over the work together, and he had tried hard to redeem his promise of creating " a knight of love who never broke a vow," as she could not forgive him Marmion's villainy.

Again, as in *Marmion*, we have a narrative in six cantos, but the action extends over six days only. More than any other poem this has been made use of by producers for the stage, for in it Scott achieves theatrical effects by pushing every incident to extremes. The bearer of the blood-

131

stained cross forces the son to leave his father's corpse, and his weeping mother takes the bridegroom from a bridal procession.   It has surprises too—a loud whistle and bare heights and empty valleys are filled with armed men : FitzJames's Highland guide turns out to be Roderick Dhu ; FitzJames the king of Scotland.   It is a hymn of praise to Scotland and the Scottish people.   All Scots, high and low, have their hearts in the right place—Scotland is displayed as a harmonious and heroic whole.

Scott was specially pleased with the fourth canto, and certain passages were singled out for universal admiration ; the Spenserian openings to the cantos, the Stag at Eve, songs such as the Coronach, the passage of the Fiery Cross.   *The Lady of the Lake* reached Adam Fergusson in the Peninsula.   His men were lying in a trench at Torres Vedras on ground exposed to the enemy's artillery.   He knelt up and read aloud to them the lines describing the battle, and they cheered whenever a shell struck the bank above them. Other persons reading it in more pacific situations seized on its dramatic possibilities.   Mrs. Henry Siddons arranged it as a melodrama, and played Ellen at the Edinburgh Theatre, in too Columbineish a way to please Scott.   Both she and Miss Smith of Covent Garden found the part much to their liking.   Two other actor managers put it on in London and Dublin, and later it was made use of for Opera.

In this poem, more than in the *Lay* or *Marmion* one feels that the story itself could have been told better in prose, punctuated by verse.   There is no exquisite use of words nor is there exquisite insight to express.   Any phraseology will do that pulls the rather lumbering narrative along, and yet the pictorial descriptions are such as to have made it the most popular of all his poems.

Neither political nor literary critics seemed to be able to keep their hands off Scott at this time. The more popular he became as an author the more they pricked him. The more Marchionesses ran after him the more Grub Street grumbled. Just as *The Lady of the Lake* was in the press Leigh Hunt made a venomous attack. In the *Feast of the Poets* he depicted the arrival of the minstrel.

> ... diners and barmaids all crowded to know him
> And thank him with smiles for that sweet pretty poem!
> However he scarcely had got through the door
> When he looked adoration and bowed to the floor,
> For his host was a God—what a very great thing!
> And what was still greater in his eyes—a King!
> Apollo smiles shrewdly and bade him sit down
> With, " Well, Mr. Scott, you have managed the town ;
> Now pray, copy less—have a little temerity—
> Try if you can't also manage posterity.
> All you add now only lessens your credit ;
> And how could you think too of taking to edit ?
> A great deal's endured where there's measure and
>   rhyme ;
> But prose such as yours is pure waste of time—
>
> .   .   .   .   .
>
> " Be original, man ; study more, scribble less ;
> Nor mistake present favour for lasting success ;
> And remember if laurels are what you would find,
> The crown of all triumph is freedom of mind."
>
> Apollo's advice : Pray be as portly
> And rich as you please but a little less courtly.

There was nothing for it but to turn a blind eye and a deaf ear to lines of this sort, and indeed the obvious and enviable success of *The Lady of the Lake* was a great consolation.

Susan Ferrier gives us a glimpse of life at Ashestiel soon after the publication of *The Lady of the Lake*. Daniel Terry the actor was there at the same time. In the evenings plays were read aloud and ballads recited from memory. The weather was very stormy during the visit, and everyone was a good deal indoors, Scott as usual working hard at his writing table. As Susan was leaving he wrote in her autograph book a few characteristic lines which she treasured through life :

> For me the blast, or low or high
> Blows nought of wealth or poverty ;
> It can but whirl in whimsies vain
> The windmill of a restless brain,
> And bid me tell in slipshod verse
> What honest prose might best rehearse.

Always careful to send copies of his new works to the right people we find Scott sending a copy of *The Lady of the Lake* to Mr. Croker at the Admiralty, and under the same cover a copy for Mr. Canning. In return Mr. Croker begged to forward Walter Scott his *Talavera* and the recipient thanks " very sincerely for the eighth edition of your beautiful poem." " Many a heart," he adds, " has kindled at your *Talavera* which may be the more patriotic for the impulse as long as it shall last."

It was all the fashion to write topical epics and moreover they were enthusiastically read. John Murray in printing a ninth edition of *Talavera* said, it exceeded in circulation Mr. Heber's *Palestine*, and *Europe*, and even Mr. Canning's *Ulm*, and *Trafalgar*. In April, 1811, Scott imparted to Lady Abercorn his sudden determination to write " a sort of rhapsody " upon the affairs of the Peninsula. He will do it for the suffering Portuguese. " Silver and gold have I none but such as I have I give unto thee " . . . " My friends the Ballantynes have very liberally promised me a hundred guineas for this trifle."

One night in Castle Street after dinner when " Mamma " had retired to the drawing-room a magnum of Marmion claret was placed on the table and Scott began to read *Don Roderick* aloud. " I have derived amusement from writing this ditty," he said, " merely because it is in a kind of measure that I have not tried before and it was pleasant to find the Spenserian stanza more easy of execution than I had anticipated." After the reading the men went upstairs for coffee. Scottish airs were played on the harp, family jokes indulged in, and after a *chasse-café* Scott went back to his desk inviting his guest Robert Gillies to look at pictures and books in the drawing room until ten o'clock supper when he would leave off work. He expected to have ten more stanzas written by breakfast time.

The Vision of Don Roderick came out a few weeks later, some people were indignant that though

> . . . Albuera thunders Beresford
> And Red Barossa shouts for dauntless Graeme

there should be no mention of Sir John Moore. Others found the ninety-three Spenserian stanzas intolerably dull, but Lady Wellington in gratitude for her presentation copy wrote an appreciative letter to the poet.

The outstanding success of *The Lady of the Lake* made its author feel magnanimously towards the critics who had not really affected the circulation of the poem. There was no doubt he was prospering exceedingly, not only was he the idol

of the reading public, but he was enjoying
enhanced remuneration as Sheriff and £1,300 a
year as Clerk, since Mr. George Home had retired
under the new pension scheme, which Scott described as " one of the last labours of poor Lord
Melville whose steady friendship for me was active
in my favour to the very verge of his life." The
well-paid shadow of Dean Swift haunted his leisure,
but he escaped occasionally from that uncongenial
presence by editing *The Secret History of the Court
of King James I*. He was beginning, however,
to tire of research-work and to consider that it
was not remunerative enough to spend time on.
Verse paid marvellously well, and since the
rebuilding schemes for Abbotsford would run into
money, he planned a new poem, dealing with the
Civil War, to provide funds for carrying them
out. The setting of this poem was to be the
Yorkshire home of his friend Morritt. It is
characteristic of him that he at once wrote for
a Gazetteer describing the district. Perhaps
Morritt would act as guide and tell him about
the ghost of Mortimer, the legends of Teesdale
and Barnard Castle ? Morritt replied with a
guide-book letter and suggested a visit, so in
July, 1812, the family set out for Rokeby.

Charlotte drove in a carriage with the luggage,
and her husband was on horseback, while Sophia
and young Walter rode ponies. They halted
at Flodden, where an innkeeper begged to re-
name his inn the " Scott's Head," in recognition
of the custom that had come to him from *Marmion*. The weather was fine, and the approach
to Rokeby through Barnard Castle delighted
Scott, as did the George Inn, well placed on the
banks of the Greta, at which all the coaches
stopped. One of the gates of the hall faced the

village, and a short avenue led to the house
with all its reception rooms on the first floor
and a low hall as entrance. It was curiously
situated on a tongue of land between the Greta
and the Tees. Scott was fascinated by the
Greta, a strange river running over a limestone
flooring between walls of rock overhung with
trees. Immensely old yews bordering the stream
gave the walker, then as now, a feeling of horror
and of gloom. A few huge firs piercing through
the canopy of sable enhanced the dismal aspect
of the ravine. To the romantic heart of Scott this
Gothic gloom "impervious to the sun," was the
perfect setting for tragedy. Soon after he arrived
at Rokeby he selected a shallow cave, high above
the stream, as his study. There he wrote the
descriptive passages of his longest poem so
accurately that they still remain true. No
better examples than *Triermain* and *Rokeby* can
be found to display his meticulous method of
piling detail on detail. Placed within the cave
for his convenience was a rustic table which is
now chipped of all its reed surface and is protected
by a wire netting. Except for the rushing stream
there is no noise ; yew needles muffle every sound,
and the neglected urn and headstone stumbled
on by explorers of the glen accentuate the feeling
of a day that is dead. Mortham Keep was
above and behind Scott as he sat in his cave ;
Rokeby, veiled by trees, faced him, a guide
book and a map were spread before him, and he
worked with the celerity for which he was famous.
Many places in the vicinity are introduced into
his lines ; Wycliffe, Winston, Barnard Castle
and most specially Brignall are mentioned. Bri-
nall valley, forming the upper waters of the
Greta, Scott adored. To every spot of historic

interest that could be reached with a pair of
horses Morritt took his guest, and every possible
item of local colour was worked into the mosaic
with extreme care.   Other ruins, like Risingham
by the Wall, that he had visited previously, were
also dragged in.   He loved the grassed ruins of
Eggleston Priory, and the view of the Tees to
be obtained from the new bridge built by his
host.   The plot of *Rokeby* is most complicated,
but it is not by the far-fetched narrative that
the lines will live, but by the actuality of the
descriptions and the observation of the scenery
and country displayed in it.   Scott consulted
Hollinshed, Lediard, gazetteers and road-books,
and by every means in his power tried to get
accuracy into his scene, and he succeeded, for
the poem may be used now to reanimate a country
which no other eye has in the poetic sense per-
ceived.   Were it not for Scott Greta and Tees
might have gurgled out their lives with no
audience than that of the local villagers and the
gentry of the Hall.   Scott has made a present of
the place to the world as well as of all the history
and legend connected with it.   There is no amber
so fine for preserving the past as a poem.   Morritt
observed with great interest that Scott worked
with a note book wherein he entered observations
on geological strata as well as the names of
flowers and shrubs.   He expressed surprise that
the poet did not trust more to his imagination,
and it was perhaps even a greater surprise to hear
Scott saying : " Whoever trusted to imagination
would soon find his own mind circumscribed and
contracted to a few favourite images, and the
repetition of these would sooner or later produce
that very monotony and barrenness which had
always   haunted   descriptive   poetry   in   the

hands of any but the patient worshipper of truth."

We must not forget that from the age of eighteen Scott had idolized Crabbe and he probably imbibed from him the habit of describing precisely what he saw. In acknowledging *The Parish Register* he said, " With respect to the comparative view of my own labours and yours I can only assure you that none of my little folks, about the formation of whose taste I may be supposed to be naturally solicitous, have ever read any of my own poems while yours have been our regular evening's amusement." By 1812 the whole Scott family had adopted Crabbe as their favourite reading. Two sets of his works were kept in use, one at Castle Street and the other in the country.

Extremely pleased with his visit to Rokeby, the bard returned with his lyrics complete to Scotland and finished the three first cantos. These he submitted to Morritt for geographical corrections. He had set himself the usual measure of six cantos, and in producing them worked so hard that the inspiration gathered at Rokeby fizzled out. The rest was task work. " I *must* turn," he told Gillies, " the three hundredth page ; and *heu me miserum*, have only arrived at two hundred and ten ! I assure you I am so sick tired of this *grewsome* tale that I can hardly persuade myself to drag it on any further."

Rokeby was published in January, 1813, by John Ballantyne. The first edition was a quarto at two guineas ; the second edition, six thousand in octavo, appeared in March. Of the 3,250 copies eighty were left the next morning. This sounds like an enormous success, but Tom Moore, who did not at this time know Scott, put a spoke in the wheel of the retail trade by a squib in the *Twopenny Postbag*. His joke soon caught on, and people in London began to say Scott's poems could be used as handbooks:

Should you feel any touch of poetical glow
We've a scheme to suggest . . . Mr. Sc'tt you must know
(Who we're sorry to say now works for the Row)
Having quitted the Border to seek new renown
Is coming, by long Quarto stages to town
And beginning with Rokeby (the job's sure to pay)
Means to *do* all the gentlemen's seats on the way.
Now the scheme is (though none of our hackneys can
  beat him)
To start a fresh poet through Highgate to meet him ;
Who by means of quick profit—no revises—long coaches
May do a few villas before Sc'tt approaches.
Indeed if our Pegasus be not curst shabby
He'll reach, without foundering at least Woburn Abbey.

Having planted his dart, he made haste to finish sugary diamantine *Lallah Rookh* before the fashion for verse was killed by ridicule. *Rokeby*, he said, had given him a renewal of courage, he felt he could not do worse and secured a promise of 3,000 guineas from his publishers, a little more than Scott had paid to himself for *Rokeby*.

Thomas Campbell read *Rokeby* aloud to the Princess of Wales. He felt ill and had no opinion about it, but the Princess and her ladies thought it very fine. Wordsworth was not above applying a stupid epigram to the poem :

He writes his verses with huge speed,
  Faster than printer-boy can set them,
Faster far than we can read,
  And only not so fast as we forget them.

Harriet Shelley read it aloud two or three times in Edinburgh and in the coach to the poor bored

Bysshe who took refuge, it is to be hoped, in his own dreams. A line for line parody appeared and curious-minded Mr. Thomas Tegg, its publisher, went sightseeing to Abbotsford. Meeting the laird he began : " I am sorry to say, Sir, that I happen to be the publisher of *Jokeby*, a burlesque of *Rokeby*." " Glad to see you, Mr. Tegg," said the genial laird, " the more jokes the better ! "

It was evident to Scott that he had come to the end of his poetical vein. Not only had Byron got him " bet," but he was like to be superseded by a Scottish shepherd. Fantastic lovely *Kilmeny* came out in 1813. Even Jeffrey recognized in James Hogg a poet in the highest acceptation of the word.

Forty-eight hours after the publication of *Rokeby*, the anonymous *Bridal of Triermain* was issued.

Part of it, but not the introductions to the cantos, had been printed before in the *Edinburgh Annual Register*. How Scott and Charlotte must have joked over the letters he wrote to his friends to advertise the work. He begged Morritt to give " the raw author a hoist to notice," and asked Lady Abercorn to note " the spirited imitation of his manner." To Lady Louisa Stewart he wrote, " As to my imitator the Knight of Triermain I will endeavour to convey to Mr. Gillies (*puisque Gillies il est*) your ladyship's very just strictures on the introduction to the second canto. But if he takes the opinion of a hacked old author like myself, he will content himself with avoiding such bevues in future, without attempting to mend those which are already made." It was a joke after Scott's own heart, and he probably would have laughed a good deal to find Lockhart in the biography disapproving of the introductions to the cantos because they seemed to plagiarize the introductions to *Marmion*. No one realized how poignantly autobiographical was the *Bridal*, though it sold fairly well, as did at that epoch all narratives in verse.

From internal evidence it seems almost certain that *Harold the Dauntless* was in part another very early essay in versification. *Ennui* was a word Scott had had no experience of till he met Charlotte and discovered it was the bugbear of her life. Forthwith the writer made play with it :

> Ennui !—or, as our mothers call it Spleen !
> To thee we owe full many a rare device ;—
> Thine is the sheaf of painted cards I ween,
> The rolling billiard ball, the rattling dice.
>
> .   .   .   .   .
>
> And now, Ennui, what ails thee, weary maid ?
> And why these listless looks of yawning sorrow ?
> No need to turn the page as if 'twere lead,
> Or fling aside the volume till to-morrow.—
> Be cheered—'tis ended—and I will not borrow,
> To try thy patience one more anecdote
> From Bartoline or Perinskiold or Snorro
> Then pardon thou thy minstrel, who hath wrote
> A tale six cantos long, yet scorn' to add a note.

Harold the Dauntless was projected as a second volume to *The Bridal of Triermain* and published by Longman as a duodecimo in 1817. It is very rough and unpractised in places and is obviously early work.

Scott paid himself £3,000 for *Rokeby* in long dated bills which he found it difficult to negotiate. He was forced in the long run to realize that three inexperienced people are not likely to make a success of any business. Mainly owing to Scott's very large self-payments for *The Lady of the Lake* and *Rokeby*, which were additional to any ordinary profits he might divide with his partners, the firm of John Ballantyne soon found itself in difficulties.

It is not altogether easy to disentangle and lay out the threads of the Scott-Ballantyne business. Such evidence as can be put together goes to show that the printing house under James Ballantyne made good profits, though it was often handicapped by having on Scott's mandate to deal with books that could never pay their way, such, for instance, as an edition of Beaumont and Fletcher, edited by Scott's German *protégé* one Weber, an edition of Defoe in twelve volumes, *Tales of the East* in three volumes, and, worst of all, the venture known as *The Edinburgh Annual Register*, a biennial Tory organ he founded. Apart from the fact that Walter Scott was a very poor judge of literature, he had a passion for dabbling in finance. Far from being the innocent victim of extravagant partners that Lockhart makes him out to be, he was himself the conjuror who passed money from pocket to pocket, never letting anyone see the true movement of his hands.

Directly he had established the second Ballantyne Company under John's name, he found he had raised up for himself difficulties with the first Ballantyne Company under James's name. Capital to set up the publishing house in Hanover Street had to come from somewhere, and James saw the carefully earned profits from the printing house go to bolster up the publishing house. The publisher saw the profits of the publishing house disappearing in the enormous fees which Scott insisted on taking. Each brother saw his particular interest jeopardized. It was most unsatisfactory, as neither of them had capital, and they were to this extent dependent on Scott's good will. It would appear that in neither business was money paid to capital account—all bills received being treated as current trading account. John Ballantyne, after seeing the business saddled with a £5,000 debit for *The Lady of the Lake* and *Rokeby*, protested in March, 1812, telling his master that he must alter his ways or wind up the publishing business.

Scott, who had confided to no one but Willie Erskine the extent of his business commitments, talked the situation over with his old friend and then went hat in hand, to Archibald Constable. Explaining that the " capital " he had provided had somehow been frittered away by John Ballantyne, he asked whether Mr. Constable would come to his rescue. Could he, for example, take over the *Edinburgh Annual Register*, or even some of the Ballantyne stock ? Constable was not eager to deal ; but his visitor stated that *Rokeby* was about to be published, and hinted that a share might be forthcoming, if Constable were in any way accommodating. In talking of the interview afterwards he reported " nothing but a share in *Rokeby* barbed the hook." In return for a one-quarter share in this poem and the winding up in due course of John Ballantyne's publishing business, Constable agreed to advance £2,000. In addition to the concessions mentioned he took over the Beaumont and Fletcher, an edition of Defoe, *The Tales of the East*, *The Popular Tales*, and eight hundred copies of *The Vision of Don Roderick*. For this rubbish he afterwards realized from a half to a third of the price he paid. As to further credits, Mr. Constable would not consider them without examination of the accounts of John Ballantyne and Co.

Scott was a persistent fellow, and in the month of May, being, one presumes, pushed for payments on Abbotsford, he offered Constable an *unwritten* poem for £5,000. This was declined. In August he applied for £2,000 or £3,000 on Ballantyne's account. Mr. Constable suggested that Mr. Scott should get some of his grand friends to guarantee the sums he required. Mr. Scott applied to the Duke of Buccleuch, who guaranteed £4,000. Gillies says " he accepted pecuniary aid from friends." Morritt, Charles Erskine and others lent him money which it is to be feared they did not see again. Meanwhile Constable went into the ledgers of John Ballantyne and reported that £4,000 would not clear them. " The vexation to me in this business," wrote Scott, " has been John's sanguine temper, who perpetually fixed some point where he hoped to get on well, and as regularly disappointed me, something like the spoiled children in Princes Street whose maids have to carry them twenty or thirty yards in hopes they will be able to walk, when behold, whenever they are set down, the rickety brats roar louder than ever and will not budge a step." So much for the way Scott envisaged the failure of the business. Ballantyne's view was of course different ; he put the failure down to Scott's predilection for publishing unsaleable books and for grasping colossal fees.

The upshot of the Constable negotiations was that John Ballantyne was set up as an auctioneer, while Scott was required to cut his losses and wind up the business as the occasion offered. No one, Constable least of all, guessed that Scott was about to turn into a novelist, whose books would have the power of the philosopher's stone.

K

CHAPTER VIII

THE NOVELS

NO trumpet heralded the entry into the literary lists of the historical novel. Modestly enough *Waverley* ambled its way to victory. In a sense its progress was as curiously fortuitous as that of its author.

The manuscript had a long and mildewed past. Its first chapters were written about the time of the publication of the *Lay of the Last Minstrel.* On the advice of Willie Erskine it was thrown aside and is said to have lain forgotten in a desk with some fishing-tackle. Before completing it five or six years later, Scott had taught himself a good deal about the presentation of old days, for in 1807 he had, at John Murray's request, edited *Queenhoo Hall,* an unfinished historical romance by Joseph Strutt, the scene of which was laid in the reign of Henry VI. The book was written for the purpose of illustrating the manners, customs and language of the people of England at that period. Strutt was an antiquarian first and last, and Scott in going over his work discovered that in displaying his accurate knowledge of the period too consistently he had raised up an obstacle, not only to his own popularity, but also to his own acceptance ; there was no common ground as it were between him and his public. In other words the book, owing to its precisely archaic language, was not easy to read, and it must be patent to everyone that a

work designed for amusement should be expressed
in a language that is quickly understood. It was
by the study and completion of this novel that
Scott learnt to avoid the pit-falls into which Strutt
had fallen, and to write in a lighter and more
obvious way. He also decided, on seeing with
what indifference the tale was received by the
reading public, not to deal, in the beginning,
with periods of history already remote ; but to
describe events bridged by living memory. The
sub-title of *Waverley* was " 'Tis Sixty Years
Since."

The novel must have been more than half-
finished in 1810 when James Ballantyne read it
at Ashestiel with but languid interest. It was
entered in the publishing list of John Ballantyne
and Co., in 1811, but never appeared. A few
sheets were set up by James Ballantyne in 1813
and, at Scott's instigation, were circulated quietly
among people of taste in Edinburgh. Two local
novelists, Henry Mackenzie and Mrs. Hamilton,
highly approved of the pages submitted to them ;
but it was not till the middle of January, 1814,
that Scott showed these sheets to Constable.
Constable did not care about the early chapters,
but offered £700 for the copyright. The author
stood out for £1,000, and fortunately for himself
was not successful in obtaining it. He finally
agreed that the novel should be issued on a
profit-sharing basis. Pressure of work for Constable's *Encyclopædia Britannica* caused Scott to
postpone finishing it till June. The latter part
was written at great speed, for he found imaginative prose-writing almost a trifle after rhymed
romances and critical reviews. Though everyone
tried to persuade him to put his name to *Waverley*,
he resolutely refused ; he had suffered enough at

the hands of an unkind reviewing-world. It was
far more amusing to launch " a love-child," as
he called it, and see what happened. He had
enshrined a good many memories in the romance,
childhood tales of Prestonpans, Prince Charlie's
march, the executions at Carlisle. Let the reviewers pull the story to bits if they wanted
without the possibility of referring to him for
explanations. It would amuse him to discuss the
book and draw people out as to its merits.
Nothing anyone said would persuade him to
forgo this pleasure ; Morritt, Erskine, Constable
and the Ballantynes, the only people in the
secret, all tried hard to make him change his
decision. " I *will* not own the book, I won't, you
Piccaroon ! " was his answer to John Ballantyne,
and to Morritt he said " he would deprive himself of the pleasure of ever writing again if he put
his name to this romance." In adhering to
anonymity Scott was often to find himself awk-
wardly involved. " The tangled web we weave
when e'er we set out to deceive " was sometimes
very hampering. It may have been the fashion
in Edinburgh, as Lockhart suggested, to wink at
the great man's subterfuges, but in England
plain unequivocal denials had to be produced to
satisfy enquirers. Mr. Guthrie Wright, an intimate friend, tells a story that throws light on
Scott's conscientious scruples. " I called one
day," he says, " at the Edinburgh post-office and
began to read in the lobby a letter from Lady
Abercorn in which she gave an answer to some
arguments I had stated to her in proof that Sir
Walter was the author of *Waverley* ; while thus
employed I stumbled on Sir Walter himself.
He immediately enquired about whom I was
reading so busily. 'About *you*,' I replied, and

put the letter into his hands. I soon observed him blush as red as scarlet and recollected that Lady Abercorn in her letter had said, ' I am quite sure you are wrong for Sir Walter Scott declared to me *upon his honour* that he was not the author of *Waverley.*' On reading this Sir Walter exclaimed, ' I am sure I never said so. I never pledged my honour—she is quite mistaken.' Then perceiving he had thus betrayed himself he stammered out some unintelligible sentence and then continued, ' Well, Mr. Wright, it is a very curious question who can be the author of these novels. Suppose we take a walk round the Calton Hill and lay our heads together to find out.' The friends went off arm-in-arm, and after discussing the possible authors and dismissing each in turn, Scott felt he was being cornered. Unloosing his arm he said, ' Mr. Wright, the author of *Waverley* whoever he may be, gets people to buy his books without a name ; and he would be a greater fool than I think he is, were he to give a name. Good morning.' "[1]

Some distinction evidently existed in Scott's mind, as it does in that of every schoolboy, as to statements made with or without the qualifying " On my honour." He could declare calmly enough to an importunate unknown female, " I am *not* the Author of *Waverley* nor in any way connected with these very successful novels," (see p. 13), and he could tell Samuel Warren, the author of *Ten Thousand a Year*, " I am not the author of these novels which the world chooses to ascribe to me." Such a categorical denial caused him no misgivings, but he must needs blush over the honour clause to Lady Abercorn, the one person in the world whose good esteem he did not want

[1] *Old Times and Distant Places.* Sinclair. p. 23.

to forfeit. Faithful James Ballantyne used to second him by saying " It is inconceivably strange that people should insist on fathering these novels on an individual who obviously and clearly has no time for such employment."

Because *Waverley* had no author's name to recommend it, Constable dared not venture on a first edition of more than a thousand copies. Though a certain atmosphere of expectancy had been created in Edinburgh, he would take no risks, the book was a novelty and might prove a complete failure. After all the fashion was in favour of verse. *Waverley* came out on July 14th, 1814. At first the sale was not rapid, but after some five hundred persons had read the story word went round of its extraordinary interest. In six weeks a second edition was called for, and by Christmas five thousand had been sold. It shows Scott's magical power of enthralling people that two years later the first editions of his books were issued in no less than ten thousand copies.

Constable, who had been so frigid over the manuscript of *Waverley* was beside himself with joy over its success, and at once made a good offer for *The Lord of the Isles*.

Mrs. Skene, who obtained *Waverley* from the circulating library at Aberdeen, knew from the very first by whom it was written. It was redolent of Scott, it contained his very expressions, his way of narration on every page, but then Mrs. Skene was among the first to indicate that Scott used every circumstance and incident of his own life when writing his novels. The description of the hare and hounds cut in toast that ornamented the dish of spinach in the Introduction of *Quentin Durward* he had told her once was a dish prepared for him by his French master. The blessed bear in *Waverley* was like the lion beaker he had been forced to drain by Lord Strathmore's factor the first time he visited Glamis. Even Boisguilbert's death was taken from that of Mr. Elphinstone of Glack. Morritt told him he might as well admit the authorship of *Waverley*, for everyone ascribed the novel to him, and Jeffrey said that if the novel were not by Scott, Scott must look to his laurels. The *Monthly Magazine* openly named him as the author. It is certain that everyone who knew Scott at home at once recognized his hand. As time went on, and other romances were poured out, many people recognized in them anecdotes they had heard Scott tell and conversations in which he had taken part. Miss Grant of Rothiemurchas, a beauty of the 'twenties, used to read the Waverley novels in order to pick out the anecdotes and " good things " purloined from Clerk and Fergusson without acknowledgment.

Scott could afford to laugh at all attributions, but he clung more tightly than ever to the figment of anonymity :

> Steal ! Foh ! a fico for the phrase
> Convey the wise it call.

" When I convey an incident or so," he says, " I am at as much pains to avoid detection as if the offence could be indicted at the Old Bailey."

In reflecting over the novels as a whole one is occasionally disposed to wonder whether Scott invented any detail or any conversation, or merely drew from the depths of a retentive and continually replenished memory. Sometimes his imagination worked on, or altered, the material collected but quite as often not. With regard to his much discussed selective faculty it is interesting to compare how his mind worked in the *Fortunes of Nigel* and in *Napoleon*, both historical subjects, though in the one case we have a work of art and in the other a chronicle. In the first memory has made him automatically selective, in the second neither memory nor imagination had any play. He pushed out all that he collected straight on to paper, there was no chewing the cud, no assimilation, and therefore very little Scott in *Napoleon*. This is the reason, perhaps, why some of his essays are not very good. Though Scott was an antiquary interested in precise details, thrilled by deserted keeps, roofless abbeys, battle lands, every item gathered was sorted and packed away in his mind, not for immediate but for future use, and during this period of gestation something happened and dry bones were made to live. He would not have given a fig, one surmises, for landscape as such or architecture as such, had no gallant or cruel human action irradiated for him the scenery or building. He had his parallel perhaps in Madame de Staël, who used to say she would not open her window to see the Bay of Naples but would go leagues to meet an intelligent person.

The life that Scott drew from inanimate things he was most miraculously enabled to impart. Think of his power of carrying men off their feet ! He records that crossing Magus Moor near St. Andrews, the spirit moved him to describe the assassination of Archbishop Sharpe to a few travellers in whose company he chanced to find himself. One of them who knew the story well, told him the next day that his lurid account had banished sleep.

Usually it appears to have been some external impulse that released the creative function—as it were a finger pulling haphazardly at an

organ-stop, and his response—*vox humana, bourdon*,
or other sound—swelled and flowed immediately.
He wrote without hesitation and without cor-
rection—for to him creating was in reality
remembering.

It is worthy of note that some sure instinct
prevented him from making an historic personage
the principal figure in any novel. It is Waverley,
not Prince Charlie; it is Ivanhoe, not Richard
Cœur de Lion; it is Quentin Durward, not
Louis XI; the Abbot, not Mary Stuart. History
for its own sake, the historical novel and the
picture it made of an epoch as a sufficient end
subordinated all sentimental interest. Young
lovers are supplementary for Scott, but they serve
a useful purpose in linking up the scenes in the
narrative. Take *Waverley* for example, there
certainly is the love-story between the young hero
and Rose Bradwardine, but all Scotland is the
setting with its fratricidal wars, and its periodic
risings to restore the Stuart dynasty; we may
find the cause empassion us, but not the lovers.
The Abbot is not written to tell the love-story of
Catherine Seyton and Roland Graham, neither is
Quentin Durward written to tell of his pursuit of
Isabella. It is pleasant to know that his love-
affair goes well, but how trivial and uninteresting
it appears compared with the weaving of the
Royal Spider. The real interest lies in the
machinations of the King of France and the Duke
of Burgundy.

One notes too, as in the narrative poems, how
much attention is given to local colour, what pains
Scott takes to represent faithfully the customs of
the country and of the epoch in which he places
his action. The animated painting of manners as
from the inside gave contemporary readers,

accustomed to stilted accounts of the past, an
impression of great originality. He made them
feel he knew the places he described and had
lived through the events that happened in them.
His many-faceted personality seemed to permeate
every character in every book.

History, indeed, is no back-curtain for Scott;
it is the very medium in which he works, and
since the interest of his novels does not lie in the
passionate intrigues of young persons of opposite
sexes, the historic element takes the first place,
and the great novelty and distinction of the
Waverley Novels are that their interest lies in
general interests, public passions or concerns, in
short the drama of an epoch or a nation. Saxon
Cedric is irascible because of Hastings and its
consequences; he is representative rather than
individual.

Scott has been impugned for inaccuracy; but
in a sense all historical romances are a contradic-
tion in terms, and for this reason it seems unjust
to submit them to the rigid test of historic
accuracy. The readjustments made by Scott in
Kenilworth and other books were for the most part
dramatically justifiable. There is no reason to
suppose him ignorant of facts. In the Prefatory
Letter (1822) to *Peveril of the Peak* he admits to
having fetched the Countess of Derby out of the
cold grave in which she had lain some twenty
years, and to making her a Catholic instead of a
Huguenot. In his 1831 Preface he meets Dr.
Dryasdust's charge that he misleads young persons with "crude uncertain often false statements,"
by saying that even a tale may impart knowledge,
to say nothing of a Shakespearean play. Had
not the great Duke of Marlborough admitted that
Shakespeare's historical plays were the only

English history he had read in his life ? and though
he himself was but a pygmy by comparison with
Shakespeare might he not also serve the purpose
of interesting people in history ? Victor Hugo
pointed out that the Duke of Burgundy's fool
made a remark when Louis XI arrived at Peronne
which correctly belonged to the fool of Francis I,
who uttered it when Charles V came to France
in 1535. He added that the Order of the Knights
of the Holy Spirit was only instituted under
Henry III, and the Order of St. Michael by Louis
XI after his coronation. But then a novelist is
not a chronicler. It is possible that Scott's
memory sometimes played him tricks, but it is
probable that most of his re-arrangements are
intentional. He had an extraordinary and almost
unique faculty for keeping the centuries distinct.
His first three novels are set in the eighteenth
century ; then came *Old Mortality*, a dip into the
seventeenth, and then three more with the
eighteenth again for setting. In his tenth novel
he was very bold, and jumped right into the
twelfth century, an epoch he exploited further in
the *Talisman* and two inferior tales. In his best
books the tenebrous past is lit up for us and re-
animated ; the setting is always more rather
than less right, and the figures move within it and
have their proper being as truly as do our
contemporaries.

Never has any writer so equipped himself with
all the essentials for pouring out stories of the
past. By nature he was a born story-teller : by
instinct he cared more for the past than for the
present ; in fact, the present never interested
him at all, except in so far as it gave him the end
of a golden thread to lead him back into the
mazes of the past ; by taste he was an omnivorous

reader, by habit he was a laborious editor and critic. All his activities seem to have converged and concentrated in the writing of historical romance.

It is still something of marvel to see this strong outdoor, genial man tied to his writing table for hours and hours on end, releasing himself after self-prescribed toil to gallop a horse or spear salmon in the Tweed. In liveliest fashion, at full tilt he wrote untouched by any desire for artistic success or scientific exactitude, yet with an antiquary's enthusiasm making his humorous, hearty pen scamper over the white sheets of foolscap ; for he composed much faster than he could write, and what he wrote because of its rapidity and spontaneity was full of life and throbbing with interest. He was *perfectly* right when he said he wrote best when he wrote fastest.

Public attention was focussed on Scott at this time in a way he had not before experienced. He was asked by the Lord Provost of Edinburgh to draw up an address to the Prince Regent from the city.[1] The member, Mr. Dundas, revealed its authorship to the Prince, who expressed the greatest satisfaction at its elegance. In gratitude Scott was made a freeman of his native town. This occurrence, or something akin to it, put it into the Regent's head to offer Scott the laureate-ship vacant on the death of Pye the obscure. The Regent " preferred Scott's verse to that of every bard past or present." Byron in a some-what puckish mood had some time previously recounted to Scott a conversation with his Royal Highness. " He talked of you and your immor-talities . . . I told him I thought you more particu-larly the poet of *Princes*, as *they* never appear

[1] 1813.

more fascinating than in *Marmion* and *The Lady of the Lake* . . . " The Regent went on " to speak of Homer and yourself and seemed well acquainted with both." And to do the Heir to the Throne justice we must add that he read Scott's *Dryden* at Brighton with all the assiduity of which he was capable.

In considering the offer of the laureateship Scott appeared to be more concerned with the fear of absorbing another sinecure than anything else. He had two nominal positions, and felt he had no right to a third when other literary men like his friend Southey, were poor. He would ask the Duke of Buccleuch's advice in the matter. This was given with unfaltering voice. " I should be mortified to see you hold a situation which by the general concurrence of the world is stamped ridiculous. 'Walter Scott, Poet Laureate,' ceases to be Walter Scott of the *Lay*, *Marmion*, etc. Any further poem of yours would not come forward with the same probability of successful reception. The poet laureate would stick to you like a piece of *court plaster*. Your muse has hitherto been independent ; don't put her into harness."

This advice, combined with Scott's dislike of filling another empty office, and his private conviction that his rhyming days must end, since it was patent to him that in *Childe Harold* and the *Giaour* he was beaten by an abler pen, made him decline the honour in favour of his industrious friend Robert Southey, a person of impeccable morals, great facility of output and extreme poverty. Lord Byron had sent him an inscribed copy of the *Giaour*. What did this brilliant writer mean by the dedication he had written in it? " To the Monarch of Parnassus from one of his subjects." It was an odd thing to write when Byron must know as well as himself that " he hits the mark when I don't even pretend to fledge my arrow."

Three weeks after *Waverley* was out Scott went to sea with the Commissioners of the Northern Lights to inspect the lighthouses of Scotland. He undertook the voyage for two reasons : as a relaxation, and as an opportunity for getting the necessary scenic and stage accessories for a long poem *The Lord of the Isles*, designed to commemorate Robert Bruce and the Battle of Bannockburn. This had been planned and partially written before *Rokeby* was conceived ; but he had put it on one side for want of the personal observation so important to his narrative. Shelley or Coleridge might have become lyrical over the Hebrides from London, but not so Scott. He had to touch with his hands to perceive.

Bannockburn was pallid beside Flodden, and compared with *Marmion* the *Lord of the Isles* was coldly received. " What are people saying ? " he asked James Ballantyne. James hesitated for a reply, and Scott intervened with, " I see how it is, the result is given in one word— disappointment ! Since one line has failed, we must stick to something else." The " something else " was the already printed *Guy Mannering*.

With this novel he tried a new scheme of setting up an edition[1] in type at his own press and then letting publishers have what he called " a scent of roast meat." John Murray and Longman's partner, Rees, being satisfied with the savour that reached their nostrils, not only bought up the edition, but relieved the Ballantyne Company of £500 worth of unsaleable stock. The three little

[1] 3,000.

volumes in which *Guy Mannering* made his bow
were retailed at a guinea, and the first edition was
sold in two days.

A motto from the *Lay* was prefaced to the
novel :

> 'Tis said that words and signs have power
> O'er sprites in planetary hour,
> But scarce I praise their venturous part
> Who tamper with such dangerous art.

a device, as Scott said later, on, for evading the
questions and guesses of certain persons who had
observed that the author of *Waverley* never
quoted from the poetry of Walter Scott.   The
Galloway and Ayrshire traditions in the story
had been imparted to the author by a new friend
he had made in Edinburgh while passing *Waverley*
through the Press.   His name was Joseph Train,
Supervisor of Excise from Dumfries and an
antiquary.   He took an immense fancy to Scott,
and from thenceforth helped him in every way,
not only with legends of the smuggler-haunted
Galloway coast, but with information about local
customs, and also with objects for his museum,
such as Rob Roy's purse and targe.

We may regard Colonel Mannering as being
to some extent autobiographical ; and as for
the other characters they are embedded in all
memories—Dominie Sampson, Dandie Dinmont,
Meg Merrilees, Edie Ochiltree, were each studies
from life, and so was Tod Gabbie, a half-witted
vermin-killer (Tod Willie) known to Scott and
Skene. *Guy Mannering* was a contrast to *Waverley*, since it was devoid of political hazard and
wholly laid in Scotland.   The Edinburgh scenes
were much approved, and his description of
Ellangowan, now identified with Caerlaverock,

delighted many readers. Familiar with the ancient fortress and the double towers flanking its entrance, he was able to depict its most characteristic aspect.

A month after the novel appeared Scott went with his wife and daughter to London. It had been indicated to him that he should attend a *levée* at Carlton House, so he donned his Deputy-Lieutenant's uniform and made his bow. The Regent was interested to see " the fellow who had behaved in such a charming way " about the laureateship and had written the poems he found so easy to read and even in patches to learn by heart. In the flesh he looked genial enough, and would, it was likely, make a cheerful guest. Invited to dinner Scott found himself basking at once in the atmosphere created by the Regent's *bonhomie*. Almost at once it was " Wattie " this and " Wattie " that, with His Royal Highness singing songs over the port and Scott telling his best stories. A truly delightful evening entirely devoid of any stiffness or awkward etiquette. The famous provincial was completely fascinated by his dip into high life, and went away with a snuff-box set in diamonds stuffed into his pocket.

Another enjoyable evening was spent with Tom Campbell, who at that time lived in a cottage " all among the furzes " at Sydenham. The wine circulated merrily, and by 10 p.m. the host had to be put to bed incapable, but Scott and John Richardson, the only other guest, repaired to the village tavern to sup off beefsteaks and brandy. Till 3 a.m. they talked, and then as bright as ever went to bed. Next morning Campbell turned up to a beer and mutton chop breakfast. As they waited for the London coach Scott recited *The Turkish Lady* to the astonished poet, and then

told rollicking stories all the way back to Piccadilly.

The most interesting of many introductions
was that to Lord Byron. The two lame authors
met in Mr. Murray's drawing-room in Albermarle
Street, and Scott poured forth all the curious lore
with which his mind was packed, and repeated
ballads to the patient peer. One day Byrn
looked disturbed as he left the house : a friend
asked what had upset him. " Scott's rendering
of *Hardyknute*," he said. Scott also repeated
Coleridge's *Christabel* which had lain in his memory for years ; it was Byron's first introduction
to this poem. Sometimes after their confabulations
both poets stumped downstairs and hobbled
away up the street together—Byron in his black
coat and white trousers and Scott in his London
" blacks " " looking just like any other ill-fitted
gentleman." Scott got the impression that he
had the advantage of Byron in the extent of his
reading, and was surprised to gather that his rival
in public favour not only knew nothing of Scottish
literature, but had no fixed opinions in religion or
politics. Lockhart thought, and one presumes
that he echoed the man of his idolatry, that in the
Giaour, the *Bride of Abydos*, and *Parisina*, Byron
clearly though perhaps unconsciously imitated
Scott. However this may be, they were good
friends enough to talk many mornings away in
Mr. Murray's hospitable drawing-room.

Returning to Edinburgh for the summer session
of the Court, Scott like everybody was deliriously
excited when the news of the victory of Waterloo
reached him, and he determined to set out as
soon as duty permitted for the battlefield.

CHAPTER IX

GOING ABROAD

OWING to the protracted Napoleonic Wars the Continent had been closed for more than a decade to British travellers. After the battle of Waterloo they began to overrun France and Belgium like an undammed stream.

Scott who, though forty-four, had never been abroad was caught by the excitement of the hour and as soon as the Courts rose in July sped away to see the actual setting of Napoleon's defeat. Before leaving Edinburgh he instructed James Ballantyne to dispose of the series of *Letters* he proposed writing during his travels. Three thousand were to be printed, of which Murray, Constable and Longman were each to be offered one-third. In this way he hoped to cover his expenses, and confidently drew from the printing firm £500 for his trip.

Arriving at Brussels he was welcomed by Major-General Sir Frederick Adam, and rode out with young Lord William Lennox to the battlefield. Scotland was as usual uppermost in his mind, and he marked the places where Picton, Cameron of Fassiefern and Gordon fell, and where Saltoun stood at Hougoumont. In all fairness and admiration he noted the names of Ponsonby and De Lancey for the poem he meant to write, but to Lennox he spoke of Scots only, his mind always dwelt by preference on the men of his own country.

The ground over which they rode was heavy, some of it lain wheat and some new plough, and even to Scott, who hardly had any sense of smell where high grouse or ripe Gorgonzola were concerned, " the fumes " from trench and mound were " pestilential," for in his own words :

> Carnage has replenished there
> Her garner house profound.

Perhaps it is hardly fair to quote any lines from the poem *Waterloo*. It labours and moralizes through twenty-three turgid stanzas. A few couplets have remained in men's memories : notably those in Stanza XXI dealing with the individual heroes already mentioned.

> Period of honour as of woes,
> What bright careers 'twas thine to close
> . . . . .
> Thou sawst in seas of gore expire
> Redoubted Picton's soul of fire—
> Sawst in the mingled carnage lie
> All that of Ponsonby could die.
> De Lancy change Love's bridal-wreath
> For laurels from the hand of Death.
> Sawst gallant Miller's failing eye
> Still bent where Albion's banners fly
> And Cameron in the shock of steel
> Die like the offspring of Lochiel.
> And generous Gordon 'mid the strife
> Fall while he watched his leader's life.

The " Childe " could do far better than this, his rhetoric was of a grander, more arresting type and people who later read both poems could only regret that Scott had perpetrated his. Severe things, now forgotten, were said, but as usual a joke has survived.

> Full many a gallant man lies slain
> On Waterloo's ensanguined plain,
> But none by bullet or by shot
> Fell half so flat as Walter Scott.

There are terrible lines in *Waterloo*.

> On ! On ! was still his stern exclaim ;
> Confront the battery's jaws of flame !

but it is hardly worth while to extract them from
their context except to show that even after
James Ballantyne had forced on Scott certain
emendations in the proof much remained to be
condemned. As far as one can see James was on
the look out for verbal corrections, and did not
trouble his head about the sense of a line—but,
then, he was a printer. His peculiar criticisms
are of this kind :

> Never shall our country say
> We gave one inch of ground away
> When *battling* for her right.

" In conflict " ? queries James—" Warring " ?
queries John. " Are worse than the text," replies Scott. And again :

> As their own ocean rocks hold *stance*,

" I don't know such a word," says the printer,
and Scott replies, " then we'll make it one for the
nance."

Many of the couplets were echoes from the
Lord of the Isles, and " to borrow from oneself,"
as James pointed out, is hardly much better than
to borrow from one's neighbours. Mary Godfrey
writing to Tom Moore said, " Walter Scott's
Waterloo is not the Duke of Wellington's Waterloo. It is by all accounts a very poor performance. . . . I have read the *Gazette* of that grand

battle, in which it is better described and just as poetically. Money however is his object."

Whatever Scott's object may have been in visiting the battlefield, he managed to enjoy himself exceedingly, examining points of attack and defence and seeking for relics, thereby incurring the disdain of his escort. He describes the ground as littered with shoes, hats, cartridges, things the peasants thought unsaleable. Lunching at the inn he was laid siege to by dealers in carbines, cuirasses, eagles and buttons. Marketing of this sort he loved, and by evening his luggage was increased by several unwieldy packages. Early each morning and late each night he wrote journalistic notes to form the foundation of the volume which Ballantyne was to sell against his return, and for which he had chosen the clumsy title of *Paul's Letters to his Kinsfolk*.

Before returning home Scott went to Paris, and was made much of by the English, his name being at that time unknown to the French. The Duke of Wellington and Lord Cathcart were specially courteous, and Lady Castlereagh took him to a delightful picnic by Rousseau's grave at Ermenonville. Possibly—since he was not interested in new ideas—Rousseau was one of the few authors he had not read. One says this with diffidence because once, when Stewart Rose said he had never met anyone who had read through Voltaire's *Henriade*, Scott replied, " I have read it and live, but indeed in my youth I read everything." The Deputy-Lieutenant's uniform figured at various functions, and at a formal presentation to the Czar Alexander, but probably what interested him most were the morning sight-seeing excursions made in company with the

aged and famous archæologist Chevalier. His
national pride was ministered to by hearing
bagpipes skirling by the Tuileries and seeing
Highlanders broiling rations of beef and mutton
in the cuirasses of the French Imperial Guards.
To James Ballantyne he wrote : " Walking home
at night I have been challenged by a dozen
sentinels in half the languages of Europe. . . .
The works of art are vanishing fast from the
Louvre. Yesterday I observed that they had
begun to loosen with wedges the Venus de Milo
and the Dying Gladiator. . . . They have also
begun to work on the celebrated bronze horses
which were brought from Venice, but this excited
such a mob that they were forced to turn out
the Guards." These horses he described as
having been placed on the top of a triumphal
arch near the Tuileries harnessed by gilded
trappings to a gilded car, driven by a gilded
Victory.

When he got back to London, he invited Byron
to dine with him at Long's Hotel in Bond Street.
He also invited Daniel Terry the actor, and was
set on getting Charles Mathews, another actor,
as a fourth. Calling on Mrs. Mathews he learnt
that her husband was due to play at Leamington,
and that his place on the coach was taken.
Requesting her to transfer the booking till the
evening mail, Scott promised that if Mathews
would only dine with him he would accompany
him that night to Warwickshire. Mrs. Mathews
accepted the offer, and her " charming guest "
turned over engravings in a portfolio for an hour,
and then walked out into the rain. His hostess
offered him an umbrella, but since he had on his
green coatee and country breeches, he did not
accept it, and she watched him from the window

leaning on his stout stick and limping leisurely along the wet pavement. At this dinner Scott expected to have a great military talk with Byron ; but Byron showed himself to be extremely bored by the subject of Waterloo, and as Scott could think of nothing else and talk of nothing else the party was not the success it ought to have been. This occasion was the last on which the lame men met.

At Abbotsford that month Scott sat down to finish his Waterloo poem. It was brought out in a small cheap form, prudently imitated by Ballantyne from Murray's innovation with the tales of Byron, a change which was the death blow to the system of verse in quarto. He then rewrote *Paul's Letters to his Kinsfolk*. Like most undertakings with a double aim they were not a success. Instruction and entertainment were then as now, most difficult to blend, and the *Letters* became perilously like lectures when comparisons were drawn between the Restoration of Charles II in England and that of Louis XVIII in France. Quoting Burke, he said that a King of France ought to spend six hours a day on horseback, and regretted that the infirmities of " the good old Bourbon called to wear this crown of thorns makes it impossible."

The travel book was printed and paid for by the three publishing houses to which it had been sold ; so Scott achieved his primary object of paying the expenses of his journey. The revision bored him terribly. He knew the *Letters* were poor stuff, and the story of the *Antiquary* was seething in his brain. It required the greatest resolution to complete the volume. At Christmas he sent the last corrected revise to press with this note :

" Dear James :
I'm done, thank God, with all the yarns,
Of the most prosy of Apostles—Paul
And now advance, sweet Heathen of Monkbarns,
Step out, old quiz, as fast as I can scrawl."

Lockhart admired *Paul's Letters* enough to decide to imitate them with a book of his own called *Peter's Letters*. Though he spoke of " the prodigal genius displayed by Scott " in his book of travel, the world at large found it long-winded and dull.

During the autumn Scott had to wrestle with a new business situation, for James Ballantyne wished, on his marriage, to be freed from his partnership in the printing business. He had been persuaded to this step by his future brother-in-law, George Hogarth, acting as trustee for his sister's interest. Scott was apparently pleased : " It not only meets my full concurrence but is what I designed to request for my own sake to put me in the exclusive possession of stock." One infers from the alacrity with which he took over all the debts and profits of the printing business and also agreed to employ the invaluable James as salaried manager, that it was in some ways a relief to be partnerless. Alone he was free to do as he pleased about the profits of the firm as they accrued, and judging by the sale of novels those profits should be enormous. By Whitsun-tide, 1816, the formalities of discharge had been executed. At last Scott, master of his fate, could build up a business of his own.

As *The Antiquary* was published at Whitsun-tide and six thousand copies were sold in three days, Scott had every reason to be cock-a-whoop about the future. Even Constable should

dance to his piping now. The author liked this
novel very much, and when asked by Miss Sinclair
which of the Waverleys he preferred he said,
" Well I for my part enjoyed *The Antiquary* more
than any other. There are touches of pathos in it
which much affected me ; and I had many a
hearty laugh at the expense of the Antiquary
himself." By dint of great exertion and some
bullying he now endeavoured to get rid of all the
unsaleable stock piled up in Hanover Street.
It was in future to be the impost or benevolence
attached to the sale of his works. Another
condition that he insisted on was that all printing
of his own books must be carried out by the
Canongate Press—no matter who the publisher
might be. Under no other circumstance would
he treat.

Scott having instructed Constable to publish
the *Antiquary* as by the Author of *Waverley*, now
permitted himself to indulge in a new *nom-de-
plume*. There really was no end to the amusement
one could get out of authorship. This fresh
disguise had been acquired in a characteristically
casual way. Joseph Train was in Edinburgh a
few days after *The Antiquary* appeared, and while
staying at Castle Street, made Scott a present
of Rob Roy's purse together with a bundle of
" traditionary gleanings," some from a school-
master who signed himself Clash-bottom. What
a name !—what a humorous invention ! thought
Scott, as he laughed with that famous deep
enjoyment which was so remarked by the visitors
who often could not share his amusement. Train
loved pleasing him, and noticing that a portrait
of Graham of Claverhouse was the only picture
in Scott's study, he asked why Dundee should
not be made the hero of a national romance as

interesting as either Wallace or Prince Charlie ?
If Scott agreed, why should he not make Old
Mortality tell the story ? He would do every bit
as well as the Minstrel had done in the *Lay*.
" Old Mortality," echoed Scott, " who was
he ? " Train then told him all he knew about
Robert Paterson, the stone cutter, and his self-
imposed task of re-incising the names on the
graves of Covenanters. In this way did the
first *Tale of my Landlord* and its editor come into
existence.

Lockhart tells us that in *Old Mortality* Scott for
the first time worked up his story from material
found in books, *Waverley*, *Guy Mannering*, and *The
Antiquary* having all been derived from personal
experience or from tales told by friends. There
is no doubt he had to pore over tracts and ser-
mons and history in order to soak himself in the
atmosphere of the Covenanters. The book roused
a storm of indignation in the religious world, but
Kirkton, whose *Church History* was published the
following year, an honest and reasonable Coven-
anter, supported Scott. In spite of hard work
Scott got a great deal of fun out of the publication
of this, the fourth of his novels. He wrote to
Daniel Terry of his fresh start in authorship, and
justified himself by saying it was only right that
a new editor should have a new publisher.

To his dear Lady Abercorn he sends an advance
copy. He is strongly inclined to swear, though
he does not like the first story—the *Black Dwarf*,
that the volumes are " the production of the
unknown author of *Guy Mannering*, . . . about
which you are so much interested. I cannot
think it at all likely that young Harry Mackenzie
wrote these books. I know him very well and
have no idea that he has either time or disposition

to bestow it on such compositions." Hogg spoke to Scott as if he were the author and being rebuked with, " You are overshooting the mark now, Mr. Hogg. I wish it were my tale," apologized, " Na, I shouldna hae said it was your tale, for ye hae said to your best friend that it was not, an' then I was wrang."

The way in which William Blackwood and John Murray jumped at the new author showed they could be under no illusion as to who Jedediah really was. They found they had to be circumspect, however, in their dealings with him, for Cleishbottom appeared to be a queer customer. When James Ballantyne offered the book to Blackwood he said that Cleishbottom would not deal with any publisher who refused to buy £600 worth of the Hanover Street stock, as part of the contract. Blackwood wrote to Murray at once saying : " it *must* be Walter Scott for no one else would think of burdening us with such trash." The publishers agreed to the terms and Scott felt he had them on a string. He called the whole venture " a new cast of the net which has hitherto made miraculous draughts." By the terms of the bargain the book was to be handed over on the 1st of October. In the meanwhile to Blackwood's amazement *Letters upon the History of Scotland* by Walter Scott was announced for publication by Constable. Complaining to Ballantyne about this, he received a haughty message from Scott saying that all enquiries about the history should be addressed to himself. " In business one must submit to many things and swallow many a bitter pill when such a man as Walter Scott is the object in view," sighed the publisher. " The cursed mysteries " and injunctions of secrecy exasperated him almost beyond bearing.

The delay in delivering the book was so great that Blackwood surmised the author was trying to sell elsewhere.   When two-thirds of the first volume was sent to him in sheets on the 22nd of August, he was desirous of forwarding them to John Murray.   Jedediah was terribly upset by this suggestion and refused to let the sheets leave Edinburgh ; " it would hazard things I would not think of risking," he wrote.   " Mr. Blackwood's taste is just as competent as that of any man to enable him to come to a just conclusion and I will not subject the book to the refusal of another."

At midnight on the 23rd of August, William Blackwood wrote to John Murray, " I have this moment finished the reading of 192 pages of our book,—for ours it must be, and I cannot go to bed without telling you what is the strong and most favourable impression it has made upon me. If the remainder be at all equal . . . we have been fortunate indeed."   To Ballantyne he also praised the book, and Ballantyne in reply said it was no doubt a work of " tremendous splendour," but would he return the sheets immediately ?

In October William Blackwood had the temerity to criticize the *Black Dwarf* and suggest a better winding up of the plot.   This upset Jedediah, who was obviously fierce by nature.   He wrote to his agent, " My respects to your friends the Booksellers, I belong to the Death-head Hussars of Literature who neither *take* nor *give* criticism." The obligation to play up to Scott's whimsies forced Blackwood to send " the author " through Ballantyne two copies of " our glorious book " ; he hopes that " the author " will pardon him for having sent the first copy to Mr. Scott.

The edition of six thousand copies, originally contracted for being nearly exhausted by January, 1817, Ballantyne agreed to deliver a second edition provided £200 additional Hanover Street stock should be taken. Blackwood agreed to Jedediah's blackmail, but before the fourth edition was due for delivery tried to cancel it as the sale of the book had slackened. James Ballantyne referred this request " to the author," which surprised Blackwood considerably, as he certainly thought that as publisher he should be allowed to know whether a fresh edition was needed or not. Despite his protest, Ballantyne delivered the edition, stating that Cleishbottom needed the money. This was tiresome, but worse was to follow, for the advertisement of a fifth edition caught Blackwood's eye as he read down Ballantyne's list of spring publications. It was to be brought out by Constable. Naturally Blackwood, seeing that he had twelve hundred copies of the fourth edition in his store, and Murray about the same quantity in London, complained most vehemently of this imposition : " You were *not* entitled to put a new edition to the press without having first consulted me, and ascertained that our stock was nearly exhausted." In any case he and John Murray should have had the refusal. " You must instantly repair the injury." Ballantyne replied in an evasive manner putting the blame on Jedediah. " As agent for the author I transacted with you for the edition prior to that which is now advertised ; *but the author has long since changed his agent.*" Cleishbottom, it appeared, had concluded the new bargain with no reference to him. Blackwood of course was not placated by this subterfuge, but in the end the quarrel was concluded more or less amicably by

Blackwood and Murray agreeing to accept subscription price for the stock they held.

When the book first came out John Murray congratulated Scott on Jedediah's triumph. Scott denied paternity, and offered to review the book at once for the *Quarterly*, an operation which he considered the equivalent of " quartering the child." The article in question was written, it is supposed, by Erskine and Scott in collaboration, but it is more than possible that Erskine did little but make a fair copy of the manuscript.

One night in London John Ballantyne, Terry and Constable were dining with the Charles Mathews. During dinner the Waverley novels had been the theme of conversation. Mr. John Ballantyne was sometimes indiscreetly vivacious. On this occasion he felt a more than ordinary exhilaration from the generous and truth-compelling wine, which prompted him to say at the close of a speech he had made about some books for which Mathews asked him. " I shall soon send you Scott's new novel." " I shall never forget," he says, " the consternation of the Messrs. Constable and Terry, and indeed we were as much embarrassed. Mr. Constable looked daggers and Terry used some——for with a stern brow and a correcting tone he cried out 'JOHN !' adding with a growl resembling the growl made to check or reprove a mischievous dog :— ' Ah ! what are you about ? ' which made us drop our eyes in pain for the indiscreet tatler ; while wee Johnny looked like an impersonation of FEAR—startled at the sound he himself had made. Not another word was said ; but our little goodnatured friend's lapse was sacred with us, and the secret was never divulged while it was important to preserve it."

The passion for concealment which obliged everyone in Scott's confidence to unlimited prevarication became stronger as the author became conscious of his power. It may have originated in sensitiveness but it was continued from this time on out of sheer enjoyment and love of a joke.

CHAPTER X

THE ROMANCE IN STONE

MANY people in writing about Scott have deplored his purchase of Abbotsford and his passion for land-ownership, but such critics have not put themselves either creatively or financially into Scott's shoes. At the age of forty he was a made man with a steady income of £2,000 a year, apart from what he earned in writing. His tastes were those of a country gentleman ; yet he owned not a rood of land. His father, though farm-bred, had been content to grind away his life in a city ; the son was made of different stuff however, and panted for moor and forest ; nor was it only moorland that he longed for, it was the ground of historical incident that enthralled him. While he lived in the house he rented at Ashestiel by the Tweed, he was constantly considering the purchase of a small farm a few miles down stream named Cartley. It was not much of a place to look at, but it had immense historical associations, and was consecrated by boyhood dreams. The battle of Melrose (1526) had been fought in its fields, that last of feudal fights waged between Buccleuch and Angus and Home for the possession of the person of James V. One day Scott said to Gillies, when showing him a sketch of Cartley as he would like to improve it, " In sober earnest, this farm might do very well to live in."

In 1811 this property, which consisted of two

small holdings stretching along the Tweed, was
for sale. Both holdings were in Scott's eyes most
desirable, but one only could he afford to buy.
After much pondering he decided in favour of the
soil which had been the scene of Kerr's death,
where :

> Gallant Cessford's life blood dear
> Reeked on dark Elliot's border spear.

Another immense but imponderable advantage
was that a narrow Roman road leading from the
ford to Eildon Hills was comprised in the property.
The place in short to him was a little hundred-
acre park of ancient association. Uninterested
persons saw nothing but some undulating ground,
a small house almost eclipsed by a Palladian
porch,[1] and a " filthy " or " clarty " duck pond.
When Scott had purchased it for £4,000 there
really was nothing to show for the outlay. A
half ruinous building, " rendered gloomy of
aspect by a row of scattered, stunted Scotch
firs," was the way Gillies described it. The land
on which it stood had at one time belonged to
the Abbey of Melrose. There was a ford near it
just above the influx of Gala water to the Tweed,
and for these reasons he named the place Abbotsford. Later on he acquired more property, and
what a moment it was for the landlord when he
could sign himself in a letter to Joanna Baillie
" Abbotsford and Kaeside ! "

Money meant very little to Scott when the
land-hunger seized hold of him. As he told
Morritt, it " was tumbling in on him very fast " ;
and there is no doubt that the sale of *Waverley*
and the facility he had discovered in himself for
scribbling novels opened to him an entrancing
vista of almost fabulous wealth. It was not,

[1] See vignette of Abbotsford in 1812.

however, till 1816 that he acquired the most legendary and coveted spot of all, " a strange secluded ravine, full of old trees . . . with a dashing rivulet and certain large stones, which in England your cocknies would call rocks. I call it the Rhymer's Glen, as it makes part of the scene where Thomas the Rhymer is said to have met the Queen of the Fairies." He got indescribable pleasure from this ownership, and alludes to it as " happiness itself."

The Scotts took possession of Cartley Farm in May, 1812, moving all their household goods and animals in procession from Ashestiel. The estate was promptly renamed . " We have fixed our residence," wrote Scott to his brother-in-law, in a " little farm house, where our only sitting-room is about twelve feet square and all the others in proportion, so that on the whole we live as if we were on board ship. . . . we are all screwed in. . . . We are realizing the nursery tale of the man and his wife who lived in a vinegar bottle." That autumn he celebrated the victory of Salamanca with a bonfire on his own hill.

From the very first he had great fun at Abbotsford, rushing down of a Saturday afternoon from the Court of Session and staying till Monday night. His study was a window bay with a curtain nailed across to separate it from the living room. There he wrote his verses long since hammered out on the Edinburgh road or beside the well—a well he was building out of fragments of Melrose Abbey.

Charlotte, who had a love of order was no friend to the lumber with which Scott encumbered the farm—the guns, pistols, targes, which were spread on every available wall. It cannot be supposed that she liked housekeeping in so rough a place, but she was of an accommodating disposition, and sat over the fire of an evening making trout nets, while her husband stared into the embers, book in hand, and made endless plans for rebuilding the house and embellishing the the estate.

His first thoughts centred round trees; he must provide plenty of trees. When a bushel of Yorkshire acorns arrived from Rokeby Scott promised himself a " Morritt Grove." In thanking for them he says he was " never so happy in his life as in having a place of his own to create." Friends soon learnt of his proposed plantations; the Duke of Buccleuch sent more acorns; Joanna Baillie and George Ellis picked up still more acorns in Windsor Forest; the Earl of Fife sent seed of Norway pines, and Lord Montagu gave lime-seed. Scott, who realized that trees took longer to grow than houses to build, ordered three thousand laburnums, two thousand sweet-briars, three thousand Scotch elms, three thousand horse-chestnuts and loads of hollies, poplars and filberts. " We can hardly have too many birches," he remarked to the patient Charlotte as he ordered one hundred thousand of them, " besides we may plant them as hedges." Soon he had nice beds of seedlings to look at and plantations two feet high. Many men from the neighbourhood were employed, as the young trees had to be put in as soon as each batch arrived. Scott took a hand in everything; in the delicate job of cutting the grass of the young plantation with sickles, as doing less harm than scythes; in the mixing of the mortar for rebuilding the house; in the ploughing of the glebe with his huge oxen Og and Bashan, who " worked with a grace altogether bucolical." Oh happy, happy laird!

When by 1817 he had begun to feel the advantage of being sole partner in the Ballantyne Company he disposed of some of his profits by buying more land adjacent to Cartley.   On this land stood a house which Scott felt would make a perfect home for Adam Fergusson, and his sisters. It was called Toftfield, but renamed Huntley Burn by its new owner.   Fergusson remonstrated on the price his friend had paid—£10,000—and told him that if he had bargained he might have had it cheaper.   Feeling particularly successful and particularly well at the time, Scott cut Adam Fergusson short with, "Never say a word about it; it will suit you and the ladies exactly and it's only scribbling a little more nonsense some of these mornings to pay anything it costs me, more than enough."

The museum, always an important feature in any Scott establishment, received many contributions, though nothing in the beginning could be adequately displayed.   In 1813 he was fortunate enough to obtain " some of the hair of Charles I cut from his head soon after his coffin had been opened in St. George's Chapel, Windsor." Joanna Baillie from Hampstead sent him a knitted silk purse for his " heavy gold coins," and hoped that he would " rely on gifts of friends to augment his collections rather than purchase odds and ends from curiosity brokers."   In addition to buying furniture and smaller objects of interest, Scott kept his eye on the remains of old Edinburgh.   Niches for saints from the Tolbooth ; and " the fountain belonging to the Cross of Edinburgh " were acquired.   When that Bastille, the old Heart of Midlothian, was pulled down, Scott obtained enough of the stone of the entrance tower to enable him to erect it with its

" sculptured doorway " as the entrance to the kitchen at Abbotsford. Skene secured for him the Gothic portal of an ancient mansion, " Black Turnpike," which stood in the High Street of Edinburgh, and Raeburn, who was renting a house with rockery and modern ruin attached, allowed him to select from the rockery the sculptured portraits of the Kings of Scotland, which once had adorned the Cross of Edinburgh. " It will be hard," he said, " if I do not find a purpose for all that is worth carrying thirty miles." In writing of Horace Walpole, Scott, with Abbotsford in his mind's eye, said, " A modern Gothic structure may excite magnificent or melancholy ideas, it cannot excite awe as halls that have echoed to the footfall of remote generations." Could one perhaps introduce the vibrations of the past by fragments judiciously placed ?

Arms and armour he could not resist, and many of the objects were bought at Johnny Ballantyne's auction room, which he visited more regularly than Charlotte liked. The result was always more lumber. There were weapons, too, which he had come by in a different way ; a sword, for example, to reclaim which he had had to drain the well of Dunottar Castle. He confessed himself " quite feverish " about his armoury. In those empty corselets he saw knights caparisoned for the fight, and each poniard, battle axe and pike had drawn blood in some hot encounter. When it became known to Scott's admirers that he was to rebuild his improved farm house and turn it into a large manor, objects of historical interest flowed in from half the country houses of England and Scotland. Perhaps the most embarrassing present was a pair of emus sent by a settler from Botany Bay.

Sir Walter accepted the gift believing them to be small green or blue parrots which might look pretty among the armour, but when he discovered the emus "stood six feet in their stocking feet," he feared for his "nicknackets" and sent the birds to the Duke of Buccleuch.

By 1816 the remodelled farm house, now a neat mansion, was too small, and dreams of a more fanciful residence floated in Scott's mind. It was to be of grey stone and to embody all the most attractive features of medieval architecture, such as bartizans, *corps de logis*, turrets, and machicolations. Many were called in to advise and several sketches for garden and courtyard were made by Skene, and even by Scott, though he was no draughtsman. George Bullock, long distinguished in London as a collector of curios, was at first the principal counsellor. Skene made drawings for the exterior and Bullock for the interior of the house. Bullock was able, to Scott's delight, to make casts of the heads and ornaments at Melrose Abbey, which would be "delightful for cornices." Skene designed a screen for the garden and courtyard, open arches of hewn stone filled with cast-iron latticing. These supported a cornice on which flower pots were to be placed. In the end a professional architect named Atkinson was commissioned to design the house as a whole. Amateurs were all very well in their way, but it was difficult to co-ordinate their suggestions. No house of the size ever took so long to build, but no house was probably the subject of so much tinkering and improvisation. Abbotsford was every bit as much an emanation of Scott's brain as any of his books. Owing to the fact that he was constantly receiving fresh inspirations delays were unavoidable,

sometimes it was a corkscrew staircase to
the roof that held up the work ; sometimes the
painted glass, sometimes the bosses for the ceiling.
Though the walls of the new house overtopped
the old in September, 1817, the total edifice was
not completed till 1823, when a ball was given to
the neighbourhood.

There was plenty of stone on the property, as
Scott told Joanna Baillie in 1816, when he confided to her that he had a private dislike of a
"regular shaped house." When Washington Irving
visited him in 1817, he found him messing about
with mortar and enjoying himself whole-heartedly.
The baronial pile was emerging from its scaffolding, and the creeper-covered mansion beside it
looked like a shooting box. Blocks of granite
lay around, and Scott " making the impression of
a tall, powerful man," emerged from among them
to greet the new-comer. He wore an old green
jacket, " brown canvas pantaloons," stout shoes
and an old white hat. A dog whistle hung from
his button hole, and he pushed himself along at a
great rate with a thick stick. In his welcoming
way he dragged his guest into family breakfast.
They had a common friend in Tom Campbell,
whose letter of introduction Irving presented.
As they spoke of him Scott said, " Tom would
never do anything fine again, for he's afraid of the
shadow cast before him of his earlier fame. Think
of *Hohenlinden* which Tom calls d——d drum and
trumpet lines, think of the *Mariners of England*—
and then of that patchy, long poem *Gertrude of
Wyoming*," of which he quoted the finest passages
by heart. " 'Twas a pity the fellow would not
give full sweep to his genius." He had done his
best for him, had invited him to dinner soon
after *The Pleasures of Hope* was published, and

introduced him to the wits of Edinburgh. For a while Tom had become one of the sights of the town. At one time he could have been met with any day on the North Bridge at noon—a neat figure of a man, in a blue coat with brass buttons, buff nankeens, white stockings and buckled shoes. Quite a dandy in his way, he dressed up to the peruke which he did not wear from choice. He was settled and married in England now and the King had given him a Civil List pension of £200. Literature was a good staff but a poor crutch to support one. Scott never tired of saying that.

Visitors usually found the laird at work. Skene describes him as knee-deep in a mortar tub, and to Irving Scott seemed most happy among his workmen ; he described him sitting among fragments from Melrose Abbey, and particularly noticed a little red heraldic lion, someone's cognizance, which his host kept tapping and poking at with his stick. The great man's eyes twinkled beneath their shaggy eaves as he spoke of Melrose Abbey. " There is no telling what treasures are hid in that glorious old pile . . . it's a famous place for antiquarian plunder. . . . There is as rare picking in it as in a Stilton cheese and in the same taste, the mouldier the better." The little red lion got a good jab over this analogical joke, and Irving begged that it might be given a worthy place in the new house, and Scott said it should be suitably provided for.

Washington Irving grew very intimate with his host and told him of his own tragedy—the death of his fiancée, and of the devotion of her Jewish friend Rebecca Gratz, who cherished a romantic love for a Christian, but remained celibate because of her faith. The account of her fine character impressed Scott and when *Ivanhoe* came out he sent a copy to Irving with, " Does the Rebecca I have pictured compare well with the pattern given ? "

The legend park at Abbotsford did not at first appeal much to a transatlantic visitor accustomed to American forests. He walked with his host to the summit of a hill and was shown the sights, Lammermuir, Smailholm, Teviotdale, the braes of Yarrow, and " Ettrick stream winding along like a silver thread to throw itself into the Tweed." Irving gazed round on the lines of monotonous hills, all destitute of trees, and at first he saw nothing in them ; Scott, however, threw such a magic web of poetry and romance over the whole scene that it gradually assumed a greater charm for his visitor than all the verdant vistas that England could show. He told his host this. " I like the very nakedness of the land . . ." said Scott. " These grey hills and all this wild border-country have beauties peculiar to themselves . . . if I did not see the heather at least once a year, I think I should die." Many people noticed how Scott came to life in the country. He seemed like Antæus when he touched his native earth and quickened with its influence.

Another American, Edward Everett, presented himself at Castle Street one day with a letter of introduction from Gifford, and later went to stay at Abbotsford. As he drove through the streets of Edinburgh on the box seat of the Blucher, he spied *The Heart of Midlothian* displayed in a bookseller's shop. Begging the driver by whose side he sat to stop, he jumped off and bought a copy. It had been published that day. On his way to his destination, he stopped at Melrose in order to visit the ruined Abbey, " first

raised into general notoriety by the *Lay of the
Last Minstrel.*" He was deeply impressed at
viewing " through the prism of poetry the tomb
of the wizard Michael Scott and the grave of King
Alexander." That day, however, he was to meet
a still greater magician.

It was a fine Saturday as he walked from the
Abbey to Abbotsford ; he found the family at
dinner, and was welcomed with the unfailing
cordiality that Scott had a genius for expressing.
His host joked a good deal, and talked of the
prodigious effect his poems had had in causing
people to travel in Scotland and to spend money
in the poor deserted districts such as that surrounding Loch Katrine. Everett from the first
moment felt perfectly at home, and spent a quiet,
happy Sunday in driving to church at Selkirk
with Mrs. Scott and the girls. On their return
they walked through the Park and picked baskets
full of mushrooms. Sophia showed him over the
new house in building and pointed out the gro-
tesque corbels mentioned in the *Lay*. She told
him that though she suspected her father of being
the author of the Waverley Novels she was not
sure of it.

What surprised Everett most was that the
family had no copy of the *Heart of Midlothian*
and that they started reading his copy aloud after
dinner. Scott took his turn with the rest and
commented on the passages that struck him. He
seemed entirely at leisure and full of jests—
story after story poured from his lips. Everett
was particularly amused with one about a guest
who was staying in the house and kept them all
waiting for dinner. Scott sent a servant up to
fetch him ; the man found the guest cleaning his
teeth, and returned to inform Scott that " the

gentleman would come immediately, he was sharpening his teeth."

This period was the happiest of Scott's life ; ill-health had ceased for the time being to cast shadows across his path, money was easy to earn, his wife was delighted at his new prosperity, his young family appeared full of promise, and more than this, at the moment " Aladdin's palace " was rising into the air, " a place to dream of, not to tell." Every day, wet or fine, Scott went to his favourite haunts. When walking with Irving to show him the Eildon stone, which marked the place of the Eildon Tree from beneath which Thomas the Rhymer had delivered his prophecies, he said, " We are now treading classic or fairy ground," and forthwith began to recite the ballad of True Thomas. As he limped up the wizard glen in front of Irving, the deep, growling tones he emitted sounded like the breathing of an organ; he was still reciting :

> Nor hill nor brook we paced along
> But had its legend or its song.

The deep, sonorous voice, with its Scottish accent, was most impressive as they clambered on in the Scotch mist. With delight he showed Huntley Burn, the silver waterfall overhung by weeping birches and rowan trees, but on looking at Irving's face he saw that he did not look too happy in this enchanting spot ; did he perhaps mind the rain ? " We are the children of the mist," he said, " and must not mind a little whispering of the clouds any more than a man must mind the whimpering of a hysterical wife." Taking his seat under a thicket, he called his man to bring him his tartan. " Come under my plaidie," he laughed, quoting an old saying. While they nestled there together, he pointed to a hole on the opposite bank as the snug house of a grey badger. On fine days he had seen him sitting like a hermit at the door of his cell. Perhaps he was a kind of successor to Thomas the Rhymer, perhaps it was True Thomas himself under a fairy spell. Who could say?

Scott's boyish delight in legend amused Washington Irving immensely. One day they went to Cauldshields loch, "a sort of little Mediterranean Sea in his dominions," his guide hoped he was not too spoilt by the vast American Lakes to appreciate its beauty. "No transatlantic lake could have a water bull living in its depths which from time to time came forth upon dry land and bellowed." Irving was quick-witted, and as they stepped into a boat to pull out into the centre of the lake he noticed a locker under the seat painted Search No. 2. He murmured it aloud, Scott said jokingly, "That's only some of Lord Somerville's nonsense." Irving smiled and remembered the buried treasure in the *Antiquary*.

For fourteen years Abbotsford was an inexhaustible delight to Scott, for in its building lifelong aspirations were realized. We cannot look at the scutcheoned windows through which the green and golden sunlight falls upon the stone floor of the " baronial " hall, or at the shields strung along the ceiling above our heads, without thinking of the sick boy who once lay in George Square reading of feats of arms and studying the language of heraldry. As we let our eyes rest on the bust of Shakespeare, on Montrose's sword, on Byron's urn and even on the Waterloo cuirasses, we resent the knowledge that he for whom they had so great a significance is no longer there to cherish them. Sophia's harp which once

accompanied so many Scottish songs is silent.
The books stand desolate and desiccate within
their gilt cages, for who now fingers beautiful red
leathered Montfaucon or the Variorum classics?
Who would now turn the pages of the *Moniteur*?
Who but Scott would revere casts of the Bruce's
skull and of the Melrose saints? The palace of
dreams once irradiated by the vital personality
of Sir Walter Scott is now an empty shell, empty
as all secular shrines are empty, and prized as all
shrines of genius are prized.

CHAPTER XI

WEALTH AND ILL-HEALTH

THE period between 1816 and 1821, during which he wrote eleven romances, built Abbotsford and directed the Canongate Press, was the fullest in Scott's life. Secure of popularity for his novels and confident in his own power of continuing to produce them, he spent money as soon or sooner than he could rake it in. By what appeared to him an extraordinarily cunning scheme he was paid both for printing books and for writing books, and he had to account to nobody for his expenditure. Most of the profits made by the Press were drawn at once, and spent on Abbotsford. Far from being the victim of the designing and extravagant Ballantynes delineated by Lockhart, Scott himself organized the ruin of his own business. He was an astute man and did everything with his eyes open, while the Ballantynes were his faithful and sometimes foolish servants. The fact that he appeared to make money with such absurd facility made him reckless of the future. Lady Scott used to say that when she wanted a new dress or a new carpet she merely had to ask Scott to scribble some more of his " nonsense."

No apparent prosperity, however, caused him to slacken in output and we find him during the summer of 1816 grinding at a historical conspectus of the events of 1814. It was designed for the *Edinburgh Annual Register* but was used again later on in the *Life of Napoleon,* as was the pendant article written for the same magazine on the events of 1815.

So certain did Scott feel that his trade connection was a secret that he endeavoured during the winter of 1816–17 to get appointed to the Bench of the Scottish Court of Exchequer. As usual he tried to enlist Buccleuch and Dundas interests in order to achieve his object, explaining that he would like to resign his present official posts and take a Barony, since " a man may without condemnation endeavour at my period of life to obtain as much honour and ease as he can handsomely come by." He added that he felt himself to be peculiarly acceptable personally to the Chief Baron, Lord Dundas of Arniston who, as it happened, was brother to the original " architect " of his fortune. The efforts foundered, possibly because his machinations over Thomas Scott's appointment made his fairness doubtful, or else because somebody whispered the story of his commercial commitments into the Chief Baron's ear. It is extremely difficult to believe that Scott's connexion with the Canongate Press could have been hidden from everyone, any more than could the authorship of the novels. The legend however is that both secrets were well kept.

Robust health had been Scott's lot for many years, but during the winter of 1816–17 he experienced touches of " cramp." The pain passed off and was attributed to want of exercise while working in Edinburgh, as he said himself, " In the vacation I never sit down ; in the session time I seldom rise up." A dinner party in Castle Street was scared by a terrifying scream from Scott one day in March, 1817. The " cramp " had become excruciating and he staggered in agony to his bed. From his room he sent down a message to beg that the party should not break up and that it would do him good to hear Mrs. Henry Siddons sing. James Hogg, who had dropped in uninvited that evening, walked home with Mrs. Ballantyne. She said, " I do not at all like this illness of Scott's. I have often seen him looking jaded of late and am afraid it is serious." " Haud your tongue," exclaimed the Shepherd, " or I'll gar you measure your length on the pavement. You fause downhearted loon that you are ; ye daur to speak as if Scott was on his death bed ! It cannot be ! It must not be ! I will not suffer you to speak that gait ! " Hogg's voice shook with emotion.

This attack, one of many danger signals, was soon forgotten and Scott went back to his claret and his " mountain dew," an indulgence for which he was to pay heavily two years later. Unlike Englishmen, he loathed port and so was saved an earlier breakdown. In condemnation of the fashionable wine he was fond of quoting the lines :

Bold and erect the Caledonian stood,
Old was his mutton and his claret good,
Let him drink port ! the English statesman cried
He drank the poison and his spirit died.

By early May he seemed as strong as ever and rejoiced in the budding birches and hazels on his beloved estate. Life was almost too perfect in this paradise for it made sedentary work difficult to settle down to. His enjoyment of nature was interrupted one beautiful day by a visit from Mr. Constable who had driven down from Edinburgh in order to secure the Author of *Waverley's* next novel, which he understood was to deal with the MacGregor chieftain Rob Roy and the Jacobite rising of 1715. Scott told him he had not found a name for the book. "Why not call it after the hero?" asked Constable. "Never let me have to write up to a name," said Scott, "you well know I've generally adopted a title that told *nothing*!"

The two ruddy and stout gentlemen wined and dined together, and Scott became expansive over the new "Waverley"; he was sure if he "ravelled up the tale of a Glasgow weaver with Rob" he could make a hit with it. Constable went home delighted with the assurance that he might count on the book for the late autumn.

During the summer term Scott applied himself to writing an Introduction for and editing two quarto volumes on *Border Antiquities*. It was one of the many odd jobs with which, owing to his antiquarian tastes and his anxiety to earn money, he had the habit of saddling himself. Immediately the term ended he drove off with Adam Fergusson to Rob Roy's cave at the head of Loch Lomond and then passed a few days at Glasgow to study the town and its ways. Having filled his mind thus with local colour he went to Abbotsford and finished the book.

David Wilkie who stayed with him this year describes Scott's intense amusement over "The Chaldee MS." He was almost choked with laughter in reading it. The document had made its appearance in *Blackwood's Edinburgh Magazine* and startled the *literati* of the city. Publishers and writers alike were made fun of in its quasi-biblical verses. The intellectual domination of the Whigs was at last challenged, which delighted Scott who had become more and more conservative as the years passed. The persons satirized

N

were often referred to afterwards by the sobriquets given to them in this skit. Constable for example was hereafter known as "the Crafty," Blackwood as "Ebony," Wilson as "the Leopard," Lockhart as "the Scorpion," and Scott himself, as "the great Magician who dwelleth in the old fortress by the river Jordan which is by the Border."

Scott's life was full of varied interests. During the winter he served as member of the Commission appointed to search for the Scottish Regalia, a Commission of his own contriving for he had recommended its appointment to the Regent one day at Carlton House. The Regalia, it was known, had been smuggled out of Dunottar Castle in Charles II's day and at the time of the Union had been deposited with great formality in a strong chest and the chest placed in what is called the Crown Room in the Castle of Edinburgh, there to be preserved for greater security. Rumours were in circulation to the effect that the treasure had been secretly removed to Hanover. "At last," wrote Croker to Scott, "I had gotten the warrant for searching for the old Regalia of the Scottish Crown which at your suggestion and by the Prince's command I have been soliciting so long. . . . I know that both the Regent and yourself have hopes of finding something."[1] When the old chest in the Crown Room in Edinburgh Castle to which they had been traced was solemnly opened by the appointed Commissioners on the 4th of February, 1818, Scott with histrionic instinct, caused the regiment drawn up on Castle Hill to cheer the discovery. Deeply moved when he first saw the sceptre, and jewels, and above all the crown which might once have rested on the head of Bruce, he alludes to the

[1] *Croker*, Vol. I, p. 113.

occasion as one of the " central moments " of his
life. John Kemble afterwards asked him whether
the crown was not splendid. " The last time I
saw you as Macbeth," replied Scott drily, " you
had a much grander one."

While the first edition of ten thousand *Rob
Roys* was being turned out by the Canongate
Press, Ballantyne received a command from his
master to dangle a new story edited by Jedediah
Cleishbottom in front of Mr. Constable's nose.
This was intolerably irritating, for Constable
could never get over Scott's absurd humour for
concealment. Of course it was subtly commercial
in origin and designed to prick him into offering
competitive prices for any work by the author of
that extremely popular tale *Old Mortality*, of
which he had as we know only secured the fag-
end of the interest. How maddening Scott was
with all his subterfuges ! And yet how could he
afford to let Miller or Murray or Blackwood get
away with another success like the first *Tales of
my Landlord* ? Forthwith he made an offer for
Cleishbottom's new book. Ballantyne replied
but it was Scott's ultimatum that he voiced. The
book would be sold to Murray and Blackwood
unless Constable put down five thousand guineas
to clear all the unsaleable stock from the Hanover
Street publishing house. It was a hard bargain
but it was concluded. Constable found it
" abominable " to have to negotiate with the
Ballantynes and held himself in to avoid a quarrel.
Dealing with principals over the port was one
thing but dealing with subaltern agents in the
cold morning light was another. Would he ever
see the value of the good money he had been
forced to part with ? Scott didn't look too well.
Perhaps he would be on the safe side if he insured

his life.   During 1818 he did so.   Jedediah's new book *The Heart of Midlothian* came out in June : it was stupendously successful.

To the pleasure of his family and retainers and friends Scott at this time accepted a Baronetcy at the hands of the Regent.   He did not actually receive the accolade till 1820 but all the prestige that went with such preferment was his from this time onward, and as all Scott lovers know Tom Purdie was quick to brand the sheep in his charge with an extra S., so that they bore S.W.S. upon their skins instead of plain W.S.

Health appeared to desert him altogether in 1819.   The cramps recurred and he was dosed with calomel and ipecacuanha ; sometimes two hundred drops of laudanum, six grains of opium and three grains of hyposcyamus were given in a day.   He vomited, he was bled and in spite of all treatment the agonizing pain continued for eight or ten hours at a time.   During these trials he took up a fine and humble attitude, indeed at no time is his essential manliness more manifest than in illness.   " I should be a great fool and a most ungrateful wretch to complain.   My life has been . . . as fortunate perhaps as was ever lived. . . . I am already a sufficient debtor to the bounty of Providence to be resigned to it."   At the back of his mind and often in his current thoughts appeared the image of Job.   " If the Lord send good things shall He not also send evil ? "   Often he kept his spirits up with an old ballad quatrain :

> O blesséd Virgin, quoth Robin Hood,
>   That art both Mother and May,
> I think it was never man's destiny
>   To die before his day.

In consequence of the excessive drugging, he became despondent about money and future work. In a fit of gloom he sold all his copyrights to Constable for £12,000 in order to pay outgoings connected with Abbotsford. After a terrible winter Scott felt " totterish," jaundice supervened and he assumed " a golden hue which after a while gave place to a silver complexion." " When I crawl out on Sybil Grey, I am the very image of death on the pale horse, lanthorny jawed, decayed in flesh, stooping as if I meant to eat the pony's ears and unable to go above a foot's pace." His clothes hung on him as if he were a potato bogle, and he lived on rice puddings, toast and water. Writing tired him abominably, and he had to make use of other hands. He lay on a sofa and between groans dictated either to Willie Laidlaw or John Ballantyne. Most of the *Bride of Lammermoor*, and all the *Legend of Montrose* were written in this way. The translated ballad known as *The Noble Moringer* was dictated at the rate of forty-three stanzas a day to Sophia and Laidlaw.

He went back to Edinburgh in May for the opening of the summer session but was too ill to attend. Friends were shocked by his looks and when the *Legend of Montrose* came out in June people said it was his last book, for he was still in bed. The eccentric Lord Buchan, thinking he must be ripe for gathering to his graveyard— Dryburgh—called at Castle Street. The knocker being tied up he made his way by the area up to Scott's bedroom door. Sophia, who was in charge, bade Peter Mathieson escort the Earl downstairs. Words failed to modify his importunity and Mathieson, lest his master should hear the argument, pushed him out of the house.

Scott, who was a very courteous man, was distressed to learn what had happened and sent James Ballantyne to apologize for this affront. Lord Buchan was irate. He stated that his visit had been well intentioned. " I had wished to embrace Walter Scott before he died, and inform him that I had long considered it as a satisfactory circumstance that he and I were destined to rest together in the same place of sepulture. The principal thing however was to relieve his mind as to the arrangements for his funeral, to show him a plan which I had prepared for the procession, in a word, to assure him that I took upon myself the whole conduct of the ceremonial at Dryburgh."

Scott in June bade farewell to his family and turned his face to the wall. A deep sleep overtook him, his last sleep as watchers thought, but to their joy he awoke from it, renewed and with conviction that the crisis was overpast. July found him partly dictating and partly writing *Ivanhoe*. During his convalescence he might sometimes be seen riding on a Highland pony in Charlotte Square " for the wholesomes." He looked almost a skeleton and sat slanting on his horse. In August he was at Abbotsford negotiating for still more land. Convinced that he was going to live, since he was putting on flesh again, he determined to buy Faldonside, remake the loch and stock it with fish. By November he was to all appearance well and strong as ever and enjoying the Abbotsford Hunt. With health came back his boyish sense of humour. He would certainly bring out *Ivanhoe* as the work of another new editor Mr. Lawrence Templeton. The story in no way resembled the Waverley series and it was half printed before Scott gave in to Constable on the question of ascription.

James Ballantyne annoyed him a good deal over the proofs of this novel. We find Sir Walter writing, " Your correctors might save much trouble by observing how proper names, etc., are corrected on the return proofs ; it is very hard to send me the same blunders again and again, always Brian-de-Bois Guilbert for Brian de Bois-Guilbert, Athelston for Athelstane, etc. I have corrected about twenty or thirty times."

Ivanhoe was destined, though no one at first realized it to widen Scott's circle of readers by half the Continent, for he had at last written a picturesque narrative which since it had no Scottish dialect, even foreigners could understand. The novel was a revelation to Dumas of the way history might be presented. In reading all the amazing scenes he began to perceive new horizons. In a month he was trying to imitate " this wonderful Scott ! "

Ivanhoe came out just before Christmas, 1819, and Constable was so pleased with the way it sold that he contracted at once for two unwritten works, *The Monastery* and *The Abbot.*

In the following March Scott went to London to receive the Baronetcy conferred on him eighteen months previously. As usual he made use of the Dumergue's Piccadilly residence, but more than ever the doors were assailed by persons of distinction wishing to do Sir Walter honour.

Among the many callers was courtier-like Sir Thomas Lawrence, commissioned by the King to paint Sir Walter for the gallery at Windsor, and Allan Cunningham, who at the bidding of Mr. Francis Chantrey came to request sittings for a bust. Cunningham found Scott buttoned up into Court dress about to proceed to the King's *Levée.* The red uniform was stiff, there were lace ruffles falling over the big brown hands, and once more as in courting days he wore a queue, a sword and a cocked hat. As he made obeisance and kissed hands George IV remarked, "I shall always reflect with pleasure on Sir Walter Scott's having been the first creation of my reign."

Scott was the only man Chantrey ever asked to sit for him. His request was immediately acceded to. At the first sitting Chantrey found that when the great man was not talking he seemed to sink into himself and assume a lethargic air. As the sculptor could not talk when engrossed in work he begged Scott to bring two or three friends with him to beguile the tedium of posing. At the second sitting Richard Heber, Lord Lyttleton and Croker were present. In all there were seven sittings and the bust when finished was universally acclaimed the living image of Scott. With Chantrey Scott got on remarkably well, they were rubicund countrymen both of them and devoted to salmon fishing. The sculptor made sitters feel at home as he welcomed them to his studio in his fine deep voice and his native tact and intelligence in conversation compensated for his want of book learning. Not that Scott cared whether a man was learned or not provided he was a good listener and enjoyed a joke.

By this time Sir Walter was a well-known figure in London much in request at dinners, picture exhibitions, and first nights. People found his hearty kindness of manner was peculiarly delightful in a sophisticated metropolis. His baronetcy called more attention than ever to his person, but no amount of public notice changed his simplicity of demeanour. He carried about with him a breezy atmosphere for his heart remained ever true to his own country. Croker gives us an idea of his way of entertaining Londoners : " Walter Scott called on me ; he looked older and not so well as I had hoped to find him, but his spirits are excellent and he had not been ten minutes with me when he repeated some stanzas of a ballad made on some laird or laird's steward in the west of Scotland, who is represented as sending out the tenants to catch a mermaid which was rumoured to be on the coast. I recollected but one stanza :

> Some they fished with long lines
> And some they fished with sma',
> And they caught him plenty of whitings
> But the devil a mermaid at a'."

Everyone in London was impressed by his simplicity. No matter how much he was lionized he never betrayed a sign of impatience or conceit. People in the metropolis found the provincial touch quite charming. Haydon, to whom he sat for a head, happened to be exhibiting a large picture, *Christ's Entry into Jerusalem*, at the Egyptian Hall in Piccadilly. One morning before the doors opened who should be found sitting on the stairs but " the mysterious Author of *Waverley* "! His simple good-nature and patient air made Haydon say that he looked as if sitting on a bank in the country. To the painter's delight not only Wordsworth and Mrs. Siddons but Scott also thought his Christ " successful." What between his talks with Haydon and his discussions with James Northcote the Academician, Scott almost began to feel himself an art connoisseur. One day at dinner Lawrence objected in a most genteel way to persons criticizing works of art who were not themselves artists. " Nay," said Sir Walter, " consider, art professes to be a better sort of nature ; and as such appeals to the taste of the world, surely therefore a wise man of the world may judge its worth and feel its sentiments though he cannot produce it. He may not know how it is produced ; yet I see not but that he may estimate its beauty." Sir Thomas smiled and said " Certainly," and gave the conversation another turn.

Charles Leslie, who was later on chosen to paint Sir Walter's portrait at Abbotsford, was taken by Washington Irving to breakfast with Scott in Piccadilly. It was a profuse meal and " quite in the Scotch tradition." Sir Walter on this occasion was dressed in a brown frock coat, blue trousers and black cravat. Though but forty-six his light hair was of silvery whiteness. Sir Walter liked associating with artists and actors and appeared to all the guests as in " full enjoyment of his high and increasing reputation." Leslie invited him to his studio to see his picture " May-day." Advice from the celebrated is always treasured, and when Scott suggested the introduction of " a few archers " into the landscape Leslie painted them in with alacrity. He was so excited by the visit of this great personage that he could do no work for the remainder of the day.

During this jaunt to London Scott had left Charlotte in Edinburgh making preparations for Sophia's wedding to Lockhart. The poor woman was far from well but he hoped to find her " quite in beauty " on his return. He tells her in letters that he has been " coaxed by very pretty ladies " and has dined in company with the Duke of Wellington who fought over Waterloo and his

other battles with great good humour after dinner.
Is it not a fine thing to hear politics discussed by
Ministers of State and war spoken of by the Iron
Duke ? Can he bring her back any finery from the
dressmaker ? To Sophia he writes of coronation
chatter. " They say the peers' robes will cost
£400 apiece, that ermine has been cornered," it is
going to be such a grand affair that he really will
be tempted to come up for the occasion. " Indeed
I don't see why I should not *stay* here as I seem
to be forgotten at home. The people here are
like to smother me with kindness, so why should
I be in a great hurry to leave them . . . ? " He
understands that Sophia and Anne have gone
through the ceremony of confirmation in the
Episcopal Church.

Rather piqued at finding his family so occupied
with Lady Scott's health and Sophia's engage-
ment to Lockhart that they find no time to write
to him, he says in a letter to his future son-in-law :
" I am very angry with Castle Street, not a soul
has written to me save yourself, since I came to
London."

The wedding was fixed for the end of April and
he hurried home to give his much loved daughter
away. Walter attended in " full regimentals "
and very proud did his father feel of him as he
decided to have William Allan paint him standing
beside his charger. In May he informed his son
he had bought more land, under Eildon, to round
off Abbotsford.

Almost everyone Sir Walter met in England
received an invitation to Scotland. One of the
first London guests to arrive was Haydon, who
at Scott's instigation had arranged to display his
big picture of *Christ's Entry into Jerusalem* in
Edinburgh. He called in Castle Street and Sir

Walter stumped down the stairs shouting, " Welcome to Scotland, Haydon ! " and then gripping his visitor's hand, " How d'ye like Edinburgh ? "

Scott, though always the countryman, was at his best as a host. One guest likens him to a prosperous farmer, another to a bonnet laird, but all agree in lauding his extreme geniality. Much preferring the society of his native town to that of London " because the literary and fashionable circles were more mixed together," Sir Walter entertained all kinds of company from princes to peasants. At 39 North Castle Street all distinguished visitors to Scotland left their letters of introduction. Shelley, who as we know was in Edinburgh in 1811 and again in 1813, never crossed its threshold, but then Scott had never heard of this young man and the young man had had a surfeit of *Rokeby*.

Lady Scott's five o'clock dinners were often very amusing in the hilarious sense. People sat at little tables in the drawing-room when the dining-room was too small for the party and story telling and chorus singing were the order of the evening. The Miss Edgeworths went there an hour or two after they arrived in Edinburgh. Three men servants sounded their names from hall to landing. The loud singing stopped suddenly when they entered the drawing-room. Maria, after the usual introductions had been made, said " do not let us interrupt," and was given the end of a silk handkerchief to hold. The Laird of Staffa began to roar a Gaelic boat-song to which all stamped in time, repeated the chorus, and waved their handkerchiefs. Supper followed at a round table and everyone was very jolly.

At no time did Scott care about conversation as such. He made statements, jokes, narrations, but never extended himself in discussion. Sometimes his elder son, who was of quite a different temperament, tried to get away from these gatherings at home. One night when Edward Everett was dining in Castle Street young Walter asked his father's permission to slip out to the theatre, but it was refused. One of Scott's friends says that it was next door to impossible to inveigle him into a colloquial dispute, and his habit of introducing the phraseology of Shakespeare half theatrically into ordinary conversation made any kind of serious discussion difficult. Sinclair gave it as his opinion that though Sir Walter told stories inimitably well, he was not so great an acquisition in general society as might have been expected ; " for when he had finished a story, few had courage to begin another,—hardly anyone would have been listened to ; " thus Sir Walter often had no alternative but either to let the conversation drop, or relate a second story and a third throughout the evening. " I was sometimes reminded," says Mr. Sinclair, " of the discouraging speech addressed by a German to his next-door neighbour when Dr. Johnson was of the company ; ' Wait a moment, Sir, I think that Dr. Johnson is about to speak.' "

Haydon, of course, was invited to dine at Castle Street where he met the complete Scott family, Daniel Terry and William Allan. To him Scott appeared a prudent, kind, deep man. Haydon told him he had climbed up to Salisbury Crags. " Ah," said Scott, " when I was a youth I have often sat there, thinking of my prospects in life. It is a glorious place ! " which remark went to swell Haydon's conviction as to the identity of the Author of *Waverley* with his host, for he remembered the opening of the *Heart of*

Midlothian and " that wild path winding round
the foot on the high belt of semicircular rocks
called Salisbury Crags, and marking the verge of
the steep descent which slopes down into the
glen on the south east side of the city of Edinburgh." This path, Scott said, used to be " my
favourite evening and morning resort when
engaged with a favourite author or new subject of
study." Raeburn, Haydon found " a glorious
fellow," even more boisterous and jolly than
Scott. How wonderful was Princes street in
those days ! In a clear sunset light a visitor could
watch limping Sir Walter talking as he walked
with Lord Meadowbank. Then Jeffrey, restless,
fidgety, keen, tripping along much faster, and
then Lockhart, William Allan, Thompson, Raeburn and other men of note. It was a good place
to be in, and then as now the most beautiful city
in Europe.

Though Scott was cheerful and happy enough
at this time, Constable was none too pleasant,
being disappointed with *The Monastery* and
uncomplimentary about its sequel *The Abbot*.
Really he must insist on a more popular subject—
a story about Elizabeth, for example, which
might, if Scott thought fit, be called the *Armada*.
Scott agreed to write a story about Elizabeth but
suggested naming it *Cumnor Hall*. Constable
liked the sound of Kenilworth, and *Kenilworth*
was the title decided on.

Honours at this time began to fall fast upon
Scott's shoulders, for he had got to the stage
when men, as in the Shagpat legend, are invited to
be crowned king of the apes or donkeys. When
Sir James Hall of Dunglas resigned from the
Presidency of the Royal Society of Edinburgh,
Scott was asked to fill the Chair. He was also

appointed Professor of Ancient History at the Royal Academy in London and invited to receive honorary degrees from the Universities of Oxford and Cambridge.

Sir Walter's fears of revolution involved him about this time in rather an annoying predicament. The scandal of the Queen's Trial had led to much political bitterness and some people, fearing lest the prestige and authority of the Crown might be undermined, strove to re-adjust the situation by means of propaganda. In January, 1821, Scott became guarantor for a new Tory newspaper to be published in Edinburgh. It was called *The Beacon*. He was in good company since the Lord Advocate, the Solicitor-General, the Lord Provost, another Sheriff-depute and two Advocates-depute, were among the fifteen persons who, in giving their bond for £100 to the banker Sir William Forbes, had made themselves proprietors of the paper. Eight hundred subscribers had been whipped up and the periodical started under the happiest auspices. No one of the guarantors seems to have been responsible for the contents and the *Beacon* was so libellously and improperly conducted that actions were brought against it and the scared guarantors, on learning that the Whigs had found out the carefully concealed secret of their names, withdrew their support in August, 1821. To make matters worse some of the libels eventuated in challenges and two gentlemen lost their lives. Public opinion was incensed against the legal officers of the Crown who had given their support to so scurrilous an attack on Reformers and in June, 1822, the *Beacon* scandal was thrashed out in the House of Commons. Curious facts came to light during the debate, for example, it was

alleged that though the Lord Advocate professed
never to read the paper and to know nothing of
its contents, his speeches had been intelligently
anticipated in its columns ; Scottish Ballads had,
it appeared, been made the vehicle of the worst
gibes and attacks ; and the Sheriff-depute of
Lanarkshire was found to have contributed
articles. Sir Walter in supporting the *Beacon* had
merely hunted with the pack and indulged his
violent anti-reform sentiment, but he disliked the
exposure involved in the debate, and the imputa-
tion that as a law officer of the Crown he had
been entirely incorrect in supporting such an
organ of defamation. As with other disagreeable
experiences, however, he soon threw off the
memory of it and applied himself to the spinning
of new tales.

During the summer of 1821 " jocund Johnny "
died. It was a great grief to Scott, but such was
the elasticity of his temperament that in July he
set sad thoughts aside and started off with
considerable excitement for the Coronation. He
had proposed taking James Hogg as his companion
and had written to Lord Sidmouth to secure seats
for himself and the Ettrick Shepherd. Lord
Sidmouth supplied the tickets and invited both
the bards to dine with him at Richmond Park
to meet the Duke of York and " a few other
Jacobites." Sheep fairs detained Hogg in Scotland and Scott alone went to Leith to board the
new nine-knot steamship *City of Edinburgh* which
in fair weather made London in four days. He
broke his usual custom of staying with the
Dumergues and in order to be in the centre of
things paid a visit, to his friend Stewart Rose,
who lived in Old Palace Yard, Westminster.

He witnessed the rumpus when the Queen tried

to get into the Abbey, and wrote to James Ballantyne "the Bedlam Bitch of a Queen you cannot imagine the contempt she is held in. . . . She retired amid groans and cries of Shame ! Shame ! Home ! Home ! and the still more disgraceful acclamations of her own blackguards who exclaimed ' That's it, Caroline ! Go it, my girl !' I really believe she is mad. Mad or not, the common people of England were strongly on her side."

Scott was immensely impressed by the Coronation ceremony. There was enough feudalism and pomp about it to please him and awaken all sorts of reflections. He adored seeing the King and the Duke of York embrace, " pressed to each other's bosoms." The effect produced by the peers placing their coronets on their heads struck him as really august. It is a gesture that always commands the admiration of spectators.

A minor sensation was created by the publication of Adolphus's *Letters,* which set out to prove that the author of the *Lay of the Last Minstrel* and other poems was identical with the author of *Waverley.* Mr. Adolphus in quotation after quotation produced irrefutable arguments and points of resemblance. He found the moon " waded " both in the *Antiquary* and in the poems ; he discovered that autumn winds made " bugle sounds " both in the *Lord of the Isles* and the *Bride of Lammermoor* ; he noted that hinds led their fawns from coverts to open ground in *Ivanhoe* and *The Lady of the Lake.* He compared the waning poet with the waxing novelist, and wrote of " the talent so unaccountably withdrawn from the depths of lyrical composition now pouring out its exuberance in another region of literature." It really looked as if the Great

o

Unknown had been cornered at last. Scott smiled on the detective work and proceeded to deal with the ingenuities of Mr. Adolphus in the Introduction to a new romance, *The Fortunes of Nigel*. This, the fifteenth of the Waverley novels, was published in May, 1822. Scott had immensely enjoyed writing it. Just after he had scribbled the first chapter he rushed out to Terry and Lockhart who were talking in the courtyard outside his study window at Abbotsford. Waving a bunch of manuscript in his hand he said : " Well, lads, I've laid the keel of a new lugger this morning, here it is. Be off to the waterside and let me hear how you like it." Terry took the papers and walking up and down by the river read the first chapter of *Nigel* aloud to Lockhart. " I could see," said Lockhart, " that according to the Sheriff's phrase he smelt roast meat . . . there was every prospect for a fine field for Terryfication." *The Fortunes of Nigel*, despite the fact that the hero is but a dull young man, is a very interesting book introducing us as it does to the Court of James I, seventeenth-century London, and all the manners and ways immortalized by Ben Jonson and his fellows. We get to know the King, Heriot the wealthy goldsmith, melancholy Charles, proud Buckingham. As a picture of manners it is remarkable, for Scott wrote it with great speed and in great excitement. It was acclaimed as of high merit, but as we know, no literary success ever elated the Laird of Abbotsford.

Writing to his old friend Jane Cranstoun, Countess Purgstall, he reveals a good deal of his constant state of mind. . . . " I promise you my oaks will outlast my laurels ; and I pique myself more upon my compositions for manure

than on any other compositions whatsoever to
which I was ever accessory. . . . For my own
course of life I have only to be ashamed of its
prosperity and afraid of its termination, for I
have little reason . . . to hope that the same
good fortune will attend me for ever.   I have had
. . . more of fame and fortune than mere literature ever procured for a man before. . . . Should
things change with me . . . ?   I trust I shall be
able to surrender adventitious advantages as I
would my upper dress, as something extremely
comfortable which I can make shift to do
without."

There was a philosopher hidden in that jovial
burly form.

CHAPTER XII

THE PLAIDED PAGEANT

THERE had been a time, before the Prince of Wales became Regent, when good Tories circled round the Princess of Wales and good Whigs round the Prince of Wales, and both sets held each other's idols in abhorrence. We find Scott writing apprehensively to Lady Abercorn in 1806, the year of the Delicate Investigation, when sympathies were acutely alienated from the Heir to the Throne. "We have been threatened with a visit of the Heir Apparent, a very serious business to the poor Scottish nobility who might have deemed it necessary to receive him and somehow not very acceptable to the people at large. It certainly requires ingenuity in a personage whose very smile is a favour and therefore has popularity so much at his own command to contrive so totally to get rid of what naturally attaches to one from whom much might have been hoped and little feared if he had chosen it should be so."

A readjustment of loyalties took place in 1811–12. The Princess, abandoned by the Tories was adopted by the Whigs. "Did you ever see anything so like a game of commerce," Scott enquired of Lady Abercorn, " as the Opposition picking up the Princess of Wales so soon as they had lost the Prince Regent ? "

After Perceval's assassination the Regent supported Lord Liverpool's new administration, and

Scott wrote once more to Lady Abercorn : " The present ministers while out of office held the Princess in their hand—a court card to be sure but of no great value. They have the luck to take up the Prince, lost by the blunder of their opponents and they discard the Princess as a matter of course." Scott, who as we know had once, like Lawrence, Campbell, Lewis and many more, been a courtier at Montagu House, was now attracted into the Carlton House orbit and took to praising the Regent as consistently as he had formerly depreciated him. The Princess was called very ugly names while her husband was exalted as the enlightened patron of Art and Letters. By the time he ascended the throne as George IV the wheel had gone full circle ; the flirtatious Queen was neglected by all, while the King with wonderful dignity reigned.

But a few weeks had elapsed since Sir Walter had presented James I to an admiring world when he was called on to present George IV to his Scottish subjects. In July, 1822, it was intimated to him by the Lord Provost of Edinburgh that the King proposed to visit his city, he determined that Auld Reekie's reception should not be unworthy of the Monarch he had seen so augustly crowned.

The notice of the visit was short, and the Lord Provost was only too glad to turn to the friend of royalty, Sir Walter Scott, for advice. Immediately he put his literary work on one side and took on his shoulders the organization of a pageant such as no one of his fellow townsmen had dreamt of. Within a few hours his mind was bubbling over with notions of how best to enable Scotland to display herself robed in typical glory and pride. To him the enterprise was almost like

conceiving a new novel, but unlike a novel it
required collaborators.   At his instigation a committee of five was formed, consisting of the Lord
Provost, General David Stewart of Garth (author
of the *History of the Highland Regiments*), Sir
Alexander Keith, Knight Marischal of Scotland,
and Mr. Skene of Rubislaw. This committee
met daily at Scott's house, which for the time
being was converted into an office.   There was
much to be planned, a court to be held at Holyrood, Highland chiefs and clansmen to be summoned to pay their respects, the tradesmen of the
town to be marshalled to manifest loyal dutiful-
ness, processions and banquets to be organized,
a cathedral service to be conducted, and the
foundation of a war memorial to be laid on Calton
Hill. The committee listened while Scott pro-
pounded his varied schemes. It was evident that
he had *Waverley* at the back of his mind, with
King George playing the part of Prince Charlie.
Great enthusiasm was required to carry the scheme
out with success, for it was easy to make a man of
twenty stone look ridiculous in a romantic rôle.
The Hanoverians were stalwarts, however, and
did not shrink from the ordeal of the kilt ; had
not the Duke of Sussex displayed his pink knees
at Scotch Masonic banquets in London and given
toasts in Erse and drunk them in usquebaugh out
of shells *à la* Ossian ? There was no limit to royal
good nature or versatility, Scott was convinced
of that as with ardour and loquacity he swept the
committee along in his wake. As there was little
time for thought his suggestions were accepted
and put into execution. In order to popularize
the visit, Scott wrote a ballad, which was distributed as a broadsheet. The verses made it
appear that King George IV was a sight for sore

eyes, the " sonsie " countenance all Scotland
ached to see.

> Auld England held him lang and fast
> And Ireland had a joyfu' cast ;
> But Scotland's turn is come at last—
> Carle, now the King's come !
>
> Auld Reekie, in her rokelay grey
> Thought never to have seen the day ;
> He's been a weary time away—
> But, Carle, now the King's come !

Somehow or another the Highland chieftains
were convened and persuaded to appear in the
capital with their tails of clansmen. Some were
men of magnificent appearance and proud bearing. Their romantic figures have been fixed for
ever for us in the canvasses of Raeburn and his
imitators, and by calling up the Cock o' the
North, the McNab, or Sir John Sinclair against
their wild mountain backgrounds we may get an
idea of the kind of persons Scott had to conciliate.
It was most difficult to decide on the Highlanders'
order of precedence in the projected procession,
for they stood on their relative positions at
Bannockburn, about which battle Scott luckily
knew as much if not more than they did. With
immense tact and good humour he secured their
good will and co-operation and introduced their
order of battle into his broadsheet. After all
it was he who had caused the Scotland they stood
for to rise blazoned with glory from the grave,
and they owed him much. Their natural leader,
General Stewart of Garth, who supported Scott
in these negotiations, found himself at last in
charge of a peaceful though haughty band of
three hundred kilted gentlemen who, since they

could not take orders from each other, decided to submit to Scott's decrees.

The house in Castle Street was thronged, not only by touchy chieftains, but by clergy, conveners of trades, furnishers who were to set the scenes at Holyrood and the Parliament House, and master tailors commissioned to produce traditional costumes.

A foreign writer calling on Sir Walter at this time made notes for his compatriots of what he saw in Edinburgh. As he stood on the doorstep of 39 Castle Street, staring at the brass plate bearing the words, " Sir Walter Scott, Advocate," his ruminations were curtailed by the door being smartly opened by footmen with powdered heads and blue and yellow livery. Announced into the study he found the author at his writing table and was greatly struck by his majestic head and charming smile. Scott had looked so bourgeois in the street the day before in his country clothes, with sweat running down his face ; but now the stranger was confronted by a dignified gentleman. They spoke of *The Lord of the Isles*, for which poem Sir Walter said he was under great obligations to the old poet Barbour.[1] Amedée Pichot went up to the drawing-room and found Lady Scott most agreeable. She was delighted to meet a French man of letters and so glad he was staying to luncheon. Did he know he was going to meet the English poet Crabbe who was staying with them ? It surprised her to hear that Crabbe was appreciated or even at all read in France. "How did Monsieur figure him ? " "Little, morose—*enfin* —miserable," hazarded Pichot. " Oh, dear, no," laughed his hostess, "that is quite a mistake, he is amiable, plump, and a great admirer of Scott's ! "

[1] 1316?-1396, author of *Brus*.

They went on to discuss food and Dr. Johnson's *Tour in the Hebrides*. " You are a friend of Monsieur Charles Nodier," said Lady Scott. " Do you know that he said his whole journey to Scotland was lost as he had not seen Sir Walter Scott ? " Lady Scott was a merry talker and much amused at the ungallant way in which Nodier had described Scottish ladies.

The Reverend George Crabbe, who had been cordially but vaguely invited to stay, turned up a day or two before the King was due. He had not intended that his visit should synchronize with the Royal Progress, but he was begged to stay for it, and proved a happy though rather fussy guest, asking for a lamp and writing materials to be placed beside his bed each night. Lady Scott told him that she wondered the day was not long enough for authorship, and he replied : " Dear Lady, I should have lost many a good hit had I not set down at once things that occurred to me in my dreams ! "

Lady Scott, like every other loyal body in Edinburgh, was practising curtseys with a train four yards long. The reverences were to be very profound and each lady was to be saluted on the cheek. Sir Walter showed Monsieur Pichot his Deputy-Lieutenant's uniform ; it really was rather fun to be behind the scenes like this, but how depressing to hear of Lord Castlereagh's suicide on the very day the King had sailed ! There was no doubt in the Frenchman's mind that Sir Walter would be made a peer for his pains.

Somehow Scott found time to dress up his homely groom, Peter Mathieson, in a flaxen wig, three-cornered hat, and embroidered livery, to drive his sociable and four about the city, for he was determined not to cut an unworthy figure

himself in the pageant. Perhaps his worst
moments were gone through with the advance
guard of English courtiers, who wanted everything
done in the English way, as had been the case
in Dublin some twelve months previously. They
did not seem to understand that by the Articles
of Union, Scotland, in the event of a King's visit,
was free to display itself as an independent King-
dom. They even went so far as to suggest that
the Highland guard should have the flints taken
from their pistols! Scott preserved his good
temper even with these impertinent persons, but
it was very hard, fussing work, and what between
worry and the mortal illness of his beloved friend
Willie Erskine, he broke out into an irritating rash
which mercifully confined itself to the covered
portions of his body. Just about the time
the King was due to arrive at Leith, Sir Walter
ran into his friend Sinclair, who seemed annoyed
and complained of the " absurd " things he had
heard were planned in honour of the Royal visit.
" There is one good thing which you must not
forget," said Sir Walter, with inimitable gravity,
"the King is coming *suddenly* upon us and thus we
shall be saved from pre-meditated absurdities."

At last the great day came. In a curtain of
rain the *Royal George* anchored at dawn in Leith
Roads. The members of the reception committee looked dejectedly out of the window and
deputed Scott to go aboard the yacht and humbly
request His Majesty to postpone landing till the
following day. Forthwith the sociable was ordered to the door and rattled off to Leith. Just
as he left Lady Scott handed him what she called
the pretty *cocarde*—a St. Andrew's Cross in silver
—set with pearls and cairngorms picked up on
the shores and estuaries of Scotland. The ladies

of Edinburgh had charged him to present it to the
King before he set foot on Scottish soil. Away
Sir Walter rattled to Leith. The King, genial as
always, on being told of the visitor's arrival, ex-
claimed, " What ! Sir Walter Scott ? The man in
Scotland I most wish to see. Let him come up ! "
More than equal to the occasion, the ambassador
addressed the King in a humorous speech :

" Impatient, Sire, as your loyal subjects are to
see you plant your foot upon their soil, they hope
you will consent to postpone your public entry
until to-morrow. In seeing the state of the
weather, I am myself forcibly reminded of a
circumstance that once occurred to me. I was
about to make a tour of the Western Highlands.
. . . I wrote to the innkeeper of a certain hos-
telrie . . . to have rooms prepared for me.
On the day appointed it rained ceaselessly . . .
we were met . . . by our Boniface with bared
head. . . . ' Gude guide us, Sir Walter ! This is
just awful ! Sic a downpour ! I really beg your
pardon ! I'm sure it's no fault of mine ! I cannot
think how it should happen to rain this way just
as you, o' a' men of the world, should come to see
us! It looks amaist personal ! I can only say for
my part I'm just ashamed o' the weather.' I
do not think," concluded Sir Walter, " that I can
improve on the language of the honest innkeeper. I canna think how it should rain this
way, just as your Majesty, of all men in the
world, should have condescended to come and
see us. I can only say in the name of my
countrymen, ' I'm just ashamed of the weather '."
The King laughed and called for a glass of
cherry brandy, in which Sir William Knighton
watched him drink the poet's health. With
courtier-like gravity, Sir Walter begged that the

glass touched by royal lips might be given to him. He was thinking of Abbotsford and his historical museum. The glass was wrapped up and stuffed into the skirt of his overcoat. After presenting the St. Andrew's Cross, Scott bowed himself out of the royal presence and hurried back to his colleagues to report on his visit. He found his home in Castle Street thronged as usual. Full of excitement Sir Walter rushed into the sitting-room, welcomed his guests warmly and sat down with a bump on a chair. Shrieking, he started up again. Lady Scott thought he must have sat upon scissors, but it was the historic glass, no longer fit to figure in the museum. Crabbe, who led a very quiet life, was present and a little bewildered by the bustle around him. Though he was handed over to Lockhart to entertain, Sir Walter found time to take him to St. Anthony's chapel, to spend an hour with him at Muschat's Cairn, and to instruct him in the history of clans and tartans. The silver-haired parson with his snuff-taking habit and his quiet ways was a calming influence in the agitated household in Castle Street.

The next day dawned brightly. Sir Walter reviewed the Celtic Club at six in the morning and invited some of the members to breakfast at nine o'clock. Retiring to his library for a while in the interval before breakfast, he entered the dining-room to find his clerical guest, dressed in silk stockings and knee breeches, expressing regret that he could not converse in French with some resplendent Scotsmen. They took him for an Abbé, and he thought they could talk nothing but Gaelic and possibly French. A joke from the Sheriff put everyone at his ease.

After breakfast the kilted Celtic gentlemen

marched to their assigned posts, and Scott drove out in his sociable to see that all was ready for the royal entry into Edinburgh. It was estimated that some 60,000 people were drawn up along the line of the route and on the adjacent rising ground. The clans represented by three hundred Highlanders paraded at the pier of Leith, together with an escort of Midlothian Cavalry and the Archers of the Body Guard. Among the kilted figures on the pier was that of an Englishman, Sir William Curtis, maker of sea-biscuits at Wapping, ex-Member of Parliament and ex-Lord Mayor of London, a favoured subject who had entertained George IV on his gorgeously appointed yacht and in his seaside house at Ramsgate. Sir William was a very tall and fat man of seventy, but he enjoyed adorning himself in the gay Stuart tartan and marching into Edinburgh in the procession. Charles Young, the actor, saw him pass amidst the laughter of the crowd. The goings on in the streets before the multifarious groups solidified into escorts and avenues amused Young vastly ; it was less like a scene in Auld Reekie than a Continental carnival, with the sun pouring down and everyone in fancy dress. Arthur's Seat was bedecked with snowy tents, the unfrequented road up Salisbury Crags was sprinkled with moving scarlet, and the old Castle had banners flaunting from the outer walls. Archers in Lincoln green, disdainful Highlanders with plumes on their heads and parti-coloured plaids about their bodies—women in summer finery, vistas of bunting and covered scaffolding—everything contributed to give the old city an air of fantastical gaiety. Monsieur Pichot enjoyed seeing lovely ladies smiling from their bonnets and waving handkerchiefs.

Dense walls of human beings watched the marching men and the crawling carriages as they moved into Edinburgh. It was noted that Glengarry's men, who immediately preceded the royal conveyance, suddenly struck up " The Campbells are coming oh—oh! oh! oh! " It was also noticed that the King's face showed astonishment as he caught sight of Arthur's Seat—a huge hill of humanity and blanched perceptibly as he looked down Princes Street and saw the welcoming thousands. Emotionally he rose in his carriage and then sank back and burst into tears. The battered beau of Carlton House was not accustomed to such manifest adoration.

The royal party slept at Dalkeith Palace, six miles from the city, but almost every day saw a scene of the planned pageant enacted in Edinburgh, and every day added to the principal producer's glory. There was the visit to the Castle—the booming cannon on Arthur's Seat, the Castle guns belching out smoke in reply; and the King, a tiny figure viewed from below, waving his hat from an embrasure. " Never King was better received by his people, never King felt it more," said George IV to Scott. The *levée* at Holyrood was a ceremony after Scott's own heart. That forsaken and ancient shell was brought back to life by the Scottish Officers of State in their rich antique dresses. Drawn broadswords, shields and banners, hidden since '45, reappeared. How Scott's heart rejoiced in it all, and how he liked seeing his boy Charles act as page to the Knight Marischal and himself to shepherd his smartly dressed, reluctant family to curtsey and be kissed by the portly, staid figure in the royal Stuart tartan! " Mamma, Sophia and Anne were dreadfully frightened and I, of course, though an old courtier, in such a court as Holyrood was a good deal uneasy. The King, however, spoke to them and they were all kissed in due form. . . . " Even Crabbe enjoyed being recognized by the royal eye. To Scott, if to no one else, the palace was packed with memories, and for him the " desolate, stripped apartments were worth a hundred of Carlton or Buckingham House." He felt " strong emotion " at this strange, histrionic revival, and great exhaustion of body.

Humorous incidents, of course, were bound to occur in such an improvisation, and not the least of them was the appearance of Sir William Curtis stalking in to do homage at the *levée*, again dressed in the eye-compelling tartan—though this time in trews. The King flushed up in anger, for he knew that his old friend was perilously near making a fool of him. No one smiled, however, and the incident was soon effaced from the monarch's consciousness as subject after subject claimed his attention. A laird arriving late for presentation asked those coming from the presence what he had to do. " Oh," said some one, " there is no difficulty about the matter. It's very plain sailing. You have only got just to go in, make your bow—lower, by the bye, than you would make to anyone else—and pass on and pass out." The old laird glided sideways across the room before the King, nervously bowing himself towards the exit. Hearing Lord Erroll in a loud aside saying, " Kiss hands ! Kiss hands !" the bewildered man retreated backwards kissing both hands to the King, as if wafting an affection-ate greeting to an old friend. This episode entirely restored the King's good humour.

In organizing public functions it is impossible

to please everyone and a Mr. Stuart wrote to his friend Fergusson of Raith, " I have been much disappointed with the *levée*. A vast crowd . . . . The King did not seem to move a muscle and we all asked each other when we came away, what had made us take so much trouble. He was dressed in tartan. Sir Walter Scott has ridiculously made us appear a nation of Highlanders, and the bagpipe and the tartan was the order of the day."

Almost every day Sir Walter drove to Dalkeith, and one evening he attended the King to a command performance of *Rob Roy*. He also inspected the Parliament House to see that it was decently hung with tapestries and pictures for the banquet to be given to His Majesty by the magistrates of the city. He saw to everything and took nothing for granted.

On Sunday the Monarch repaired for divine service to the Cathedral of St. Giles. To some spectators this was the most edifying sight of the pageant. The same people who had cheered him madly on foregoing days now stood silent with bowed heads, conveying in this manner their reverence for the Lord's Day and their homage to the King of Kings. As Sir Walter wrote to Lady Abercorn " not a single whisper was heard. . . ." The King told Scott that " the silence of such an immense concourse of people and for such a cause seemed to him the most impressive thing he ever witnessed."

In one of the processions, the Regalia of Scotland were paraded before the King, and Scott felt no incongruity in the event, for he had somehow assimilated the Fourth George as the representative of all Stuart traditions. It was the sort of curious transmutation of which his mind was eminently capable. He had the power of

believing things to be as he wished them to be.
It was to be one of the causes of his financial
imbroglio.

Mr. Robert Peel walked up the High Street with
Scott early one morning before the day's cere-
monies began. There were crowds everywhere
and all greeted his companion with enthusiasm.
The Minister said later that " it was the first
thing that gave him a notion of the electric shock
of a nation's gratitude."

The royal fortnight was one of nervous tension
for Scott, nervous tension and great self-control.
Willie Erskine had been buried on one of the
gayest days of the pageant, and Scott had hurried
from a grave to a banquet. He was tormented
physically and perforce intensely active. It was
an immense relief when the last ceremony was
over and he saw the King re-embark from
Lord Hopetoun's house on the Firth of Forth.
Before leaving Scotland George IV, on Sir Walter
Scott's advice, knighted Adam Fergusson, Keeper
of the Regalia, and Henry Raeburn, painter of
portraits. With a contented sigh the novelist
returned to Castle Street and resumed his metho-
dical desk life. The house had been no better
than an office for weeks past, but the parade
had been an unqualified success. Scotland had
been lifted high in English eyes.

The Poet Laureate had spurred himself to
support the efforts of his friend Scott by inditing
one of his deadly royal odes.

> At length hath Scotland seen
> The presence long desired
> The pomp of royalty,
> Hath gladdened once again
> Her ancient palace, desolate how long !

.   .   .   .   .

P

Land of the loyal, as in happy hour
Revisited, so was thy regal seat
In happy hour for thee
Forsaken, under favourable stars, when James
His valediction gave,
And great Eliza's throne
Received its rightful heir
The Peaceful and the Just.

And to support the illusion of the Hanoverian re-incarnation of a Stuart King, he wrote :

Nor hath the sceptre from that line
Departed though the name hath lost
Its regal honours. Trunk and root have fail'd ;
A scion from the stock
Liveth and flourisheth. It is the Tree
Beneath whose sacred shade
In majesty and peaceful power serene
The Island Queen of Ocean hath her seat.

No poet laureate ever earned his fee more con-scientiously than Southey, as he sank to every occasion of royal birth or death. He pæaned forth the arrival of distinguished visitors to our shores and trumpeted the King's visits to the sister kingdoms. It was a terrible task to have undertaken, but he never winced, and was always grateful to his friend Scott for having secured for him the reversion of the office.

Mere words, however, could never shadow forth the unparalleled success of the Plaided Pageant. It displayed Scotland as the land of romance and loyalty and we are left wondering whether in Sir Walter was not incarnated the greatest scene producer of all time.

CHAPTER XIII

THE CASTLE OF HOSPITALITY

IF a man achieves success in any walk of life, but more especially in literature, the world soon wears a path to his door. Some authors discourage this form of hero-worship, to others it is a stimulating incense. Scott, who was the least vain of men, derived a sort of pleasure from the chance contacts fame brought to him, and real enjoyment from the company of invited guests. Besides the many tourists who drove up to stare at Abbotsford and watch for the owner—sixteen coachloads a day at one time—there were always friends from Edinburgh and neighbours from the vicinity to be welcomed. The house was seldom empty of guests, indeed Lady Scott used to say, it was a hotel in all but pay.

It was inevitable that people so hospitable should from time to time be imposed on. One day two young Americans attired in Macgregor tartan called. Scott was out and his wife did not think to ask them for their credentials, but merely gave them luncheon and allowed them to wait for their host. When the laird came in and heard their accent, he asked what letters of introduction they had brought. None were forthcoming, but, unabashed, they explained that one of them was a lawyer and the other a Unitarian preacher from Massachusetts. Proceeding to question him preposterously about the house, the family, the ages of Lady Scott and the children, the Sheriff was obliged with rather a wry smile to dismiss them. Sometimes sight-seers hid in the park or in the glen in the hope of watching the great man as he walked. On one occasion a group stood round him as he slumbered ! Publicity then as now was an almost unmixed evil though Scott was slow to find it out.

Sir Walter, as we know, dealt out invitations freely during his visits to London. Samuel Rogers was requested to stay at " Conundrum Castle " and see the " Gothic Museum "—" such a contrast by the way to Rogers' classical collections "—full of " rusty iron coats " and " jingling jackets ! " Tom Moore was also invited, and Mrs. Coutts and Lady Alvanley and the Duke of Wellington and Chantrey and Lawrence, indeed almost everybody he met. When he was on his death bed, his failing mind was busy with arrangements for the reception of the Iron Duke at Abbotsford. Scott's hospitality was unbounded by ideas of expense and sometimes of accommodation ! He liked his sideboard to groan under good fare at all times and his table to be furnished with silver plate. Visitors were always struck by the breakfasts they found at Abbotsford. One or two guests made an inventory of the food set before them. Besides tea, coffee, chocolate, there was porridge, white bread, bannocks of barley meal, and rolls. On the sideboard a venison pasty, a ham, some collared eels, kippered salmon, reindeer tongue and a flagon of claret. Scott ate enormously at breakfast, having his own loaf by his side, from which he cut and cut again. Lady Scott grew accustomed to store up plentiful provisions in the house as she never knew what the day might bring forth. She was thus fully prepared if told on waking that Prince Leopold of Belgium would dine that day, or that Prince Gustavus Vasa, Crown Prince of Sweden, would spend the week-end under her roof. Money it seemed was plentiful, and provisions, especially meat, were comparatively cheap. What need therefore for economy? If the supplies were not consumed on the premises, there were always the cottagers on the estate with whom she was intensely popular and to whom she was a constant gift-bringer.

George Ticknor of Boston was at Abbotsford with his wife in March, 1819. Like his compatriots Irving and Everett, he was struck by the vitality Scott appeared to draw from contact with the soil. In their walks together, every stone, every hillock seemed to evoke a traditional story or a ballad from Scott's fecund mind.

Ticknor commented on the " good-looking, self-satisfied dog " dressed in Highland costume, who played the pipes during dinner. Some guests complained they were unable to enjoy their food because of " the droning notes of the bag-pipe which never intermitted till the cloth was about to be removed." The sounds interrupted conversation and irritated nerves ; indeed everyone except the host was thankful when the performer, who had paraded up and down in front of the windows, was summoned to drink his bumper of Glenlivet, bow to the company and disappear. There were many evenings when he re-appeared and the house party danced reels till the small hours. Scott was quite unmusical, but he adored the skirling of the pipes and the singing of Scottish songs. He used to say he had a " reasonable good ear for a jig " but that " solos and sonatas gave him the spleen." It was amusing to observe his face when visitors sang Italian or

German songs. The other guests might be enthralled, but Scott sat absent and abstracted
with his lips drawn down, his chin on the crutch
of his gold-headed stick, his eyebrows contracted,
his whole countenance denoting a " sad civility."
The moment, however, that Sophia uncovered
her harp and played *Charlie is my Darling*
a change came over the host. His eyes lit up,
he smiled, blood mantled his cheek, his big chest
heaved with relief, and unable to contain himself
he would hobble across the room, and then brandishing his cane with animation shout, " And a'
the folk came running out to greet the Chevalier !
Oh ! Charlie is my darling ! "

Sophia seemed to sing Jacobite ballads with as
much pleasure as her father listened to them. He
is described as following them " with eyes, lips,
mind, his whole being as if a religious rite were
being performed." His taste was for the comic
or the sentimental, and he joined with gusto in
*Bannocks o' bear meal, bannocks o' barley, Ken-
mure's on and awa'* and *Auld Lang Syne*. One
evening Lady Home asked Sophia to play *Rob
Roy*, a song from the play at that time being
performed in Edinburgh. This was a little embarrassing, and she went across the room to ask
her father what she should do. " Yes, my dear,"
he said, " play it to be sure if you are asked, and
Waverley and the *Antiquary* too, if there be any
such ballads."

Evenings were not always spent in the saloon
at Abbotsford. Sometimes the gentlemen, after
absorbing their quantum of wine repaired to the
armoury for coffee and were there joined by the
ladies. Scott would seat himself in a high-
backed chair and would lead the conversation
for a while, telling tales of mystery and second

sight; and when he thought he had filled the stage long enough he would get up and call to occupy the high chair another guest, it might be histrionic Charles Young, who from memory would give them *Tam o' Shanter*, or Charles Mathews, who would impersonate an old Hieland body telling stories in dialect, or Adam Fergusson, who would carol, *Hey, Johnny Cope, are ye wauking yet?* or *The Laird o' Cockpen* or *Wha wad na fecht for Charlie?* As each person abdicated the chair, someone else occupied it and contributed to the common stock of social amusement. Sometimes Scott read aloud from Shakespeare, Crabbe or Byron. One evening he took down *Christabel* and seating himself in the midst of his guests read it right through : another evening it was Thomas the Rhymer's adventure with the Queen of the Fairies. Sometimes he read passages from his own unacknowledged works. Mr. Adolphus speaks of him as a charming host, and says that his silver hair, rubicund face and ever changing expression were a pleasure to look on. How admirable too was the range of his voice in reciting *Bonnie Dundee*. The first dawn of a humorous thought would show itself sometimes in an involuntary lengthening of the upper lip, and then, as with Walpole, came " the heart's laugh." Sometimes on fine warm evenings guests were sent to see Melrose Abbey by moonlight. Perhaps someone would recite Gray's *Elegy*, or Scott on daylight visits would read out the epitaph he loved with what Mrs. John Ballantyne called " awe-striking solemnity " :

> Earth walketh on the earth
> Glistering like gold ;
> Earth goeth to the earth
> Sooner than it wold,

> Earth buildeth on the earth
> Palaces and towers.
> Earth sayeth to the earth,
> All shall be ours.

The company of his charming women guests
was specially enjoyed by Scott, though sometimes he got into difficulties in entertaining such a
variety of types. On one occasion Lady Compton and Lady Alvanley were enjoying a happy
visit when " the mistress of millions," Mrs.
Thomas Coutts, suddenly announced her arrival
from Edinburgh with a lady companion, two
physicians and two maids. This visitation was a
heavy trial to Lady Scott, but Sir Walter beamed
at everyone and everyone was fitted in somewhere.
The Ladies Compton and Alvanley, who loathed
the ostentation of the banker's widow, were
inclined to give her the cold shoulder, but a word
from Scott persuaded one of them to play her
accompaniments after dinner and the other to
behave with polite urbanity. When Scott was
uncertain in matters of precedence he adverted
to a ruse, and in the case of Lady Grey and Lady
Cockburn, he engaged the attention of both ladies
just before dinner was announced with a diverting
anecdote, and then, as if in a fit of absent-
mindedness, he continued his tale and offered one
arm to one and the other to the other and carried
them off to the dining-room while still telling his
story. Lord Cockburn, who was often at Abbotsford, said of Sir Walter, " no bad idea of his
conversation will be found by supposing one of
his Scotch novels cut into talk, not so much
conversation as a joyous flow of anecdote, story,
character and scene, mostly humorous, always
graphic and never personal or ill-natured."
Where Abbotsford was concerned no detail was

too insignificant for Scott to adjust, in fact, he
attached significance to every detail. The pictures, the wall-papers, the curtains, the wainscoting were all carefully chosen. The library,
perhaps the finest room in the house, was forty
feet long and eighteen feet wide with a carved
oak roof. It had quite an ancestral air with its
20,000 volumes in beautiful bindings, its books
given by the King and by Constable, its bust of
Shakespeare on a porphyry stand, its silver urn
containing Attic bones given by Byron, its mantel
surmounted by a portrait of Captain Walter
Scott and his charger, its crimson curtains woven
in Galashiels from Sir Walter's own wool. Sir
Walter's kinsman, Hugh Scott of Harden, gave rolls
of " a splendid Chinese wall paper," green with
figures on it and enough to cover the walls of the
drawing-room and two bedrooms. How beautiful it looked when hung, though Lady Scott
would spoil perfection by insisting that two
" ugly blank spaces " should be left bare for the
mirrors she adored. The crimson damask curtains assigned to this room seemed to Sir Walter's
eyes " very handsome " with their golden fringe ;
and well-varnished doors and window frames of
Jamaica cedar wood (" the colour of ginger-
bread ") were a source of great pleasure in library
and drawing-room. The dining-room had crimson walls and was hung with historic canvases—
the portraits of Lucy Waters and her son Monmouth, a picture of Essex on horseback, and the
head of Mary Stuart, painted by Amias Cawood
the day after decapitation.

With some old beams from Robroyston or
Rarbiston, where Wallace was betrayed to death
by Monteith, he had a chair made " as a memorial
of our most patriotic hero with a feeling somewhat

similar to those who remember their Saviour in the crucifix." It was copied from a carved chair at Hamilton Palace. The library table was made by the village carpenter under Scott's supervision. Painting, graining, plastering were seen to by the laird who had strong views on decoration, abominating pale blues, pinks and even white and loving gold and wainscot real or imitation.

The hall was the subject of much cogitation. One entered it through a porch copied from Linlithgow Palace. At first it made rather a gloomy impression, as its windows were filled with heraldic devices of the clan Scott. The walls were made of carved oak from Dunfermline, for the magistrates of that place had bestowed on him the pulpit and repentance stool from the old kirk, and when the oak failed he had the bare surfaces painted to imitate panelling. The chimney piece of dark red free-stone was copied from a cloister recess at Melrose. The roof was oaken and bore sixteen shields running along the centre, Scott's own quarterings, " eight on my father's side but five only on my mother's," the rest were nebuly. The scutcheons along the cornice were charged with the devices of the Border Clans, and plaster images of dwarfs and saints and monsters after originals at Melrose and Roslin peeped from the corners. The floor was of black and white marble, two full suits of armour stood on guard at one exit, while the walls were hung with cuirasses, spurs, swords, helmets and thumb screws. The most treasured object in the armoury was the sword of Montrose.

Sir Walter's own sanctum opened out of the library. It contained a writing-table, the leather chair in which he sat to write, and one other chair. A half length of Claverhouse and a small

full length of Rob Roy were the only pictures.
He was of course surrounded by books, reference
books in the lowest tiers, and above, in a little
gallery made accessible by a light stairway, were
more books. He could escape by this stairway
if necessary to his bedroom. The landing formed
the top of what he called his " oratory," though
Atkinson the architect had missed what his idea
was in ordering it. Scott had thought of a
recess to contain such relics as the cast of the
Bruce's skull, or anything that appealed to him as
sacrosanct. Lady Scott had very little to do with
the decoration—though it seems possible that she
was allowed to choose " the Bannockburn carpet " for the drawing-room ; however, she was an
admirable housewife and saw to it that not only
were the " nicknackets " dusted but that the
recessed tables in the library and the bedrooms
were well supplied with *porte-feuilles*, paper, pens,
ink and sealing wax. Matches and tapers were
rendered unnecessary by the jets of gas which,
turned low, remained lit throughout the day.
This illumination by coal-gas was something in
which Scott really delighted. It was as up-to-
date in its way as were the water-closets, of which
he was so proud. Some of the family and less
acclimatized guests noticed the smell of escaping
gas, but this did not trouble the laird, to him it
had " no smell whatever " and afforded a bright
overhead light in which he basked. At dusk,
when the dining-room chandeliers were turned on,
he rejoiced in the " Aladdin-like effect," without
noticing the corpse-like pallor it produced on the
lips and cheeks of even the youngest at the table.
The glare was dreaded by all ladies, but Sir
Walter loved the sun to shine full on him as he
wrote by day and the gas to shine full on him as

he worked on a winter's morning or quaffed his quaigh in the evening.

Occasionally a carping guest criticized Abbotsford and spoke of its absurd architecture and its irreconcilable ornament, its skimpy courtyard. Some were even so captious as to be depressed by their surroundings. One gentleman talks of pulling on his socks in an armchair embroidered by Mary Stuart, facing a portrait of Henry Darnley. By him was a table which had belonged to the Earl of Essex and on the table lay a mirror which had reflected Anne Boleyn's features. He noted that all the furniture had little copper plates with inscriptions affixed. To him they were but sinister souvenirs of a hideous past.

Some guests said the merriment on big occasions at Abbotsford was too forced. Captain Hall found the duty of being jolly at Christmas and New Year very depressing. Hogmanay to him was a ponderous evening, though he danced reels like a lunatic and squealed and snapped his fingers with the best. Supper ended at midnight with bumper drinking, crossing of hands and songs, but even Sir Walter's jollity could not save the roar of a noisy toast subsiding into an unwelcome silence.

After *Quentin Durward* was published, Abbotsford became the haunt of foreigners. No visit to the British Isles was complete unless Scott was included among the sights visited. One French traveller said, " As Scott was not at home, I only saw Scotland." Sir Walter never cared very much about foreigners. " I do not like them, I hate fine waistcoats and breastpins upon dirty shirts. . . . They are seldom long in making it evident that they know nothing of what they are talking, except having seen the *Lady of the Lake* at the Opera."

The visit of " warbling little " Tom Moore gave great pleasure to all the Scotts. He was slightly surprised to find his host completely unmusical, and that he knew nothing of Greek and had only read Homer in Pope's translation. By way of excusing these deficiencies, Moore told him that Lord Byron knew nothing of music either. During his stay the usual nightly choruses were sung, and Moore trilled a few of his own songs to the piano for the benefit of the ladies.

It would be tedious to give even a partial list of the guests at this most hospitable home. Kemble, Mathews, Southey, Wordsworth, Chantrey, Turner, Wilkie, Landseer, Leslie, all were there—Chantrey very much pleased to catch salmon, and Wilkie to make the picture of a rustic group of the Scott family.

Lady Scott sometimes showed off the beauties of the house and talked in what was considered a very droll way about her husband's genius. One visitor, who was studying the bosses of the cornice, was begged not to look on the floor at the worn carpet. " I am ashamed of it," she said. " I must get Scott to write some more of his nonsense books and buy me a new one."

Guests to Abbotsford were often taken for excursions by road. As they drove along, Scott would point out the old Border keep of Smailholm and quote the lines describing how it :

> Looked over hill and dale
> O'er Tweed's far flood and Mertoun's Wood
> And all down Teviot-dale,

and tell them it was there, at Sandyknowe farm, that he had spent his childhood and learnt to

love the Border and all its legends " of witches'
spells, of warriors' arms, of patriot battles won of
old." He used to say he had often thought of
buying the place, repairing the old tower and
making it his home. Then Bemerside was indicated to visitors, a place that had almost a wizard
spell cast on it by Thomas the Rhymer :

> Betide, betide what'er betide
> Haig shall be Haig of Bemerside.

Dryburgh Abbey, he would add, was not only the
burying place of the Haigs, but also that of his
father's people, the Haliburtons. It was of
special import to Scott as containing the family
tombs and monuments of his ancestors. Lord
Buchan, the owner of the ground, had often
expressed a lively anticipation of one day burying
Scott amongst the sepulchral relics of the past and
raising a memorial worthy of him. As we know,
in 1819, when he believed Scott to be dying, he
had endeavoured to arrange the funeral, though
Scott was as yet no corpse. He was an eccentric
man and Scott disliked him intensely. Henry
Crabbe Robinson, when visiting Scotland, had
hoped to pay his respects to Scott, but since the
only letter of introduction offered him was one
from Lord Buchan, he gave up the idea, on hearing
that they were not on speaking terms.

Among Scott's author friends none was more
liked than Joanna Baillie ; he admired her person,
he admired her plays and he helped her to produce
The Family Legend in Edinburgh. Another woman writer he liked immensely was little, active,
slight Maria Edgeworth. She and two of her
sisters stayed for a fortnight at Abbotsford,
and though she had already seen him in Edinburgh, she greeted him in the archway with,

" Everything about you is exactly what one ought to have had wit enough to dream ! " They picnicked and told stories and saw sights together in lovely August weather. Her society was intensely congenial to her host. The friendship had opened when she wrote to the " Author of *Waverley*, care of Ballantyne and Co.," expressing her delight over the novel *Waverley*. The letter was headed *Aut Scotus, aut Diabolus*. Ballantyne replied to it on behalf of the " great Unknown," and the great Unknown then carried on a correspondence that lasted till the end of his life. Maria was most impressionable. Pope once said : " The finest minds, like the finest metals, dissolve the earliest," and she often listened with tears brimming her eyes to some of Scott's remarks. " We shall never learn to respect our real calling and destiny unless we have taught ourselves to consider everything as moonshine compared with the education of the heart," he once said. Maria, brushing aside her facile tears, commented on this saying to the company assembled, " You see how it is. . . . Dean Swift said that he had written his books in order that people might learn to treat him like a great Lord. Sir Walter wrote his books in order that he may be able to treat his own people as a great Lord ought to do." The deduction gave great pleasure and was felt to be particularly apt.

Miss Edgeworth is one of the few people who commented on the excellence of Lady Scott's house-keeping and the manner in which she brought up her family. She told her hostess that she had been in Scotland in 1803, and Lady Scott thought it so odd that they had not at that time made each other's acquaintance. " Why, you forget, my dear," slipped in Scott, " Miss

Edgeworth was not a lion then, and my mane, you know, had not grown at all ! "

To Maria he denied categorically the authorship of the novels—and in referring to the " unknown author " he said, " I think highly of many of his works and expect to be gratified by those which are still promised from the same abundant and concealed source. I do assure you I am quite an impartial judge upon the occasion and that you do me too much honour in supposing that I have any interest in these narrations." Miss Edgeworth was perspicacious and stuck to her intuitions, being in no way taken in by Scott's disclaimer.

No visitor's book was kept at Abbotsford, but the guests who basked in that genial atmosphere must have numbered hundreds. Lady Scott was the chief sufferer. At one terrible moment she had to find accommodation for thirteen ladies' maids ! It had become a necessity to cater for the house on the most generous scale, never must she be taken unawares, expenditure was bound to be lavish, but as money was plentiful, what did it matter ? The princely entertaining, the concourse of visitors, who that contemplated it could doubt the identity of the " great Unknown " ?

CHAPTER XIV

THE APPROACH TO CATASTROPHE

GREAT capacity for enjoyment and great confidence in his own powers probably led Sir Walter to ignore the unreal nature of his wealth. So long as bills were discountable, so long as Constable was indulgent over credits, so long as the circulation of his books increased, so long as he could by means of the airy machinery of his brain build a large house and acquire an estate (costing it is said £70,000), he was content. Credit as we know is based on confidence and the shaking of confidence is the quake that brings all fortunes to the dust. Sir Walter had not our bitter experience to enlighten him, and the financial juggling of his day satisfied his sense of security. And yet, as we see from time to time in his letters, a little doubt obtrudes itself—not of the system, but of his fortune. Will his luck always hold?

We must allude again to the death of John Ballantyne which had the curious effect on his brother James of making him desire to be readmitted to partnership in the Canongate Press. To Sir Walter, as he became more and more engaged in public duties, it was not an unwelcome suggestion. Why should he not shift some of the responsibility for " this now so flourishing business " on to his old friend's shoulders? At once he prepared a draft of the conditions under which he was prepared to delegate part of his authority to his faithful henchman. One must assume that Ballantyne was actuated by a wish to save Scott from catastrophe; nothing else would account for this self-sacrificing offer. With " jocund Johnny " dead, and Willie Erskine prematurely feeble, there was no lifelong friend left to speak plain truths to the Great Unknown, or put a brake on his personal expenditure, and he had become more and more unmanageable over money.

If we look at the notes made by James in August, 1820, we can see how his mind worked. It evidently worried him to death to see his name being used to raise funds, while Scott's name was never pledged at all. It was natural and correct enough that financial transactions should be carried out in the name of James Ballantyne and Company, but the advances so obtained were ruthlessly applied to the sole partner's private expenditure and uses, without consideration of the firm's solvency; and the manager was always haunted by the fear that he might be held responsible, in the event of an enquiry, for the extraordinary way in which the business was run. " When I reflect," he says, " how many bills I have paid for Sir Walter Scott on verbal orders or mere notes . . . I absolutely quake for the aspect under which I might be considered were he to die. Thousands upon thousands might be brought against me." As partner, he surely ought to be in a position to protest, and if necessary refuse to obey mandates to pay the house-bills at Abbotsford. No one not in the secret could credit the way in which Sir Walter ran his affairs, or the muddle from which, as manager, he was sometimes called on to extricate Lady Scott.

The mandates were after this kind : " Please settled enclosed account. Faulkner and Co., £94 odd. . . . I will be obliged to you for £24, being a fortnight's support of my family. . . . Be pleased to settle with Messrs. Blackwood, mercers, an account due by my family to them, £218. . . . I will be obliged to you to send £22 odd to the Scottish Insurance for my premises at Abbotsford. I think I will want about £100 more for wages and other Martinmas demands. By'r Lady, you may make it some £150. The enclosed (bill) for oil-gas."[1]

If there happened to be no money in the till, Scott used the name of the firm for raising it. The building of Abbotsford, young Walter Scott's captaincy, and other outgoings were, as they arose, paid for by bills on James Ballantyne and Co. As salaried manager, James Ballantyne was no better than Scott's servant. He was bound to honour the sole partner's overdrafts, no matter how they were couched, but, as co-partner, surely he ought to be, he felt, within his rights in refusing to allow the current account to be depleted, or loans raised for reckless personal expenditure, in this hopelessly unbusiness-like way.

From such fragments of Lady Scott's handwriting as have been preserved, it is possible to see that she did not always keep within her housekeeping allowance, or confess to Scott the amount of her expenditure. She also was apt to draw on this too convenient bank. A clear exposure of her want of method is revealed by the following note, obviously one of many similar demands. " Lady Scott, with best compliments to Mr. Ballantyne, takes the liberty of enclosing him two

[1] *The Ballantyne Controversy.*

of Miss Scott's bills, which have been omitted being added with her own, and might occasion some difficulty in the settling of them, as Messrs. Jollie and Brown are giving up business. Lady Scott has many apologies to make for giving all this trouble, and having also to request that when he is so obliging as to settle her account with Mr. Pringle, the butcher, that he would also settle her last account with him. Lady Scott thinks that her second account will amount to nearly £40."[1]

No wonder James Ballantyne was worried, and took what he believed to be the only steps in his power to save his friend and master.

Sir Walter's "missive letter" defining the terms on which he was willing to re-admit James Ballantyne to partnership show how level-headed he could be when he chose. Probably he was always level-headed, though prone to be thrown off his balance by the opportunity of acquiring land and giving substance to his baronial dream.

Nothing could be more reasonable than the way he deals with the situation existing between himself and James. He points out that on the dissolution of partnership in 1816, Ballantyne had owed him £3,000. He reckons £1,200 of this sum to be discharged by an assignment of Ballantyne's share in the profit of certain novels.[2] For the remaining £1,800 he is willing to accept the surrender of a share in the profits of three novels contracted for. On the £3,000 debt he demands no interest, as he accounts it "compensated by the profits of the printing office which I have drawn for my exclusive use since 1816."

[1] *The Ballantyne Controversy.*

[2] Under the first agreement James Ballantyne had retained a one-sixth interest in each novel.

He was careful to indicate the ways in which he had improved the business. The whole stock of the printing office had been renewed (£1,700); the overdraft to the Bank of Scotland had been paid off (£500); the feus affecting the Printing House property had been acquired (£375). The value of these assets was £2,575, for half of which James must give him a bill or bond to bear interest at 5 per cent. as from Whitsunday, 1822. For the floating debt of £36,000 he accepted full responsibility. £27,000 had been incurred by him on account of private expenditure; the balance probably represented "renewals" or accommodation bills, for no single bill was current on account of the firm.

It is easy to see what an advantage it was to Scott to shelter behind a trading concern. On his own name he could have borrowed little, but on the name of a house known to be engaged in an excellent business he could acquire a mountain of paper money. When, after the crash, the firm of James Ballantyne and Co. was taken over by trustees it was run by the same manager at a comfortable profit.

Lockhart's explanation of the relations between Scott and the Ballantynes is, as everyone knows, fantastically unfair. In the second edition of the *Life of Scott* he had to withdraw some of his statements, but enough remain to show how warped was his judgment in dealing with those, to him, common people. Not for nothing had this handsome, satiric, half-deaf man earned the sobriquet of " Scorpion." And yet his fault was not hate but love; he loved too jealously. His devotion to Sir Walter knew no limits and his great biography was written with the " sole object of doing him justice." That he did less than justice to the Ballantynes was possibly the outcome of his desire to burnish the shield of his paragon till it shone like the sun.

It can hardly be too clearly insisted on that Sir Walter was no vague literary dreamer who refused to occupy himself with money affairs. Neither in love nor in business was he as feeble as his devotees have depicted him. He was a practical man, and at all times was aware of the state of his business. Once a month the red morocco account book or private ledger was carefully checked over against the office-ledger by Scott in the presence of Ballantyne. A statement of the bills falling due for the ensuing month was shown, and the means of retiring them discussed. The balancing of the account often resolved itself into a series of new bills.

There is plenty of evidence of Sir Walter's methods of supplying himself with funds. We will look at a typical note written in May, 1821. " I cannot reconcile your statement for May with my book. There are about £10,000 or under in my book, add wages, etc., £500,—then a new novel for £3,500, for which publishers' bills have been received, and the printing of *Nigel* . . . at least £2,000. Total £5,500, leaving only £5,000 to be found." Then again let us look at a monthly settlement after partnership had been resumed. Scott writes, " My plan is to provide for a £12,000 debit by selling £6,000 (partly *Peveril of the Peak* and partly printing of same)." The other £6,000 he proposes to raise by " accommodation " with Constable. At no time was Scott ignorant of the extent of his liabilities, and we can see how frivolously he regarded them when as late as May, 1825, we find him " meditating a new purchase (of land) to the extent of £40,000."

It is almost impossible to exaggerate the value of the service rendered by James Ballantyne to his employer both in managing the business and in seeing books through the press. Endless hours were spent by him in drudging over proofs ; Scott's slap-dash way of composition made this necessary. One has only to look at the page proofs of *Waterloo, Redgauntlet, Woodstock* and *Napoleon* to be surprised at the emendations, additions, and clarifications suggested by this faithful, industrious friend. Ballantyne wrote once to Hogg : " I assure you if he had nobody to correct after him, there would be a bonny song through the country. He is the most careless and incorrect writer that was ever born, for a voluminous and popular writer ; and as for sending a proof sheet to him, we may as well keep it in the office."

The Waverley novels could never have been the success they were except for James's unostentatious plodding. Lockhart sets it down against him that he was correcting proofs when he should have been minding his business, as if any amount of business-minding would have stopped Sir Walter's overdrafts ; but Lockhart never realized the vital part Ballantyne played in transforming those apparently effortless manuscripts into readable books. In some novels there is no page of proof uncorrected, and James's " Please read this " is on every sheet.

At Whitsuntide, 1822, when the partnership had become operative, the following books were in course of printing against Lammastide :

Peveril of the Peak.
Gwynn's Memoirs.
Bellecoeur's French Exercises.
Chronological Notes.

Hydriotaphia.
Boece's Livy.
Rome.
Blackwood's Magazine.
The Novelists' Library.

All profits from these books were earmarked for Sir Walter, as was *The Fortunes of Nigel,* soon to go to press.

James Ballantyne was permitted to share the profits in a " miniature " set of novels and a " miniature " set of poetry by the author of *Waverley,* as well as in the *Edinburgh Annual Register,* which always ran at a loss.   His pickings for the first year were not to be very large.

The Novelists' Library mentioned in the list was a set of English novels with biographical prefaces by Scott.   Studies of Richardson, Fielding, Smollett, Cumberland, Sterne, Mrs. Radcliffe and Horace Walpole figure in the series, which is very well worth reading.   It is evident that in the last-named author Scott found his most congenial subject, for Walpole loved to " gaze on Gothic toys through Gothic glass," and his mind, like Sir Walter's, was tinged with love of pedigree and appreciation of family honours.

Though unpleasantly set up in double columns of small type, *The Novelists' Library* crept along to a tenth volume and then petered out.   The venture had been intended to benefit poor John Ballantyne, " a person whom no one could know without being desirous to oblige him," and had been undertaken by Scott as an act of friendship.

In a way it is not to be wondered at that Sir Walter spent easily ; for he earned easily, and money for its own sake he did not prize.   Publishers in those days seem to have flung bills about. In June, 1822, Mr. Cadell, Constable's financial manager, pressed £1,000, or over one pound a line, on Sir Walter for a dramatic sketch *Halidon Hill* ! It had only taken him two days to write. At this rate of work and this rate of payment he felt it really could not signify what expenses he let himself in for. Delighted with his bargain, Mr. Cadell gave an order to the Ballantyne Press to print an edition of 10,000 copies. He had no doubt but that it was the beginning of a new dramatic lode in the Scott gold-mine. Poems, Novels, and *now* Plays ! " I am quite happy," he wrote to his father-in-law, Archibald Constable, " to have such a nice little thing to blaze out with now at the heels of *Nigel*."

In the earlier part of 1822 Constable, who had been " resting in the milder climate of Ealing," had spent a good deal of time in concocting plans for Scott's consideration. Would he not write a Pocahontas novel ? Would he not edit Shakespeare ? Could he not bring out an edition of his own miscellaneous prose-works ? The last suggestion would be least trouble and probably would be more paying than anything else. He urged Sir Walter to think over his ideas.

Mr. Cadell highly disapproved of some of his chief's proposals. What sense was there in getting Scott to edit Shakespeare ? Why should he have been bribed with advances for four novels at a time ? Surely it was more rational to deal with one book at a time and know where they were for profits ? Sir Walter's vogue could not last for ever. For his own part he would rather be bought out of partnership than participate in such folly. Constable somehow propitiated his son-in-law, and the partnership went on as before. In the long run he even had his way over

Shakespeare.[1]   Not that Scott was any more
eager to undertake the task than Cadell was to
publish the result, but he found the copyright
money irresistible, to say nothing of the printing
order involved.   Lockhart makes no mention of
the Shakespeare, though Scott writes, "In the
event of Shakespeare going, I could have Lockhart's powerful assistance in the philological department . . . the undertaking would not
interrupt other work."   There were to be 1,500
copies and twelve or fourteen volumes, the
remuneration was fixed at £2,500.[2]

Prompted by Cadell's anxiety, Constable, who
could not bear his own books to be examined,
ordered his auditor to go through the Ballantyne
accounts, for to his thinking their presentation
was unsatisfactory.   Scott was furious and called
on Constable to get the investigation stopped.
Afraid of offending the great man, Constable
weakly gave way, and no one of his firm dared to
speak their mind to him for fear of injuring
Ballantyne's credit and incidentally their own.
David Constable was disgusted at the weakness
displayed by his father on this occasion.

Peveril of the Peak was published in January,
1823.   It was not much liked.   The morning it
came out Scott walked through the Outer House
towards the stove where young barristers were
gossiping.   On catching sight of Scott's conical
head somebody said, "Hush, boys ! here comes
old Peveril.   I see the Peak."   He asked Lockhart what the joke was and on being told said :
"Ay, ay, my man, as well Peveril o' the Peak
one day as Peter o' the Paunch," alluding to the
nickname of a fat barrister.   Scott henceforth

<hr>

[1] Ballantyne correspondence, undated.   [2] *Ibid.*

was known to the Outer House and to many in Edinburgh as Old Peveril. He would sometimes sign himself like this. In the prefactory letter to this novel Scott described his own appearance in a humorous way :

" The Author of *Waverley* entered, a bulky and tall man, in a travelling greatcoat, which covered a suit of snuff-brown, cut in imitation of that worn by the great Rambler. His flapped hat— for he disdained the modern frivolities of a travelling cap—was bound over his head with a large silk handkerchief, so as to protect his ears from cold at once, and from the babble of his pleasant companions in the public coach from which he had just alighted. There was somewhat of a sarcastic shrewdness and sense, which sat on the heavy penthouse of his shaggy grey eyebrow ; his features were in other respects largely shaped, and rather heavy than promising wit or genius ; but he had a notable projection of the nose, similar to that line of the Latin poet,—

'—— immodicum surgit pro cuspide rostrum.'

A stout walking-stick stayed his hand ; a double Barcelona protected his neck ; his belly was something prominent, ' but that's not much ' ; his breeches were substantial thick-set ; and a pair of top-boots, which were slipped down to ease his sturdy calves, did not conceal his comfortable travelling stockings of lamb's wool, wrought, not on the loom, but on wires, and after the venerable ancient fashion known in Scotland by the name of *ridge-and-furrow*. His age seemed to be considerably above fifty, but could not amount to threescore, which I observed with pleasure, trusting there may be a good deal of work had out of him yet, especially as a general haleness of appearance, the compass and strength of his voice, the steadiness of his step, the rotundity of his calf, the depth of his hem, and the sonorous emphasis of his sneeze, were all signs of a constitution built for permanence."

The rather discouraging reception of *Peveril of the Peak* decided him to cross the Channel. As he wrote to James Ballantyne :

> The mouse who only trusts to one poor hole
> Can never be a mouse of any soul.

Since American agents had been trying to buy advance sheets of *Peveril* from workmen engaged in the Canongate Press, *Quentin Durward* went through its preliminary printing without a title. For this novel Scott had derived help from Mr. Skene's accurate and lively journal kept in France. He got " dreadfully stuck " all the same for want of topographical books. He calls Plessis-les-Tour " a vile place " because he cannot find any description of it or locate it on the map, though he spent hours in the Advocates' Library poring over charts and gazetteers. Philippe de Comines, however, was the very key to the manners of the period, and he drew copiously from his history. For some reason *Quentin Durward* did not score an immediate success. Maybe, thought Robert Cadell, the public would not stand for a new novel every six months. Scott, quick to realize the danger of over-production wrote, " I am sorry to find our friend *Quentin Durward* is somewhat frostbit which I did not expect. If on consideration it is thought necessary to have greater intervals betwixt these affairs, which I think may be the result, we must keep the mill going with something else."

Cadell advised Constable that it would be

judicious to stop further advances to Scott, and reminded the author that £20,000 was owing to his firm from Ballantyne and Co. ; it was politely urged that the sum should be reduced to £8,000 or £10,000.

Understanding only too well the significance of this manœuvre, Sir Walter replied briskly by enquiring whether the request had been made because *Quentin Durward* was not a success, or merely in the way of ordinary business. In any event he promised that payment for his next book, *St. Ronan's Well*, should be applied to debt reduction. Hardly had he fenced off Constable's demand, than *Quentin Durward* became a raging success and brought greater profits to Constable and more reputation to Scott than any of his other works. France had discovered him, and from France the enthusiasm for his romances spread over Germany and the rest of Europe, even to Russia. This was indeed a pleasant surprise. Scott could now return care-free to Abbotsford " with a better portion of health than he had had before."

Even without the continental conquest 1823 had been a good year. It saw the publication of three novels and the penning of a fourth, *Redgauntlet*, as well as a demand for a second edition of *Swift*. During its course Scott had been elected to The Club, and the Roxburgh Club, and had founded the Bannatyne Club. He had also been elected chairman of the Oil Gas Company of Edinburgh. The scare of over-production was allayed ; he could go calmly ahead with his scheme for *Tales of the Crusaders*, and enjoy the now almost perfected amenities of his beloved retreat.

During 1824 he did but little writing and was

disposed more and more to give himself over to the outcome of celebrity—unceasing hospitality. Towards the end of the year he arranged a marriage for his elder son, with Jane Jobson heiress of Lochore, and decided to settle his estate on the young couple. In the intervals of practical affairs he read up the Crusades and meditated on his projected *Tales*. While he was occupied in this peaceful way his publisher Archibald Constable was especially active. It is not unprofitable to observe his moves as he tried to advance the business of his firm.

Though portly and hobbling with gout, the Czar was not a man to sit still in his armchair and let things slide. He was always up and doing. One gets a notion of his personality from looking through his early letters to Murray and his later correspondence with his London agents Hurst and Robinson. Writing to him in December, 1824, they deplored the number of " remainders " offered at John Murray's annual sale. Books, albeit recently published, had sold for little above the price of waste paper. It made them fear that the bookselling trade was falling on bad times. Mr. Robinson takes the opportunity of reminding Constable that he still holds £40,000 worth of "Waverleys," and therefore is apprehensive about the Scott " sets " which the Edinburgh firm is issuing, for it is plain that they must affect adversely the sale of the individual novels. If he decides to buy any of the forthcoming *Tales of the Crusaders* he must be granted liberal terms.

Constable in his characteristic bluffing fashion deplored that books should go so cheap. If he held £40,000 of "Waverley" novels he " would lay them up snugly in a warehouse," and " sell quietly

as the occasion arose." Mr. Robinson's stock in
Scott works is certainly heavy, but had he not
sold £100,000 worth of individual novels before
ever the " sets " were thought of ? Schemes for
getting rid of the remainders of these books are in
process of being devised ; he has " sundry plans
in cogitation," but as for liberal terms for the
Crusaders, he refuses to give 15 per cent. discount
on any account whatever. . . . "It is altogether
unreasonable your demanding such on an article
actually sold before it reaches you. . . . The
Crusaders will not be out for some months," . . .
and then, as if conferring a favour, he adds, " If
you don't ask too great a pennyworth, you may
likely have the greater part of our share." He is
glad to hear that Robinson is not proceeding
further with the publication of *The Novelists'
Library*, " the book was on a bad plan as I have
often told you . . ." He informs him that the
biographical sketches prefixed to each novel have
been sold to him by their author, and would be
added to the *Miscellaneous Prose Works* which he
was bringing out in six volumes, and of which he
cynically suggests that Robinson should take a
thousand (the whole edition consisted of a thous-
and sets). He begs to enclose the first sheet of
Scott's Shakespeare, it is to come out in ten
volumes. Constable's letter concludes on a note
of false *bonhomie*. " Now, my good friend, on
looking at your stock of books, I think, considering the extent of our dealings, it is wonderfully
small. . . . Don't be hasty in making waste
paper. What about the American market ? I
drop the hint."

Constable was always turning over ideas in his
head for making new money. It is pretty clear
that he had been over-trading for years, and could

only maintain himself by tapping fresh sources of supply. Hurst and Robinson were probably also insufficiently capitalized ; but owing to the issue of notes by private banks, long-dated bills and renewals of bills, no one could have exactly known how they stood for real money at any particular moment of time.

One day Constable journeyed to Abbotsford to divulge to Sir Walter a plan for producing cheap books for the million. Young Disraeli saw him on this occasion and thought him a wind-bag—" as much puffed up as if he had written the ' Waverleys ' himself. . . ." He explained his plan—a comprehensive *Miscellany* to be issued in monthly instalments at 2s. 6d. or 3s. a volume.

If the publisher made but one half-penny profit on each volume the sale of a million or two would make him " richer than all the quartos ever hot pressed." Having tumbled on the idea of mass production and profit cutting, and viewing Scott as his chief asset, he arranged that the first number of the series should consist of half *Waverley*, and the second of a section of a new *Life of Napoleon*, to be written in four parts by the " Author of *Waverley*." So enormous was his belief in Scott's saleability that he decided that until all his novels had been published in this way, the *Miscellany* must be kept going in alternate months by historical and biographical works by the same author. It was his intention to fill up gaps as they arose with works from his general reserve by Miss Edgeworth, Captain Hall, Lockhart, and Gleig. But the broad back on which the scheme was based was that of Scott.

Both Sir Walter and his son-in-law approved of the *Miscellany*, and gave their blessing and support to an undertaking of which they did not even partially realize the implications. Constable found less malleable material when he expounded his bright idea to the booksellers who held stocks of "Waverleys." With curious indifference to their protests, and even to their solvency, which must be seriously endangered if he pushed his plan through, the Czar went ahead with his project. It was imperative for him to raise new money.

Hearing in London that the *Life of Napoleon* was being written Robinson wrote to Constable suggesting that the first edition should be in two handsome quarto volumes, to be quickly followed up by an octavo edition. The Czar in his reply disclosed his scheme for a weekly *Miscellany*. (This was a new development, for when he spoke to Scott it was to be issued monthly.) Enclosing a five-year plan for Mr. Robinson's consideration he informed him of the arrangements made for the first two numbers. Part of *Waverley* was to form volume one, and part of Captain Hall's *Loo Choo* volume two. *Waverley* would be spread over six numbers and Hall over nine. He hints at another innovation, that of engaging a traveller to find out what numbers of the *Miscellany* could be sold in the different districts of England. He questions the wisdom of making all sales through London, for he had come to the conclusion that he could arrange big sales direct with the provinces.

Mr. Robinson was appalled by these disclosures, and wrote satirically of the effect Constable's scheme would have on his business. " No doubt the *Miscellany* will succeed, and no doubt can exist as to its entirely destroying an immense property now in our hands, i.e. £8,000 worth of detached works by the 'Author of *Waverley*,'

R

and £30,000 worth of " sets," to say nothing of
Hall's *South America*, of which we lately bought
quantities." Such a project meant ruin to him,
for even the publication of the prospectus submitted would stop all sales of works by the
"Author of *Waverley*." He entreats Constable to
take no further steps without consulting his firm.

Constable acknowledged the " short, abrupt
letter evidently written in a panic," and explained
that the *Miscellany* was not intended to be detri-
mental to the works of the Author of *Waverley*;
indeed it cannot " in its effect produce anything
but good to all concerned. . . . It is for another
class who cannot afford to purchase any edition
now in existence." He assured Robinson that
his plan will not lessen the sale of the original
editions by five per cent. He will see whether the
prospectus can be modelled to allay " his ground-
less fears." . . . Well-accustomed to beating down
opposition, he added : " As for my *Miscellany*,
abandoned it cannot be."

Quite obviously such a letter was no comfort to
Robinson, and after consultation with his partner
Hurst over Mr. Constable's " *extraordinary* proposals," he made a further protest. " We have
£40,000 of works by the Author of *Waverley*, can
you make me believe that an edition issued at
one-third to one-quarter the price of our present
stock would not be injurious ? Would you propose
the *Miscellany* if you held all the stock we do ? "
To cap everything he suddenly caught sight of an
advertisement of the *Miscellany* in the *Gazette of
Literature*, whereon he urged that, " In no case
must you in your prospectus refer to the ' Waverley ' novels or other books in which we hold a
large stock."

After deleting his advertisement from the

Gazette, Constable replied to Robinson's ill-timed question whether, if he held vast quantities of the old stock, he would publish the *Miscellany* by writing the word ASSUREDLY. Bluffing mendaciously he added in a postscript, "Instead of being a preventive, possessing such a stock would be an additional and urgent inducement." The Czar was not a merciful man, and soon took the opportunity of informing the unhappy Robinson that, "Nothing can promise better than the *Miscellany.*" Of all these goings-on Scott was kept in ignorance. Everything appeared on the surface to be going as well as possible in the bookselling world ; so well that Sir Walter decided to take a holiday in Ireland.

At the close of the summer session, he crossed, in the company of Anne and Lockhart, to Belfast with the plan of visiting Walter Scott junior and his bride in Dublin. At Drogheda they were shown the battlefield of the Boyne by a dragoon officer. As they rode over the ground Scott recited *The Crossing of the Water.* In Dublin the great man was half suffocated with attentions. The Archbishop of Dublin, the General Officer in Command, the Attorney-General and other official personages hurried to call. "They treated me like a Prince of the Blood," he said, when recounting his adventures. Invitations arrived from the Lord Lieutenant, the Royal Society, and the Provost of Trinity College ; each morning he held a *levée* of distinguished people at his house in St. Stephen's Green, and as he drove through the streets shopkeepers bowed and their wives curtsied, while crowds cheered his every appearance. He visited Lord Plunket at his seat near Bray and little Miss Plunket sat on his knee. She has survived this honour for over a century.

To Scott St. Patrick's Cathedral was merely the tomb of Swift, and it vexed him that no ladder was available to enable him to examine the bust by Roubilliac set high upon the wall. His remark that " the severity of Swift's countenance was much increased by the absence of the wig " has been preserved.

On looking at the folio *Clarendon* with the Dean's still legible, though pencilled, marginal notes,[1] he observed, " Very savage as usual on us poor Scots everywhere ! " In Trinity College Library an official said rather fishingly, " I have been so busy that I have not yet read your *Redgauntlet*." He answered very meekly, " I have not happened to fall in with such a work, Doctor." At the theatre the actors could get no hearing owing to his presence in a box. A thousand voices shouted " Sir Walter Scott ! " until he pacified them with a speech.

At Glendalough Sir Walter insisted on climbing into St. Kevin's bed, and then drove to Edgeworthstown, taking Walter and his daughter-in-law Jane with him. The weather was hot. Scott " sweltered." On touring farther South they found the historian Hallam lying at Killarney with a broken leg. " So much for middle-aged gentlemen climbing precipices," said Scott, as he remembered the face of St. Kevin's cliff, and his intended scramble up to the top of Blarney Tower to kiss the stone, an adventure depicted by a young observer—Daniel Maclise.

When he got back to Abbotsford he told Charlotte that his tour had been " one ovation." After recounting some of his adventures in detail he settled down once more to grind at French history. Friends noticed how different was the

---

[1] In St. Sepulchre's Library.

tired expression of his face while coping with
chronicles and newspaper reports, to the buoyant,
happy expression with which he had scribbled
The Talisman. A story he had heard in Dublin
was rather a comfort to him. It was that of
Sir Boyle Roche's dream-conversation with his
own decapitated head. ' Quite separabit,' said
the head. ' Naboclish ' (no matter) says I,
in the same language." This expression delighted Scott and when things were bad " Naboclish " was the word that came to his lips and was
written in his *Journal*. The humour of it enchanted him.

We learn from John Richardson who stayed at
Abbotsford in the autumn of 1825 that the shadows
of insolvency were beginning to fall darkly across
Scott's path. It is best to let him tell his own
story : " The house was full of company. . . . It
was a beautiful moonlight night and I walked
with Sir Walter to the terrace towards the Tweed.
The thriving holly hedge was glistening in the
moonbeams and the library which we had left was
gay with brilliant light and high and happy guests
—everything contributed to inspire me with admiration for Sir Walter's efforts and success and
merited station and happiness and I could not
refrain from expressing that sentiment. I dare
say I did so as fervently as I did it sincerely :
I was thunderstruck when instead of responsive
acquiescence he uttered a deep sigh and said,
' I wish to God I had the means of providing
adequately for poor Anne.' Knowing that his
life was insured, I observed that that fund was
ample. He made no explanation and was silent ;
but I could not but feel when his misfortunes
were soon afterwards disclosed, what a pang I
must have inflicted,—the fund I had alluded to

and all he had being absorbed in his overwhelming pecuniary ruin."

On his return to Edinburgh for the winter session the laird found Constable more set than ever on making his *Miscellany* a success. He had a favour to ask of Sir Walter Scott, but he could hardly muster courage to mention its nature. " It is a dedication to the King," he said. " I do not mean a mere inscription ; but such an address as should explain the nature and object of the undertaking in suitable language, addressing the King as the real friend of knowledge, the enlightened promoter of intelligence among all classes, as the head of the world of letters." Could Sir Walter advise him whether such an idea would meet with Royal favour ? The friend of royalty promised to make enquiries in the right quarter, and before Christmas was able to inform the publisher that such a dedication would be acceptable and that he would draft it himself.

To be allowed to use the Royal name as an advertisement for his wares was indeed a triumph. Mr. Constable was most thankful for the favour, and sat in his armchair dreaming happy dreams of a future piled high with millions of plain volumes in the hands of millions of plain people. The awakening when it came was vastly unpleasant.

CHAPTER XV

CATASTROPHE

WHILE Sir Walter was wrestling manfully with French newspapers and official Gazettes, and involving himself in an ever more complicated maze of bill-discounting, the Czar forged ahead with his baneful *Miscellany*. Fatuous in his self-esteem he continued to deride the grumbling of old customers in London. If the dunder-headed booksellers could not dispose of their existing stock let them lay it up or ship it to America if they liked, he really could not be expected to be responsible for the distribution of his own consignments. He had quite enough on hand without that—new schemes to further cheap editions to be disseminated through the agency of provincial houses, illustrated sets with fresh introductions that would supersede (he hoped) all other editions. No doubt there was a great deal of new money to be made in pioneer work of this kind.

Mr. Constable's reveries were interrupted by Hurst and Robinson's demanding of him a loan with which to carry on. How annoying they were with their insistence that he had affected their credit and purchasing power! It was all stuff and nonsense; he would go to London and tell them so. In London it was made unmistakably clear to the Czar that Hurst and Robinson's stability was shaken. There are none so blind as those who won't see, and he assured himself that it was in no way due to him that they were in a bad way ; they had brought that on themselves. Gossip had it that they had been speculating in hops. All the same he must do everything possible to help them, as their failure would certainly affect his credit since he had backed many of their bills. Forthwith he made a melancholy round of such bankers as he was acquainted with ; London was not like Edinburgh where he knew everyone, and unfortunately Mr. Carstairs, the Scottish banker, was out of town. He found Dixon at home and was alarmed to hear that Hurst and Robinson could not expect the consideration that would be accorded to an older firm like Longmans. And then he heard talk of overtrading and speculating, of a private bank being about to put up its shutters, and of the Bank of England only lending money from day to day. A worse moment for borrowing money could not have been chosen. Feeling rather downcast, he visited Mr. Robinson, and was in no degree cheered by this gentleman's indifference on the subject of the *Miscellany*. He did not seem to care in the least what happened now. Much perturbed in mind, Mr. Constable drove back to Edinburgh, a dreadful fit of the gout was coming on and he longed for his comfortable bed at Polton, and the advice of his son-in-law as to the support of Hurst and Robinson.

He was hardly tucked up in bed before he heard that Sir Walter had paid a panic call on Cadell.[1] It appeared that the great man had received intelligence from London of the most definite and unpleasant kind. Hurst and Robinson were said to be on the rocks, and Constable

---

[1] Lockhart represents the call as having been made on Constable, but the Constable correspondence does not support his statement.

was reported as rushing back to Edinburgh to try to save his own firm.

This was awful. Everything seemed crumbling. It was imperative that the Czar should get round to see his chief asset and restore confidence. Even now the situation might be saved if Scott could be reassured sufficiently to be cajoled into raising £10,000 on Abbotsford, and into signing a contract for those new forewords which were half-promised for a collected illustrated edition of his novels. In a few days the Czar rose from his bed and went smiling to Sir Walter. So optimistic, so overwhelming was Mr. Constable during the interview that Scott was completely comforted. That florid solidity, that grip, that smile, of course the Czar was rooted and branched like an oak! What harm could come to anyone sheltering under such branches? He would certainly mortgage Abbotsford to the tune of £10,000. In some ways Scott and Constable resembled each other, both were forward-looking, successful, full-blooded, accustomed to dominate, and in some peculiar way they managed to impress each other. This is odd when we think how often Scott had spoken of Constable as " The Crafty," and " the great Swab," and how often Constable had been maddened by Scott's bullying over book contracts.

Satisfied with the promise of a loan from Sir Walter and stimulated by threatening disaster, the Czar set to work to plan out the *Magnum Opus* or complete library edition of the " Waverley " novels. It would pay him to engage the best artists, Turner, Leslie, Phillips, as illustrators ; and Sir Walter must be made to contribute bright new introductions to each romance. Mr. Cadell, who could not bring himself to be interested in anything so remote as the eventual publication of this series, applied his mind to dealing with immediate contingencies as they arose. He was of opinion that less than £50,000 would be no help to Hurst and Robinson, but how were they to set about raising so large a sum ? What really were their assets ? As he discussed the situation with his chief he was obliged to admit that Scott was still their principal, if not their only available asset. They looked to get £8,000 for *Woodstock* ; £10,000 for *Napoleon* ; £8,000 from an unnamed novel ; £26,000 in all. But were these books, with the *Magnum Opus* thrown in, security enough on which to borrow £50,000 ? They must probe the situation and meanwhile it could do no harm to assure Robinson that they would stand by him. It might prevent him doing something foolish out of panic. One feels a kind of pity for Sir Walter who unwittingly played his Atlas part in all negotiations. There he was standing under three interlocked firms none of which knew the extent of the others' liability. The mountains of paper money he was entrusted to support might at any moment collapse into a little heap of rubbish.

Perhaps Sir Walter was over-easily persuaded to exercise his right of raising £10,000 on the estate settled on his son. Weeks later, when he learned that he had been fooled into throwing good money after bad, he never shook hands with Archibald Constable again. Everything else he could understand and forgive, but this act of " treachery," as he called it, never. But we must not anticipate his experience ; for the time being he was happy, felt that he had done the right thing, and settled down to write prefaces for the *Magnum Opus* and entertain his usual Hogmanay party.

Having raised a sum of money, and recovered from his fit of gout, Constable, still retaining the full confidence of Sir Walter and Ballantyne, ventured once more to London. The journey upset him and when he got to his hotel in the Adelphi, he had to lie up again with another attack of gout. Lockhart calling on him found him fuming with nerves and temper. Precious time was being wasted ; if Hurst and Robinson " went," he " went " too, but provided Sir Walter played up the game might yet be saved. Would not Lockhart accompany him to the Bank of England to borrow £100,000 on his Scott copyrights ? Lockhart shook his head, and he swore he would go alone. Two days later he asked the unwilling Lockhart to back an application to Scott for a further £20,000. Vainly did he cudgel his brains to devise new resources, there was nothing to be done, it was far too late.

While the Czar was away in London, Sir Walter called in almost daily to find out from Cadell how things were shaping. The first real blow came when Hurst and Robinson suffered a dishonoured bill to come back upon Constable ; from this Scott inferred correctly the ruin of all their houses. A few days later it was known that Hurst and Robinson had failed for a very large sum. Their failure brought down the firms of Constable and Ballantyne. Owing to the complicated and almost unintelligible system of bills, counter-bills and " renewed accommodations," Ballantyne was shown to have a deficit of £117,000. Sir Walter knew the worst on January 17th, and faced it like the man he was. He had dined with Skene on January 16th. Next morning he sent word to his friend to come to him the moment he was up. At seven Skene found him writing by candlelight. Holding out his hand Sir Walter said " This is the hand of a beggar." He also said, " Do you know I experience a sort of determined pleasure in confronting the very worst aspect of this sudden reverse, in standing as it were in the breach that has overthrown my fortunes, and saying, ' Here I stand, at least an honest man '." He was advised by his friends Cadell, John Gibson, Ballantyne and Hogarth to create a trust of his property at once for payment of his own obligations. This was executed two days later. On the 26th a meeting of the creditors was called and John Gibson, W.S., on behalf of Sir Walter, stated that his client would work to pay everyone in full. A committee of trustees and a committee of creditors were formed. The trustees insured Sir Walter's life, taking over Constable's £15,000 policy, and Ballantyne's £5,000 policy, as well as a further £2,000 policy on their own account. Castle Street was advertised for sale.

Lord Cockburn had no idea that Scott was in trade. It had " never crossed his imagination." . . . " Well do I remember," he says, " his first appearance after the calamity was divulged, when he walked into Court one day in January, 1826. There was no affectation and no reality of *facing it*, no look of indifference or defiance ; but the manly and modest air of a gentleman conscious of some folly but of perfect rectitude and of most heroic and honourable resolutions . . ."[1]

To Lockhart, who states that he was entirely unaware of Sir Walter's commercial connection, the crash came as a terrible shock. He at once

[1] *Cockburn Memorials*, p. 402.

jumped to the conclusion that it was owing to some villainous extravagance on the part of the Ballantynes that this had come to pass, and that Scott was an injured saint. The causes of Sir Walter's failure were deeper than could be accounted for in this way, and we are left with the conviction that it would be just to blame everyone who was concerned in creating credits which had no relation to real capital. Academic judgments however are not within the province of this book ; what concerns us is that though Sir Walter was very hard hit, his head was high and he maintained a real equanimity in the crisis. Never did he complain, for in all fairness he was bound to acknowledge that through the business connection that had now ruined him he had achieved and enjoyed a fortune. He was well accustomed to the idea of financial instability, he had juggled too long with paper money to be anything else. " Methinks," he wrote in his Journal, " I have been :

> ' So constantly in ruin's sight
> The view o't gives me little fright.' "

To Lockhart he wrote, " It is easy, no doubt for any friend to blame me for entering into connection with commercial matters at all. But I wish to know what I could have done better— excluded from the Bar, and then from all profits for six years, by my colleague's prolonged life. Literature was not in those days what poor Constable has made of it, and with my little capital I was glad to make commercially the means of supporting my family. I got but £600 for *The Lay of the Last Minstrel*, and—it was a price that made men's hair stand on end —£1,000 for *Marmion*. I have been far from suffering by James Ballantyne. I owe it to him to say that his difficulties as well as his advantages are owing to me." (January 20th.)

Unlike Constable and Lady Scott, Sir Walter did not take the blow too hardly, indeed to him it was far less of a shock than it was to any other person concerned. He must have known for a long while that the juggling must have an end. Charlotte, who had anticipated no disaster, was stunned by the blow, but it really left Scott serene. "For myself I feel like the Eildon Hills quite firm though a little cloudy. I do not dislike the path which lies before me."

Rarely is a man viewed heroically by his immediate family. Anne writing to her brother Charles a fortnight after the crash says, "I hear of nothing but *money, money*, and as speaking about it won't bring it back, I wish Papa would be quiet on the subject of pounds, shillings, and pence. You can have no idea what absurd stories they have here, and crowds call every day *to condole*, and after all I do not believe he will lose so very much. I look forward to a very lively life with Mamma for six months in the year particularly as her ladyship is very cross."[1]

Willie Clerk supped with Scott one night soon after ruin was declared. They discussed the whole affair and its consequences openly and playfully, till at last they laughed over their noggins at the change, and Sir Walter observed that he felt "something like Lambert and the other Regicides whom Pepys says, when he saw them going to be hanged and quartered, were as comfortable as any gentlemen could be in that situation." He was utterly incapable of being unhappy for long. Lady Scott and Anne in

[1] *Law Letters*, Vol. IV, p. 71.

the withdrawing room listened to the laughter with great disapproval. What could Papa and Mr. Clerk find to joke about under present circumstances ?

Once the earthquake was over, Scott settled down to a routine life again. His official income was immune from confiscation, and sufficient for his needs. " I have enough left for all useful and comfortable purposes," he writes, " and even with economy can still keep a carriage for Lady Scott."[1] All he had to do was to carry on with his work at the Court of Session and grind at *Woodstock* and *Napoleon*. " Time and I against any two," was his favourite saying.

" Give me my popularity," he exclaimed, " and all my present difficulties shall be as a joke in four years." To Mr. Croker at the Admiralty he wrote, " No oak ever quitted its withered leaves more easily than I have done what might be considered as great wealth."

He was not a sensitive man in any but one respect—pride in and love of Scotland. Things that concerned his own comfort and fortune were of far less account. Captain Hall tells a story that shows him to have been insensitive to a peculiar degree. Sir Walter on arriving at an inn was told there was no bed for him. " No place to lie down ? " he asked. " No, none, except in a room in which a corpse is lying." " Well, did the person die of any contagious disorder ? " " Oh no, not of all." " Well then, let me have the other bed." Scott concluded the story by saying, " So I laid me down and never had a better night's rest in my life."

There is no doubt that personal feelings of sorrow, pleasure and pain, enjoyment and

[1] *Law Letters*, Vol. VI, 51.

privation were, after his first stroke, far colder in him than in most people. He could stand a great deal of buffeting. Whatever the cause was, virtue or indifference, he could show himself pretty stoical on occasion.

Most of his suffering came from Lady Scott and Anne, who both hated and feared poverty. Scott hopes it may " teach them a little of the frugality he had not the heart to enforce when money was plentiful." It had to be explained to Charlotte that she must pay for everything in cash. The old habit of running up accounts everywhere must be stopped. Over these readjustments there were painful scenes and tears.

When it was decided that Abbotsford was to be their only residence, the contents of Castle Street were sold. For the future Sir Walter intended when in Edinburgh to stay at the Albyn Club or in lodgings, perhaps in " the titmouse house near St. Andrews." Skene offered to put him up, but Scott felt that " few friendships stand the attrition of constant, close contact," and declined the kindness.

In spite of most generous offers of money from friends,[1] Sir Walter received but little consideration from Bank or creditors, and was aggravated sufficiently to turn on them saying that if they treated him scurvily he was under no obligation to write for them. He could always apply for legal bankruptcy and where would they be then with Abbotsford inviolate ? His work kept him going though he was vexed by the way James Ballantyne criticized the *Woodstock* page proofs. The printer's comments are on many pages: " This totally perplexes me," " Incomplete."

[1] £30,000 is said to have been offered by an Englishman and the Duke of Buccleuch made some magnanimous suggestions.

" This Marcus has already gone to press as Markham," " Unintelligible." He objects to " damned " as much too coarse, " hanged or damned," says Scott, " I care not." Ballantyne prefers "sinless clay" (of a dead body as spirit is the sinner) to " senseless clay." Scott writes " too recherché." James writes " Wildrake *had* left the room," Scott writes, " Good God ! if a man goes out can't he come back without his absence being discovered ? " James notes " There is surely some confusion here ? " Scott replies, " I think it clear as day."

When the book was complete Ballantyne wrote, " This is one of the finest, if not the very finest . . . Bravisissimo ! "

To Scott's delight *Woodstock* was sold in April (1826) to Longman for £8,228 ready money. It represented three months' work, and he hobbled out to plant three acorns, having a fancy to measure by their growth the extent of his success in eventually clearing off the debt.

Poor Charlotte pined and drooped—the spring found her hold on life weakening visibly. Asthmatic and dropsical she watched the glum faces around her till she could bear it no longer ; could they not laugh to cheer her ? This was too much for the Scottish strain in her children, and for her husband, pure Scot as he was. Death-beds were terribly gloomy affairs, one had to be French to flicker out with a joke. Scott, who was afraid of death-beds, escaped to Edinburgh two or three days before the end, just as when he was young he had escaped to London when his father lay dying. The unfortunate Anne, aged twenty-three, was left in charge. He knew Charlotte to be dying, for on the day before she died he wrote to Charles and Lockhart to

come to " us in our distress," but he did not
return to Abbotsford until her death had been
announced. Anne was in hysterics when he
returned. After contemplating the corpse he
described it in his Journal with a detachment
usually reserved for less intimate relations.
" Yellow masque," " pinched features," " sym-
metry of form " ; this is neither the language of
anguish nor of love. But then Scott was certainly cold in middle life. Nothing touched him
deeply now. Indifference is the curse of age.

Charlotte was buried in Dryburgh Abbey.
When he was courting her " Wattie " had talked
with enthusiasm of the ruins amongst which his
bones would eventually be laid—and Charlotte
had chided him for morbidity. She did not want
to think of skeletons during courtship—fie, fie,
let us be gay while we can, for the spring of life is
fleeting. Sir Walter wrote to Sophia the day
after Charlotte's death, " when we consign dust
to dust in the Church of Dryburgh Abbey, where
after such pilgrimage as may further await me
here, I will evermore be her companion on earth,
as I hope to be in a better world. Whatever were
her failings they hurt only herself and must be
weighed against one of the most sincere, loyal and
generous hearts that ever blood warmed." A
grim reminder of the Burke and Hare depreda-
tions is brought to our mind by a note from Sir
Walter to Lockhart. " My poor labouring people
have affected me much by insisting on supplying
a night guard in Dryburgh Abbey till such
precaution should be totally unnecessary. There
was something very delicate in this peculiar
expression of attachment."[1]

Three weeks after the funeral, Captain Hall called

1 *Law Letters*, Vol. VI, p. 67.

on Sir Walter Scott and found him at his writing table dressed in a suit of "blacks" with white weepers on stock and cuff. He was surrounded by volumes of the *Moniteur*, and arrested his work to talk to his visitor in an unaffected human way. To Hall Sir Walter had never looked more attractive than in misfortune. He seemed to gain stature in the process of trying to dominate adverse circumstance. Some men fight better with their backs to a wall—and it is a tribute to Scott's essential manliness to say that he was stimulated by difficulty. He seemed to write faster than ever, and was always ahead of the Press with his *Napoleon* manuscript. This is not so remarkable as at first sight might appear, for all his manuscript had to be transcribed before going to press, and we have the authority of his devoted, deaf amanuensis, Huntley Gordon, for stating that no line of Scott's own handwriting was ever seen by a Canongate printer.[1] As he always preferred to work with the sound of presses thumping in his ears, he filled in the time created for him by the copyist by turning out *Chronicles of the Canongate* and *Letters on the Currency*. The much admired *Journal* was kept during these difficult times.

The *Journal* is the record of a gradual decline. Sometimes one regrets that it did not occur to Scott to keep it in the heyday of his strength, and yet—this narrative of illness, sleeplessness, financial difficulties, deaths of friends, and funerals, has been of inestimable help to people going through a like experience. We can see exactly how Sir Walter met pain and misfortune and

---

[1] The Great Unknown would not allow *one* line of his own handwriting to be scrutinized by type-setters. I transcribed *for the press* thirty-seven volumes of the novels. (*Times*, July 15th, 1868.)

misery, and exactly how brave and uncomplaining
he was.　Many people would have found his
afflictions unendurable, but he endured them
cheerfully.　Never does Scott show up better
than when things are going desperately wrong.
He never admitted despair, he never admitted
defeat.　He smiled in the face of fate and gave
thanks that he had enjoyed life so deeply.　The
advancing years denuded him by slow degrees of
his comforts ; the body no longer functions
automatically, wine no longer cheers, friends old
and trusted die.　Exposed to the whips and
arrows of misfortune Sir Walter retained his
kindness, his good temper, and his dignity.　He
was indeed a man.

For some time before the crash Mr. Constable
had been desirous that Sir Walter should go to
Paris to collect data about Napoleon while he was
still vivid in men's minds.　Mr. Constable was no
longer in a position of authority, but Mr. Cadell,
for whom, after the crisis, Scott engaged himself
to work, approved the journey and advanced the
money for undertaking it.　On his way to the
Continent he stayed with Sophia and Lockhart
in their home at 25 Pall Mall.　His Majesty,
kind as ever, commanded him to appear at the
Lodge in Windsor Forest.　No host could have
been more hospitable, and Scott, in talking,
forgot " the prince in the accomplished gentleman."　A visit to Windsor Castle amused him
exceedingly.　It was being done up but in a
" very paltry sort of way " compared with
Abbotsford.　Paper was being painted to look
like wainscoting, and hung upon the paper were
Mecklenburg-Strelitz ancestors painted to look
like " orang-outangs."　How preferable in every
way was his own romantic building with its

heavy beams, carved oak and solid furnishings.
" *Voilà nous à Paris*," he wrote adding, " I
understand the language less than I did ten or
eleven years ago." Who would have thought he
had courted his Charlotte in French in the far-off
dancing days at Gilsland ? The courtiers who
accompanied Charles X to exile in Holyrood once
said his French was that of the Sieur de Joinville
—but even in that stiff lingo he had been able to
make his little French girl understand him.
Youth and love overcome greater obstacles than
any language can offer.

The Marshals Macdonald and Marmont, and
Pozzo di Borgo were all communicative on the
subject of Bonaparte. At the end of a fortnight
Scott, in the intervals of social distraction, had
gathered voluminous memoranda. Fenimore
Cooper was in Paris, and on several occasions
Scotch and American lions took the field together,
notably at Princess Galitzin's and at the British
Embassy. Scott was flattered in all sorts of
ways, at one party " a covey " of Russian ladies
sported tartan dresses ; at the theatre *Ivanhoe*
was playing to packed houses ; the fashionable
miniaturist Madame Mirbel took his portrait in
three sittings. At the conclusion the lady artist
had wet cheeks but Sir Walter remained " pebble-
hearted." " The pleasure of hearing Mass performed with excellent music " in the Tuileries
Chapel was one of his outings, and it secretly
pleased him to watch the blonde, lively Duchesse
de Berri, the organizer of " Waverley " balls, yawn
during the ceremony, just as it pleased him to
be greeted by the King, whom he had known in
youth in Edinburgh.

When he returned to London he found himself
in great request. Mr. Croker had him dine to

meet five Cabinet Ministers ; the Duke of Wellington entertained him, talked of battles and gave
him his notes on the Moscow campaign ; at Mr.
Robert Peel's he also met members of the
Government.   Sophia's house was pleasantly situated in Pall Mall close to his club, the Athenæum,
so he was always able to drop in and hear the
news.   Old friends too could come and see him.
Joanna Baillie seemed as attractive as ever,
though Sir Walter, having been run after by many
ladies of fashion, was more sophisticated than
in days of yore.   He found Madame d'Arblay
charming, and a new friend the Duchess of
Buckingham accompanied him to a sitting at
Sir Thomas Lawrence's studio.   In the four hours
spent by this artist in sketching the author's
hand they had a spicy gossip over the Byron-
Leigh scandal.   On another occasion he and the
Duchess were joined by Sam Rogers.   The
Duchess plumed herself over these séances and
was rewarded for her kindness by gifts of little
Pepper and Mustard terriers.   To retire for the
winter to a tiny furnished house in Edinburgh was
depressing.   Rheumatism, aggravated by damp
beds in France, worried him : chilblains distorted
his fingers :   his lameness was becoming real
infirmity.   As he sat over the hearth in the long
evenings he called up visions of Persepolis from
the sea-coal—and visions also of death.

The famous Theatrical Dinner at which Scott
was obliged to own himself the Author of *Waverley*
took place in March, 1827.   The Chairman, Lord
Meadowbank, in proposing Scott's health said :
" He it is who has conferred a new reputation on
our national character and bestowed on Scotland
an imperishable name."   Another speaker alluded
to the Great Unknown, but Scott intervened :

" The Small Known *now* Mr. Bailie ! " Sir Walter in replying, did not think it necessary to enter into the reason of his long silence, but said perhaps caprice had a great share in it.

The *Life of Napoleon* was completed in the spring. Scott missed his task-work terribly, and tried to fill up the gap by compiling *Tales of Scottish History* for his grandson. They were inspired by his friend Croker's *Stories of Children from English History*. He told each tale to Hugh Littlejohn before writing it down so as to make sure the child understood, and then they rode out together at Abbotsford and talked them over. No longer was Scott's mount a dashing black charger or a fretting grey, but a cob " Douce Davie," warranted to carry any one home safely though dead drunk. Mr. Adolphus describes the atmosphere of gentle satisfaction that Sir Walter extracted from these declining days and declining ways. Scott, as we know, was never unhappy for long. Indeed he questioned his own capacity for unhappiness at all.

It gratified him to know that he was not forgotten, that he was bidden to Ravensworth Castle to meet the Duke of Wellington, to banquet with the Bishop of Durham, to visit at Alnwick. Now that Abbotsford had become less dear, it was the sort of thing he liked best, but he could not indulge in much visiting, it wasted time, the creditors had to be put first.

By Christmas, 1827, that is to say in twenty-three months, he had earned nearly £40,000, and could pay six shillings, in the pound. It was a marvellous achievement, and even the creditors passed him a vote of thanks. The success did him no end of good. " I am restored in constitution," he said, as he got to work on the long delayed autobiographical prefaces for the *Magnum Opus*. They had been dropped when Constable failed, but now Mr. Cadell proposed to issue the series.

Things went amazingly well, second editions of *Napoleon* and *Tales of a Grandfather* were called for in January, 1828. *The Fair Maid of Perth* made her début in March and was sold for £4,200.

After a winter of hard work he set out again for London taking his chariot with him. Fenimore Cooper, walking down Pall Mall, caught sight of it standing in front of Sophia's house. There was no mistaking that crest—a mermaid combing her hair before a small mirror—and then there were the arms and the bloody hand. No doubt the literary baronet was in town !

The two authors met at a dinner party—the last time they had seen each other was in a hotel in the rue St. Maur in Paris two years earlier. At first Cooper did not recognize Scott, but soon discovered that in spite of change he had the same charm as of old. " That fellow Napoleon has given me a good lift," he said alluding to his social success. At a dinner given by Mr. Sotheby the poet they met Coleridge who told stories of the American Navy during dinner, and when the ladies retired descanted on Homer for over an hour. " Scott sat immovable as a statue, with his little grey eyes looking inward and outward and he occasionally muttered ' Eloquent ! Wonderful ! Very extraordinary ! ' " When at last Mr. Sotheby broke in and invited the gentlemen to join the ladies, Scott, Cooper says, " walked deliberately into a maze of petticoats, and as in Paris let them play with his mane as much as they pleased."

" Zounds ! " commented Sir Walter on Coleridge's table talk, " I was never so bethumped with words ! "

Sam Rogers gave a dinner in his tiny house fronting on the Green Park. To Cooper's amusement he found it had but a width of 18 ft. and a depth of 50 ft. It pleased the American to see there the original £5 agreement for *Paradise Lost*. Mrs. Siddons and Sir Walter were both guests. On this occasion Scott was silent, perhaps he was not feeling well, for the next day he called on Cooper in his lodging in St. James's Place to say he could not make an excursion arranged by Rogers to Hampton Court. Cooper having mentioned the previous evening that he held the appointment of American Consul at Lyons, but had never been to the place, Scott had pricked up his ears, and came in to tell him that Lady Scott's father was a native of Lyons, and it was important to him to get extracts made from the local registers. He had made an exact note of what was required and gave it to Cooper, who promised that entries should be looked up. This was to enable Scott to claim certain monies that should have come to Lady Scott from her mother.

London was becoming more like home than Scotland. The new house in the Regent's Park into which the Lockharts were moving proved very congenial. It was almost like being in the country. And not only were Sophia and her husband available, but Walter and his Jane were quartered at Hampton Court, and Charles was at his desk in the Foreign Office. The old friends he met were cordial. His Majesty remained faithfully kind, and when sounded through Sir William Knighton seemed pleased to accept the dedication of the *Magnum Opus*.

The Duchess of Kent smiled on him. He enjoyed " the beauties of the Palladian dome" of the Duke of Devonshire's house at Chiswick, and the sylvan loveliness of Richmond Park with Lord Sidmouth. He dined and slept at Holland House, and found that Lord Holland practised his old Abbotsford habit of sitting anywhere at his own table, a habit which made parties delightfully informal.

Everybody seemed to want to paint Scott's portrait nowadays. He had become a sort of figurehead, or as he called himself, " a weather-beaten block." In Edinburgh he had posed to Colvin Smith and Watson Gordon, now it was the aged Academician Northcote and the mercurial Haydon, whom he had to oblige.

People were so attentive, so anxious to be of service to him. Sophia was full of understanding and asked just the right people to the house. Walter and Jane were always delighted to see him and to one charming luncheon in their quarters he took Wordsworth, Rogers and Tom Moore, a wonderful party, on the occasion of which Mr. Rogers presented him with the handsome pair of gold-mounted spectacles which were such an anxiety to him afterwards.

The winter of 1828-9 was spent in Edinburgh. writing a second series of historical tales, and *Anne of Geierstein*. This novel was shown in sheets to a Christmas party at Abbotsford in 1829. The snow lay on the ground outside and everyone expressed delight with his description of Swiss scenery. His imagination, Lockhart says, had outdone the efforts of a thousand tourists. It was the last novel composed before the bad February stroke of 1830. Skene was very helpful to him over the Vehmgericht and the history and scenery of Provence. Scott said he

hated *Anne* and knew she would not be popular.
Nevertheless she sold for £4,200, and since orders
for the *Magnum Opus* were coming in fast, everything financial seemed in a good way. One day
he might again be a free man. In the spring of
1829 Lord Buchan died, and Sir Walter had the
satisfaction of attending his funeral at Dryburgh. It was close on ten years since Lord
Buchan had arranged Scott's obsequies, and the
older people grow, the more pleased they become
at surviving their contemporaries. It is almost as
if they derived from it a sense of superiority.
As he stood on the day of the burial for a moment
by Charlotte's grave, underneath the ruined arch,
he half-longed for and half-dreaded the moment
that would re-unite them in the clay. It was the
first time he had viewed her grave since her death
three years earlier.

Susan Ferrier visited Abbotsford during the
autumn of 1829. She found Sir Walter as kind
and courteous as ever and observed that he
delighted in watching the grandchildren " chas-
ing each other like butterflies among the flowers."
He was very talkative and quite himself, but a
few months later he sustained a stroke and Miss
Ferrier rushed round to Castle Street to see what
she could do for Anne. Poor Anne, whose life
had been a succession of shocks, had been scared
but Papa had rallied after bleeding and was
almost himself again. Yet another attack felled
him in April. Miss Ferrier after this found a
great change in him, he was as kind and polite
as ever but his head was shaven and he wore an
unbecoming little skull cap. Though it made her
unhappy to look at him he talked with so much
vigour that the first impression wore off. One
more visit was paid by this novelist to the castle

by the Tweed.   Sir Walter seemed almost indifferent to the beauty of his surroundings and took no interest in the trees and shrubs that he had planted.   Balmy airs blew in at the windows, birds sang, the sweetness of the early summer was everywhere, but the laird no longer took pleasure in these things: miserable comforters were they all.

Mrs. Lockhart on this occasion was confined to her room with a bad knee but Sir David Wilkie and his sister were staying in the house and the Fergussons and other friends came in to dine. One evening Sophia caused herself to be carried down to the drawing-room while the rest of the party was at dinner, and there she sat with her harp before her when the company came out of the dining-room.   Sir Walter was surprised and listened with delight as she sang his favourite ballads.   Towards the close of the evening he made all present stand in a circle with hands joined singing :

> Weel may we a' be
> Ill may we never be !

Mrs. Lockhart was unable to join in the circle ; Sir David was ill and dispirited, Miss Ferrier depressed.   She did her best to laugh and sing but the mirth around her seemed forced and unnatural, it jarred her feelings.   " It was," she says, " the last attempt at gaiety I witnessed within the walls of Abbotsford."

CHAPTER XVI

THE WAY TO DEATH

AS the minute guns proclaiming the death of King George IV reverberated in the summer air, a heavy old man dressed in a black suit might have been seen limping through the village of Prestonpans. He appeared startled by the booming shots, and leant for a while on his staff, as if to take in the full meaning of the sounds. So his royal friend and benefactor must be dead, dead like Charlotte, Willie Erskine, "jocund Johnny," Tom Purdie and others who had made living the most sunshiny and enjoyable of experiences. His face twitched nervously as he resumed his plodding progress, and Scott reflected that he too had long been walking in the shadows, and that the bourne of life's journey was in sight for him also. Well, well, Naboclish, it was the common lot.

To two friends he pointed out the gateway of the house in which he had lodged more than fifty years earlier. It was not changed in any way, but who now was left to remember the little lame boy who had dreamed the dreams that had changed the world? There was the miniature at Abbotsford to remind men of what once had been and there was his life work—the Scotland he adored and interpreted, lifted high in the eyes of all men. Her fame, at least, had been secured against the fret of time.

A great, invisible company encircled that lame

figure as it crossed the links and stood by the grave of the Jacobite soldier. Mary Stuart, Montrose, Claverhouse, Prince Charlie, Rob Roy, Monkbarns, Baillie Jarvie, Jeannie Deans, crowds upon crowds of ghosts rescued by the Wizard from oblivion, or created by him to typify his own people.

The thorn tree that was the centre of the battle-field still flourished. Nothing had changed except himself. It is depressing to measure oneself against a landscape. Presently the old man walked back with his friends and clambering into a carriage was driven away. One of his few remaining pleasures was to drive slowly to places of historic interest. Sir Walter's sociable was often to be seen crawling through the Canongate of an evening, or drawn up at some favourite view of the Castle or of Arthur's Seat. This was his chief relaxation from desk life.

Whether on account of Joanna Baillie's interest in Constantine Paleologus, or for some other reason, Scott toiled away at the history of Byzantium in order to write his latest novel, *Count Robert of Paris*. James Ballantyne, who thought nothing could be made of such material, tried to discourage him from writing about the " miserable plots and treacheries of the European Chinese." Scott certainly preferred writing about Scotland ; for one thing it was much less trouble, and for another he had a new romance, *Castle Dangerous*, lying at the back of his head ; but the public was always on the side of novelty. His venture into French history had been much appreciated, as also his skit on English society at a spa ; and after all it was money he was writing for now, not the glory of Scotland.

Disregarding James Ballantyne's advice, he

sent parcels of manuscript to him as usual. The printer showed them to Cadell, and the two men agreed that the work revealed signs of senility. It fell to James to break to the author that in their opinion the opening chapters of *Count Robert* were decidedly inferior to anything he had written. Scott was irritated and hurt, and said perhaps it were better that he should follow the example of the fathers of the novel, Fielding and Smollett, and lay his bones abroad. It was too bad of Ballantyne and Cadell to go on like that when he had cleared off such an immense load of debt—9s. in the £1—and was well on the way to pay another 3s.! He would certainly go on with the novel. The creditors had behaved very differently; they were grateful to him for his "unparalleled exertions," and had begged him to accept "the furniture, plate, linens, paintings, library, curiosities of Abbotsford hitherto held in trust on their behalf."

This put fresh heart into him. Once more, as he sat scribbling at his table, he felt the happiness of authorship—but his handwriting? well the less it was looked at the better. Then he could not help noticing a kind of impediment in his speech, and his right leg was perfectly stiff and very painful. Please God, it might not be his lot to follow in his father's footsteps, and lie for months as an imbecile paralytic. To circumvent his growing infirmity a doctor persuaded him to have a support fitted. At first it helped him, but it had a way of getting out of order, and he found himself helpless when it had to be repaired.

Scott worried terribly over the general election occasioned by the death of George IV; the Reform Bill was to him a specially dangerous experiment. Gillies says it haunted him like a spectre and that he conceived that if Lord Grey's measure were carried a Revolution like that in France would follow as a matter of course. He felt aggrieved that Robert Cadell should be a Whig, and that James Ballantyne, since the shock of his wife's death, had become sympathetic to reform. Even Laidlaw was of a Whiggish persuasion. What was coming over the world ? Why should men want to throw away the constitution, and allow the unwashed and the illiterate to select legislators ? The curse of Cromwell be on those who brought England to this pass !

Those who loved Scott most were anxious to keep him out of politics, but he insisted on attending a meeting at Jedburgh. He spoke in the Court House against " French democratic ideas." The audience booed and hissed him, but he spoke on, and though interrupted, he moved his resolution ; then, with the sudden irascibility characteristic of his complaint, he exclaimed, " I regard your gabble no more than the geese on the green," and left the hall.

A visit from his old friend Lord Meadowbank to Abbotsford was the occasion for a little party to neighbours. Scott, exhilarated by the company, felt himself again, and drank champagne. Soon after he reached his room he fell upon the floor unconscious. Copious bleeding and other rough treatment was prescribed, and after a while he recovered sufficiently to be lifted on to his cob, to take the air.

Lockhart paid him a visit in May, 1831. Scott rode half a mile along the Selkirk road to meet him. The son-in-law was deeply shocked at the change in Sir Walter's appearance. Under the blue bonnet was the black silk cap and the shaved head that had so upset Susan Ferrier. The face was drawn down on one side, and at first it was difficult to understand what he said. He seemed to have shrunk a good deal, for his green jacket hung loosely from his shoulders. But still Sir Walter smiled, still showed himself brave and manly.

He told Lockhart of Ballantyne's behaviour over *Count Robert* ; Ballantyne didn't want to print it at all—the dog ! and they were near a breach over it. Lockhart listened sympathetically, and by degrees persuaded him to lay the work aside for the time being, and begin more *Tales of a Grandfather*, this time from French history. Johnnie Hugh counted on grandpapa's stories ; he must not disappoint him. Though Lockhart influenced him to relinquish *Count Robert*, he was not strong enough however to keep Sir Walter away from the Roxburghshire election, where weavers and other malcontents were insulting all who did not wear the Reform colours. Scott's carriage was stoned, and as he walked a short way down the street a woman spat on him from a window, and men groaned and blasphemed. Shouts of " Burke Sir Walter," were clearly audible. A few days later he attended a meeting at Selkirk, over which, as Sheriff, he presided. These excursions were very upsetting, and Anne, Lockhart and Cadell were pleased when the general election was over, for he could then be set to work on something that worried him less, another tale from Scottish History : *Castle Dangerous*. Laidlaw, to whom he was dictating this novel, became reluctantly convinced that his mind was going. He had consecutive bright moments while dictating quickly but these were succeeded by dark and confused ones. It was evident that if he remained at home he would continue to write, and Cadell feared for his

T

reputation, and for the sale of his collected edition, the *Magnum Opus*. A really rubbishy book might affect the fortunes of Cadell disadvantageously. He informed the family that Scott must somehow be stopped from writing. Could he not travel abroad ? The Lockharts and Anne thought the recent appointment of Charles to the British Legation at Naples might prove an excuse to get Sir Walter away for a while, and break his old habits of regular composition. Captain Basil Hall agreed it was an excellent plan, and pulled strings at the Admiralty to get one of his Majesty's frigates put at the disposal of the author. Scott, much gratified at being officially informed that whenever he found it convenient to come south, H.M.S. *Barham* would take him to his destination, began to make plans. Cadell was studiously optimistic about the sales of his works, and by degrees Sir Walter came to think that the *Magnum Opus* would pay off all his debts. This reconciled him to abandon work for a time, and to his family he spoke of the journey with resignation.

It was a great pleasure to Scott when his eldest son appeared to escort him to Naples, and he caused himself to be hoisted on to Douce Davie for the last time in order to watch the tall hussar jumping banks and walls on his great black charger.

In mid-September, just a year before his death, Scott welcomed his last party at Abbotsford, and there was " a night of flowing cups and pibrochs loud," " once more within the Minstrel's blazon'd hall." The neighbouring gentry and some old friends had the opportunity of meeting Captain Burns, son of the poet, on leave from India.

Lockhart did honour to the guest in verse :

What princely stranger comes ?—what exiled lord
From the Far East to Scotia's strand returns—
To stir with joy the towers of Abbotsford,
And " wake the Minstrel's soul " ?—The boy of Burns.

Four days after this festivity Wordsworth and his
daughter came to say goodbye. The poet wore
a green eye-shade, but his sight was correct
enough to inform him of the sad change in his
host's appearance. Gallant as ever in battling
with physical ills, Scott accompanied his guests to
Newark's stately Tower looking down on Yarrow.
He was still able to walk " pretty stoutly." As
they crossed the Tweed on their return journey,
" a rich but sad light of rather a purple than a
golden hue was spreading over the Eildon Hills."
Wordsworth was deeply moved and wrote the
well known valedictory sonnet that evening :

A trouble, not of clouds or weeping rain
Nor of the setting sun's pathetic light
Engendered, hangs o'er Eildon's triple height ;
Spirits of power assembled there complain
For kindred power, departing from the sight ;
While Tweed, best pleased in chanting a blithe strain
Saddens his voice again and yet again,
Lift up your hearts, ye mourners, for the might
Of the whole world's good wishes with him goes ;
Blessings and prayers in nobler retinue
Than sceptred King or laurelled conqueror knows,
Follow this wondrous potentate. Be true
Ye winds of ocean and the midland sea
Wafting your charge to soft Parthenope !

Wordsworth read it aloud to Scott before leaving
Abbotsford. It was like a benediction on his
head. The two poets talked seriously and intimately of life and death. Scott spoke with
gratitude of all the happiness that had been his.
As Wordsworth travelled home and pondered on

their farewell meeting he imagined another poem
Yarrow Revisited, based in pattern on Hamilton's
ballad *The Dowie Dens of Yarrow*. It was a
ballad Scott loved, and in ballad form must
Wordsworth enshrine his late experience, for :

> —what, for this frail world, were all
> That mortals do or suffer ;
> Did no responsive harp or pen,
> Memorial tribute offer ?

On the day Wordsworth left Abbotsford the
Scotts started for London. Sir Walter stayed in
Sussex Place with the Lockharts but he was
unhappy. London was rocking tumultuously
over the Lords' Debates on the second Reform
Bill. He actually saw the Duke of Wellington's
house mobbed. How terrible was this social disorder ! Tom Moore dined with the Lockharts and
found Sir Walter very quiet. Sophia had asked
friends in after dinner, Lady Belhaven, Lord and
Lady Ruthven, Lady Louisa Stuart, the Macleods,
the Raes. Moore felt it was hardly right to
assemble so large a company to meet the invalid.
Sophia, Moore, and others sang, and Sir Walter
looking vacant waited till it was his bedtime and
then slipped away.

Preparations were made for the journey, and
at last the party took coach for Guildford. A
blind horse turning suddenly into the stable yard
threw Sir Walter violently to the ground, and well
nigh killed him on the spot. " What a fate ! "
reflected Captain Hall, " the foremost man in all
the world to be trod to death by a decayed post-
horse, and yet, upon the whole might not even
such a catastrophe have proved a blessed exemption
from much subsequent suffering and sorrow at
which the nations wept ? "

At Portsmouth, where they waited for a favourable wind, Sir Walter was waited on by the Philosophical Society of the town. On October 25th H.M.S. *Barham* sailed bearing Sir Walter Scott, Captain Scott and Anne to Naples. A verse of Lockhart's expressed hope for a calm voyage and a restoration of health.

> Through seas unruffled may the vessel glide
> That bears her poet far from Melrose glen
> And may the pulse be steadfast as our pride
> When happy breezes waft him back again !

The journey was rough and cold, and all the Scotts suffered the usual miseries incident to sailing through mountainous waves. The Mediterranean Sea was smoother, and Scott's mind became occupied with a volcanic island that had recently appeared in it. Nothing would satisfy him but to land on this excrescence. In a letter to Skene he described the experience, and noted that he had come upon two dead dolphins and a robin redbreast. They appeared to him of great importance.

Friendly hearts awaited his arrival in Malta. There was Hookham Frere, now a permanent inhabitant ; there was Skene's son, a naval officer ; there was Stoddart, a friend of Lasswade days, now Sir John Stoddart, Chief Justice of the Island ; there was Willie Erskine's girl Euphemia whom he had known from babyhood, now married to Captain Dawson of the garrison ; there was John Davy, head of the medical staff, son of Humphry Davy, and his wife, daughter of his old friend Fletcher, a brother advocate and a neighbour in Castle Street. All were set on making dear Sir Walter's stay as pleasant as they could.

Since " cholera prevailed in England," quarantine was enforced on Sir Walter and his party. Dr. Davy and other friends had seen to it that they should not be conveyed to the common lazaretto, and arranged for their accommodation in fine apartments in Fort Manuel. There in a wide doorway sat Sir Walter holding audiences for nine days. Visitors who climbed the many steps leading to the fort saw before them the Scott family, all seated on chairs, with Euphemia Dawson and her husband in the background, for they had insisted on joining themselves to the family. Scott found the quarantine regulations sufficiently ridiculous, " notwithstanding mosquito curtains and iron beds [we] are sorely annoyed by vermin, the only real hardship we have to complain of." The quarantine bar placed in front of the party made a visit very formal, as distant bows only could be exchanged. Sir Walter sat there patiently, dressed in a brown coat and trousers of a small checked Lowland plaid. His hands were crossed on his shepherd's staff, and as visitors arrived he rose, an unexpressive look on his face and in his eyes, which distressed those who had known him in brighter days. Hookham Frere was his most regular visitor ; but what between his absence of mind and Scott's natural impulse to shake hands, it was all the liveried officer of health could do to prevent contact.

When this trying exposition was over, the Scott family went to Beverley's Hotel in the Strada Ponente, and tried to fulfil the series of engagements made for them. Most unsuitably a ball had been arranged in Sir Walter's honour by the garrison at the Auberge de Provence. Every detail from music to decorations was

overwhelmingly Scottish. Well-intentioned people like Sir John Stoddart gave dinners for
Scott, and plied him hospitably enough with
" champaign " and porter. Mrs. Davy thought
him at his best when entertaining a few friends
at the hotel. He was almost his old self ; told
anecdotes, and repeated a " pretty long passage
of Frere's version of the *Romances of the Cid*,
and seemed to enjoy a spirited charge of the
Knights, placing his walking-stick in rest like a
lance to suit the action to the word." These
flickers of the old life encouraged Anne to hope
the improvement was real.

The Davys lived opposite Beverley's Hotel,
and one morning Miss Scott rushed across to
them fearing her father was about to have another
stroke ; would they come in at once. Snatching
up some views of the volcanic island they sped
into his presence. Scott flushed and lethargic
sat there in a silk dressing-gown. He rose,
looked at the volcano sketches, and began to talk
indistinctly of the life of Sir Humphry Davy
which he was then writing. The application of
leeches averted the stroke, and he was well enough
to drive out that afternoon to San Antonio,
which had been lent to Mr. Frere by the Governor,
while his own house at the Pietà was under
repair. He snuffed up the perfume of the new
oranges hanging on the trees and laughed to see
pigs rootling among the stems. Next day he
made an excursion to Città Vecchia.

After paying several visits to St. John's Church
and the graves of the Knights within it, he conceived the idea of writing a novel with the island
for setting, and with this end in view he spent a
good deal of time in the old library of the
Knights making notes for the projected romance.

" It will be hard," he said, with something of the old enthusiasm, " if I cannot make something of this ! "

H.M.S. *Barham* reached Naples a week before Christmas, 1831. Charles came aboard at once and told him that the King had waived the quarantine regulations in his father's case and they might drive straight to the Palazzo Caramanico. English visitors surged forward to do what civilities they might. Lord Hertford, Mr. Keppel Craven, Mr. and Mrs. William Ashley, Sir George Talbot and others proffered assistance, but the person Sir Walter took to most was Sir William Gell, who suffered infirmities like his own. They had known each other in happier days under Lady Abercorn's roof at Stanmore Priory, and Gell had formed one of the circle to whom Scott had read his earliest effusions. And now Lady Abercorn was dead. Naples had proved fatal both to her and his dear Lady Compton.

On several occasions Scott was obliged to go to Court, and since the appliance on his leg made the wearing of stockings impossible he attired himself in the green coat, heavily laced, and the trousers of a Brigadier-General of the Scottish Archers. He understood practically nothing of what the King and other foreigners said to him on these occasions ; he could but bow and smile at all compliments.

Idleness he could not brook so made a collection of street-ballads and broadsides, worked at the *Siege of Malta* and at a shorter tale *Bizzarro*. Friends conveyed him on excursions to Paestum, Pompeii and other places ; the remains scarcely made any impression on his mind, but certain aspects of scenery evoked the memory of Scottish ballads, and he would recite *Hardyknute* or *Jock of Hazeldean* in unexpected spots. He shambled and stumbled a good deal, but took it all in good part, though afflicted by anxiety over Sam Rogers' gold-rimmed spectacles lest they should break as they slid off his nose. A view of Lake Avernus, and of the Lucrine Lake called up some other vision of the heart—for his heart was always in Scotland, and he repeated in a grave tone and with the old emphatic diction :

Up the craggy mountain and down the mossy glen
We canna gang a milking for Charlie and his men.

He was pelted with sugar plums and confetti as he drove about Neapolitan streets during the Carnival ; perhaps it was better than being pelted by stones in Scotland, though it is to be doubted whether he thought so. More and more he took refuge in work. By April his family decided they could no longer contend with his energy, or with his increasing irritability over restrictions in diet. The experiment of making him winter abroad had failed ; there was no longer any point in keeping him away from his own desk and from the influence of physicians whom he had learned to trust.

As a first move towards Scotland the party left Naples for Rome in an open barouche which could be turned into a bed. They were provided in Rome with apartments in the Casa Bernini. Sir William Gell accompanied Scott to St. Peter's to see the tomb of the last of the Stuarts. He fixed a glove to the end of his friend's walking stick as a precaution against slipping on the marble pavement, for Scott was becoming increasingly infirm and incautious. The sightseer was also shown the Palace in the Piazza dei SS. Apostoli which bore the name of the Palazzo del

Pretendente. Another Jacobite excursion was made with Mr. Cheney to the Villa Muti at Frascati, where the Cardinal of York had lived. There Scott saw a portrait of Charles I, an ivory head of the monarch screwed on to the Cardinal's walking stick, a bust of the Cardinal, and another of the Chevalier St. George, and a painting of a fête in the Piazza dei SS. Apostoli given to the Cardinal on his promotion to the Curia. In this picture Scott tried to pick out the more distinguished followers of the exiled family and thought he recognized Cameron of Lochiel. An unkind, truthful pencil made sketches of his fallen face conveying its expression of vacancy. The intervals of intelligence and excitement were getting rarer.

Another day Sir Walter drove with Scottish intention to the burying ground outside the Porta San Paolo. It is doubtful whether he or his family knew anything much of Keats, but Anne Scott was compelled to visit the cemetery in order to see the grave of a clanswoman, Lady Charlotte Stopford, daughter of the house of Buccleuch. Sir Walter felt himself too lame that day to walk to the Scottish grave, but he could not help seeing the pyramid of Cestius, that sight familiar to all lovers of poetry.

Among the strangers he met in Rome was Thorwaldsen. Those who saw the two tall distinguished-looking men together noted their grey hair, heavily eaved eyes, marked features and bent shoulders. They had no language in common, " but they embraced with fervour and cordially and repeatedly shook each other by the hand."

" Methinks I will not die quite happy," wrote Scott in the heyday of his life, " without having seen somewhat of that Rome of which I have heard so much." He may have died happy, but Rome in no way contributed to his happiness.

Something inside Scott warned him that he should hurry home. Charles obtained leave of absence from his chief, and the party left Rome in May. The movement, and possibly the long fatiguing vista opened up by the journey, made Scott irritable and impatient. Whatever happened he must die in the country where he had left his heart. The landscape as they crossed the highest part of the Apennines pleased him. There were pines, there was snow, it was a little reminiscent of Scotland. At Bologna and Ferrara he would look at nothing; at Venice he walked over the Bridge of Sighs and scrambled into the dungeons; he would look at nothing else. He talked of Innsbruck and the armoured knights round Maximilian's tomb, but when they got to Innsbruck he again would look at nothing, and they hurried, as fast as heavy carriages could be said to hurry, through Ulm, Munich, Heidelberg, Frankfort. It was, as it had been in the ballad of *Lenore*, a race with death. Scott would have liked to travel all night as well as all day. His children, realizing that this impatience was the forerunner of another paralytic attack, caused him to be bled by his valet. At Mainz they boarded a steamer, and for a while the sight of the Rhine castles and the memory of old ballads connected with them seemed to pacify him, but when the hills subsided into flat lands a great despondency overtook him. The feared attack felled him at Nymeguen, the lancet restored consciousness and he was transported to a steamer at Rotterdam. Sooner than Sophia expected he reached London, and Charles, for fear she might be away, took his father to the St. James's Hotel in Jermyn Street and put him to bed. The family hung round the bedside, distinguished physicians were called in, and Mr. Cadell came down from Edinburgh to see if he could be of use. The patient was kept in a half-darkened room and muttered occasionally of irrelevant affairs.

On July 7th, the day it had been arranged for him to return to Scotland, he asked for light, and they dressed him in a quilted silk dressing gown and sat him at the open window. He was then lifted into a carriage and driven to the steamer *James Watt* in the Thames. Four days later they were on the road from Edinburgh to Tweed-side. As the dearly-loved landscape came before him, his eyes brightened. " Gala Water ! " he murmured, and at the sight of Eildon grew excited, and when Abbotsford towers came in view he sprang up with a cry of joy. His agitation on drawing up at his own house was ungovernable ; the dogs came jumping round him and he recognized Willie Laidlaw. It was good to be home again.

Next day he was wheeled into the garden among his roses—and then up and down the hall and library. " I have seen much but nothing like my own house," he said, " give me one turn more." He asked for St. John's Gospel to be read to him, and favourite passages from Crabbe's pedestrian poems, poems that had also solaced Fox as he lay dying. Kindly Laidlaw tried to rally him with the old favourite saw, " Time and I against any two." Sir Walter listened and then let his head fall back on the pillows murmuring " Vain boast ! vain boast ! "

For four or five days he was trundled about, and then came a request to be placed at his desk

and left to himself. Sophia put the pen into
fingers that would not clasp it—slow tears rolled
down his face as he beckoned to them to wheel him
away, " Bed," he exclaimed, " was the only place
for such as he." They had placed a four-post
bed in the library, and there he lay, still drawing
breath but living in past scenes and consorting
with ghosts. One would have expected him to
die with a refrain from a Border ballad on his
lips, but it was otherwise. Watchers by his side
heard him murmuring lines from Latin hymns,
Dies irae, dies illa, and *Stabat Mater dolorosa*—
indeed they were his last articulated words. On
a still September day, so still that Lockhart, as
he knelt by the bed, could hear the ripple of the
river dancing over pebbles, the Laird of Abbotsford died. His four children, devoted Lockhart,
and admiring, faithful Willie Laidlaw were with
him to the end.

Five days later his own horses drew the hearse
to Dryburgh Abbey. As they approached the
" Shirra's View " at the height of the road above
the Tweed, they stopped, as they had done a
hundred times before, to allow their master to
gaze over his beloved valley to the Eildon Hills.
It was a lowering windy day ; to those who
followed the coffin Nature seemed in harmony
with their mood, for the dark clouds rolling
overhead to them had the semblance of a pall.

BIBLIOGRAPHY

IN the " Life of Scott " by C. D. Yonge (Great Writers Series, London, 1888) is printed an excellent Scott Bibliography compiled by J. P. Anderson of the British Museum. It is now over forty years old and therefore incomplete, but I wish to acknowledge how useful I have found it. Another good Bibliography is printed in " Sir Walter Scott " by M. Ball, Ph.D. (Columbia University Press, 1907). I have read almost everything included in these lists as well as other more recently published works. In these days of financial stringency it hardly seems worth while to print yet a third list merely to register additional matter, more especially as we are promised an exhaustive Bibliography by a Scott expert during the course of the year.

Apart from Sir Walter Scott's own revelation of his personality in Poems, Novels, Miscellaneous Prose Works, Letters and Journal, in themselves a most formidable mass of evidence to assimilate, the descriptions and comments of contemporaries furnish us with lively pictures of the way Sir Walter lived and moved among his fellow men. Fragments of information are taken from the writings of J. D. Adolphus, Joanna Baillie, the Ballantynes, Byron, T. Campbell, F. Chantrey, R. Chambers, Lord Cockburn, S. T. Coleridge, Fenimore Cooper, A. Constable, Crabbe, Creevey, Croker, A. Cunningham, Mrs. John Davy, Maria Edgeworth, Edward Everett, Susan Ferrier, H. Frere, J. Gibson, R. Gillies, W. S. Gillies, Basil

Hall, Baron d'Haussez, B. R. Haydon, Hazlitt, Hogg, Mrs. Hughes, Leigh Hunt, Washington Irving, W. Knighton, W. Laidlaw, T. Lawrence, C. R. Leslie, Matthew Lewis, C. Mathews, T. Moore, John Murray, A. Pichot, Countess Purgstall, Anna Seward, Sinclair, J. Stoddart, Lady Louisa Stuart, W. Taylor, D. Terry, G. Ticknor, D. Wordsworth, C. Young. Some of these contemporaries give a great deal of information, others record a single meeting, a gesture, a joke. On the whole the American impressions appear the freshest, but the women novelists run them close in intelligent observation. Artists and actors have left vivid accounts of their intercourse with the great man, and there is much to be gleaned from the Ballantynes and their defenders as well as from the correspondence of John Murray and Archibald Constable. Two Frenchmen wrote amusing descriptions of interviews with Sir Walter and the memoranda of three Scots— Laidlaw, Chambers and Hogg are invaluable. The many letters written to Sir Walter by Morritt, Ellis, Lady Abercorn and numerous other friends are also of importance.

I have read and re-read many times the " Life of Scott " by J. G. Lockhart, a wonderful book from which up to date there has been no appeal. In spite of its established position as one of the two greatest biographies in our language, its numerous omissions and misstatements conduce to make it but a fallible guide to those who seek to provide for modern readers a true and intimate presentation of this man of genius.

Among the books consulted with advantage I would mention " English and Scottish Popular Ballads," by F. J. Child (Boston, 1882-96); " The Scott Centenary Exhibition Catalogue '

(1872); " The History of Selkirkshire " by T. C. Brown (1886); " Sir Walter Scott as a Critic of Literature," by M. Ball (1907); " The Life of Scott " and " A History of Criticism and Literary Taste in Europe," by Professor Saintsbury ; " Le Roman Historique à l'Epoque Romantique," by Louis Maigron (Paris, 1898); " The Age of Wordsworth," by C. H. Herford (1905); " Hansards Parliamentary Debates " (Scottish Judicature Bill and Beacon case); " British Monachism" by Fosbroke (1817) (used by Sir Walter Scott as a text-book on Catholic affairs). There is not as much literary criticism as one would expect to find, but W. Bagehot, W. C. Bryant, Carlyle, F. Doyle, A. Dumas, R. W. Emerson, Hazlitt, Heine, O. W. Holmes, V. Hugo, Keble, D. Masson, B. Matthews, Palgrave, W. Prescott, Rossetti, Ruskin, Leslie Stephen and Taine have all given their opinions on Scott's work. The best of the recent essays I have read—" Scott and Carlisle" —is by Professor Grierson ("Essays and Studies by members of the English Association," 1928).

To all mentioned in this condensed Bibliography and to many unmentioned authors I wish to express once more my sense of indebtedness.

INDEX